Defending
Community

CONFLICTS IN URBAN AND
REGIONAL DEVELOPMENT,
a series edited by
John R. Logan and
Todd Swanstrom

Defending Community

The Struggle for
Alternative
Redevelopment
in Cedar-Riverside

RANDY STOECKER

Temple University Press

Philadelphia

Temple University Press, Philadelphia 19122

Published 1994
Printed in the United States of America

The paper used in this publication meets the minimum requirements of American National Standard for Information Sciences— Permanence of Paper for Printed Library Materials, ANSI Z39.48-1984 ∞

Library of Congress Cataloging-in-Publication Data

Stoecker, Randy, 1959–
Defending community : the struggle for alternative redevelopment in Cedar-Riverside / by Randy Stoecker.
   p.   cm.—(Conflicts in urban and regional development)
Includes bibliographical references and index.
ISBN 1-56639-127-X.—
ISBN 1-56639-128-8 (pbk.)
1. Community development, Urban—Minnesota—Minneapolis.
2. Community power—Minnesota—Minneapolis.
3. Community organization—Minnesota—Minneapolis.
4. Cedar-Riverside (Minneapolis, Minn.)
I. Title. II. Series.
HN79.M63C67   1994
307.1′416′09776579—dc20   93-20331

The map on page 2, by Jim Ashley, is used with permission.

Portions of Chapter 4 are adapted from Randy Stoecker, "The Federated Frontstage Structure and Localized Social Movements: A Case Study of the Cedar-Riverside Neighborhood Movement," *Social Science Quarterly* 74 (1993).

Portions of Chapter 6 are adapted from Randy Stoecker, "Taming the Beast: Maintaining Democracy in Community-controlled Redevelopment," *Berkeley Journal of Sociology* 35 (1990).

Portions of the "Social Reproduction" section in Chapter 8 are reprinted from Randy Stoecker, "Who Takes Out the Garbage? Social Reproduction and Social Movement Research," in *Perspectives on Social Problems*, vol. 3, ed. Gale Miller (Greenwich, Conn.: JAI Press, 1992).

Quotations from the following interviews are used with permission: William Betzler, 1978; John (Jack) Cann, 1978; Robert Drew, 1978; Steve Parliament, 1978; Charles Warner, 1978; Ralph Wittcoff, 1978; Joyce Yu, 1978: Sound and Visual Collections, Minnesota Historical Society.

For the people of Cedar-Riverside,
past, present, and future,
in the hope that we may never forget.

Contents

Preface

"I JUST want you to put in your book that 'gee, we had fun,'" said Cedar-Riverside activist Tim Ogren when I told him of my plans to try to publish the story of Cedar-Riverside. I hope I have expressed in these pages just how much fun they had. Sometimes the fun was hard work, and sometimes it was even quite painful. But it was ultimately the fun of winning—of building a neighborhood and a community. Few people get the opportunity to experience the sense of community I experienced in the five years I lived in Cedar-Riverside, although those five years were some of the hardest on the community fabric. But even under the circumstances of a community increasingly disrupted by internal conflict, I too had fun. Cedar-Riverside is one of the most dynamic communities anyone can imagine, and it is hard to resist being swept up in a community that is actually winning in the struggle—not winning unconditionally, but winning nonetheless.

I ended up in Cedar-Riverside—along with Tammy Raduege, my partner—quite naively in mid-1983. Looking for housing close to the University of Minnesota, where I was about to begin my doctoral work in sociology, we found the closest, cheapest, and most spacious housing in Cedar-Riverside. Never mind that "central heat" in our upper duplex apartment meant a huge gas space heater in the center of the apartment that would occasionally singe the cat's tail when he got too close, or that the noise from the two freeways bordering the neighborhood was constant, or that the bar traffic would sometimes rouse us out of bed in the middle of the night. We were living in Cedar-Riverside, with an entire metropolitan area's worth of culture and politics all rolled into one three-hundred-acre neighborhood, and it was just a four-block walk to school.

Once we got settled, it didn't take us long to realize there was something different about this neighborhood. It was full of mature hippies —some more noticeable than others. Long hair, peasant skirts, and funky language were fashionable in Cedar-Riverside long after they had been declared out of date in the rest of the country. And Birkenstock sandals had been fashionable in the neighborhood long before the rest of the country decided maybe they weren't so ugly. Hippie dogs (gentle animal-shelter refugees—no purebreds here), who wore bandannas instead of collars, roamed the neighborhood freely and, to my amazement, looked both ways before they crossed the street. Living in Cedar-Riverside meant that, instead of unloading your junk at a rummage sale, you put it out by the street with a sign proclaiming it "free stuff." Here "cooperative" had a highly elaborated meaning: the debates were not over which capitalist-owned grocery store to patronize but over the relative political correctness of a worker-controlled organic foods co-op versus a consumer-controlled mixed organic and nonorganic foods co-op. But the weirdest thing of all was an immense complex of concrete apartment towers called Cedar Square West. The incongruity of all that concrete facing what otherwise looked like a small town with small-town housing and a small-town business district (except for the hippies, of course) demanded an explanation.

So I started asking questions—questions that led me into the heart and soul of Cedar-Riverside, introduced me to my neighbors, and helped me get my degree. I had always been drawn to alternatives— to experiments in better living, insulated from the violence of competition, hypermasculinity, and racism/ethnocentrism. Until then, however, I had only read about better places. What I discovered after I began asking questions was that Cedar Square West—that immense experiment in entombing a community in concrete—was not the story. The real story was the rest of the neighborhood, which appeared so unremarkable on the outside—except for the hippies, of course. The true experiment, the true alternative, had developed in the rest of the neighborhood.

Now, in the 1990s, the dogs are not nearly as likely to roam the streets or wear bandannas. The surviving grocery co-op is the one that tenaciously adhered to a worker-controlled, organic-foods philosophy. The people have grown into the 1990s. They no longer look like stereotypical hippies, and one realizes, in retrospect, that they were always more complicated than the media images that attempted to portray them.

It is, then, to the community residents that I dedicate this book. They were skeptical at first. They had been exploited by journalists, academics, and students before. They had been misquoted and defamed. But I was also a neighborhood resident, and being a resident gave me a bit more legitimacy as a mutual adoption took place. While most social "scientists" fear nothing more than "going native"—becoming too close to the local community—I found myself quickly and fluidly settling into Cedar-Riverside as my home. This community was attempting to overcome the problems of modern life imposed by the capitalist society I had become so critical of. It was trying to enact values of peace, justice, wholeness, participation, and *community* in its truest sense. Though none of these ideals was ever fully realized, and some have slipped farther away, few communities have come as close to realizing them as Cedar-Riverside.

I must first thank the residents of Cedar-Riverside—some of those with whom I spent the most time are listed among the interviewees at the end of this book. Tim Ogren, Tim Mungavan, Dorothy Jacobs, and Ralph Wittcoff deserve special mention. They have read much of what I have written, spent countless hours in conversation and interviews, and remained supportive even when my conclusions strayed from theirs. They became friends.

There were many other people who hung in there with me as I bumbled through the initial research process. My mentors at the University of Minnesota—Barbara Laslett, Ron Aminzade, and Eric Sheppard—didn't laugh when I told them I wanted to study a neighborhood and didn't freak out when I told them it was my neighborhood. They read my work with incredible care, and they pushed me even when I resisted being pushed. I am especially grateful to Barbara, since it was her idea to consider the issue of social reproduction, which I came to embrace as an essential ingredient of this neighborhood movement. There is also Joe Galaskiewicz, who has always been a step away from my work but has been a very important professional mentor, always reminding me (probably without realizing it) to reflect on my own sometimes overidealistic radicalism. Others, such as Ron Randall, the director of the Urban Affairs Center at the University of Toledo, helped provide the resources that allowed me to take this book four years beyond the initial dissertation by funding a trip back to Minneapolis so that I could catch up on the neighborhood. Still others provided resources without which this project could not have been completed. The Minneapolis Public Library, the University of Minnesota libraries, and the Minnesota Historical Society were repositories of essential historical documents. Scattered throughout these libraries was an entire neighborhood history just waiting to be pieced together. And neighborhood activists Deb Wolking, Tim Mungavan, and Ralph Wittcoff opened their files and their photo collections to me, entrusting me with even the last known copies of historical photos and posters.

Harry Boyte read through my entire original dissertation, giving me detailed comments on how I might turn it into a book. Steve Buechler, Scott McNall, and Craig Jenkins gave me incredible support and very detailed suggestions for improving my initial attempts at rewriting. Poor Teddie Morrissey must have read the first three chapters a dozen times to help me slowly but surely figure out what I wanted to say. When I finally exhausted her to the point where she had nothing more to say, I sent the chapters off and got a contract to publish. John Logan probably influenced me the most in terms of helping me to see the big picture of how to turn this work into a book. He made me think clearly about the themes I wanted to address and their relationship to one another. I also must thank Lisa Tracy, one of my favorite graduate students, from whom I humbly acknowledge learning more about writing than I taught. Finally, Michelle Young, Deb Groh, and John Schwartz, three of my other favorite graduate students, worked incredibly hard to compile the references for the text. John also went through the pain of index construction with me.

My thanks also go to Michael Ames, editor-in-chief at Temple University Press. When I approached Michael about this project at a meeting, his eyes lit up, he took me aside, and we had a very energizing conversation—a conversation between two people interested in the same issues and the same ideas. Michael's interest and excitement meant a great deal to someone who had no great hopes of ever becoming a "book author." His enthusiasm encouraged me to finish the project. And, apparently, the hours he spent trying to get through my thick skull how to write "organically" finally paid off. Joan Vidal, my Production Editor at Temple, was a fountain of help, gently guiding me through the production process with clear instructions and meticulous attention to detail. And Kim Vivier was incredibly thorough at the job I could never imagine doing—copyediting the prose of the overeducated and undertrained writer.

There are others who deserve thanks for the success of this project —those who built the foundation, provided the basic skills, and molded the raw material. Andrea Nye, Lanny Neider, Tuck Green, Hadley Klug, Richard Salem, and the late John Prentice took a small-town, working-class undergraduate and helped him learn how to observe and think actively and sensitively. Old friends also deserve mention, especially Michael O'Neal and Vicky Brockman, who not only put me up on my return trips to Minneapolis but helped me sort out theoretical ideas and historical events as well.

Although I did not realize it until later, Rex and Joan Stoecker, my parents, brought me up in an environment centered on neighboring in a small, traditional community. Their example of neighboring allowed me to see the depth of community in Cedar-Riverside and the shared meaning of community even for dramatically different cultures.

And finally, there is family, who often get thanked, if only for putting up with the obsessive-compulsive behavior that a project like this demands. Tammy Raduege, my partner through all, was much more than understanding. Her friends and her extended family would all regularly ask me, "How's the book coming?" She bragged to everybody and gave me much-needed encouragement and even pressure not to give up and embarrass us both. Tammy also acted as my skeptical reference point, balancing my tendency toward idealism. And then there was Cameron the cat, for whom the concept of "writing a book" had no meaning whatsoever but "getting petted" meant everything. He would crawl up on top of the keyboard and refuse to budge until he got his much deserved share of attention. He helped me keep my perspective, reminding me of what is really important. And finally, I thank our daughter, Haley, who came into our lives at the absolute worst possible moment for this book—or so I thought. There were times in the early days of colic-induced hysteria when I was ready to give up. But strangely and cosmically, it was Haley who spurred me on. When Haley cried, I turned off the computer. As a result, my writing time became much more precious and much more focused.

On the foundation of the contributions of all these individuals, and many others not mentioned, the story that follows was built. Sometimes it was painful, tedious, and depressing. But I must admit, most of the time it was fun.

Abbreviations

ADHOC	Anti-Discrimination Housing Organizing Committee
B-PAC	Business Project Area Committee
CDBG	Community Development Block Grant
CDC	West Bank Community Development Corporation
COG	Committee for Open Government
CRA	Cedar-Riverside Associates
CRAC	Cedar-Riverside Area Council
CREDF	Cedar-Riverside Environmental Defense Fund
EIS	Environmental impact statement
ERAP	Economic Research Action Project
GMMHC	Greater Minneapolis Metropolitan Housing Corporation
HoDAG	Housing Development Action Grant
HUD	Federal Department of Housing and Urban Development
MCDA	Minneapolis Community Development Agency
MCLU	Minnesota Civil Liberties Union
MHRA	Minneapolis Housing and Redevelopment Authority
MPIRG	Minnesota Public Interest Research Group
PAC	Cedar-Riverside Project Area Committee
RPTA	Riverside Plaza Tenants Association
SDS	Students for a Democratic Society
SNCC	Student Non-violent Coordinating Committee
UCPI	University Community Properties, Incorporated
UDAG	Urban Development Action Grant
WBBA	West Bank Business Association

Defending
Community

CEDAR-RIVERSIDE NEIGHBORHOOD

1. Riverbluff neighborhood area
2. Seven Corners neighborhood area
3. University of Minnesota West Bank
4. University of Minnesota East Bank
5. Cedar Square West (Riverside Plaza)
6. Neighborhood Business District
7. Cedar East neighborhood area
8. Augsburg College
9. Fairview and St. Mary's Hospitals
10. Riverside Park neighborhood area
11. Downtown Minneapolis

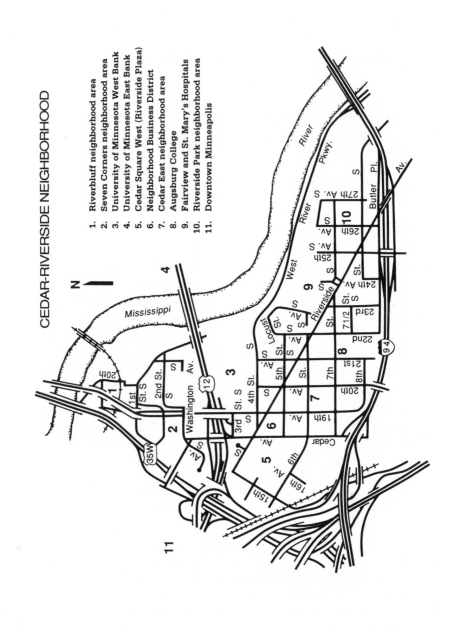

CHAPTER 1

Capital, Community, and Cedar-Riverside: An Overview

THERE we were, maybe a hundred of us, in the street clutching our gold-painted plastic spoons—our "groundbreaking shovels"—on a warm summer day in 1986. We were celebrating yet another redevelopment project beginning in our neighborhood. That we were celebrating at all was momentous. Twenty years ago no one would have given odds that this neighborhood would even still be standing. But stand it did, and the redevelopment we were marking that day was vastly different from the plans of twenty years ago. More than just the plans were different, however. Tim Mungavan, one of the leading activists in the neighborhood, walked up to the microphone and explained to us just how different it was: "The traditional groundbreaking symbol is the gold shovel. These gold spoons you are holding symbolize the fact that a lot of people came together to make this happen—a lot of people making small efforts." In contrast to urban development that is planned by the few in central offices far removed from the influence of citizens, in Cedar-Riverside we were celebrating the triumph of democracy in urban renewal planning. So there we were, occupying the street—legally, for a change—with our spoons in the air, having a good laugh and feeling the power of community.

This is the story of a community that overcame the odds against its own survival. Cedar-Riverside first triumphed by preventing the implementation of an urban renewal plan that slated the neighborhood for total demolition. And it won an even greater victory by implementing community-controlled redevelopment. This community, with initially nothing more than its commitment and savvy, was up against all the power of development capital backed by the state. Out of the encroaching concrete of a massive, high-rise housing development designed by top-down planning to serve the profit needs of a private developer rose a powerful neighborhood-based, grass-roots movement. That movement not only stopped the spread of concrete, but went on to create one of the largest community-controlled urban redevelopment projects in the country to serve the residents of the community against the profit demands of capital.

Can urban communities prevail against capital, influencing urban redevelopment to serve community needs rather than capital needs? I attempt to answer that question by tracing the history of the Cedar-Riverside community and analyzing its historical path. The Cedar-Riverside neighborhood movement expresses fully the character of neighborhood resistance in the 1960s and 1970s and the transition to neighborhood-based development in the 1980s. What happened in Cedar-Riverside happened across the country (National Commission on Neighborhoods, 1979; Henig, 1982; Mollenkopf, 1983; Checkoway, 1985; Giloth, 1985; Fainstein et al., 1986; Lenz, 1988), but rarely did the transition occur in single geographic locations, and even more rarely with such enormous stakes, involving thousands of people and millions of dollars. And Cedar-Riverside is most distinctive in that communities seldom win their defense so thoroughly. Cedar-Riverside thus provides a unique event that allows us to study fully the changing fortunes of capital and community in the struggle for the soul and turf of urban neighborhoods. Understanding Cedar-Riverside means understanding where community power comes from and how it can be used to resist domination by capital. The fact that there are regrettably few examples of successful community power (Fainstein, 1987) makes the study of Cedar-Riverside all the more important.

Community-based social movements are the least visible, least understood, and most widely practiced form of political action in North America. Small-scale, localized, community-based movements have been studied extensively by only a few (Boyte, 1980, 1984; Boyte and Riessman, 1986; Evans and Boyte, 1986; Castells, 1983; Delgado, 1986; Henig, 1982; Davis, 1991), and no common set of theoretical questions has guided that research (Posner, 1990). Neighborhood movements have not captured our attention nearly so much as the 1960s national-level civil rights, student/antiwar, and women's movements. And yet the total impact of small-scale community mobilizations in stopping neighborhood destruction in the guise of urban renewal, and expanding community control over local circumstances, has been substantial. Too many scholars continue to deem worthy of study only those social movements that are national or regional in scope and highly visible in mobilization. As a result, researchers focus on the past and the visible while discrediting the importance of community-based mobilization, even when such efforts were the genesis for their favorite movements, as Aldon Morris (1984) has shown so convincingly for the civil rights movement.

What we are witnessing is, in Charles Tilly's (1984) terms, a shift in the "repertoire of collective action." In the second half of the twentieth century we have been party to a change in the class struggle. As capitalist-labor struggles that were centered on the shop floor became institutionalized and rule-bound through the acceptance of unions, the locus of struggle moved. Increasingly into the late twentieth century, social movements and citizen protests have been neither derived from clear class antagonisms nor directly focused on class issues (Katznelson, 1981; Harvey, 1978; Touraine, 1988; Čapek and Gilderbloom, 1992). The class dynamics of capitalism continue to generate the issues around which citizens mobilize, but the issues are generated at the output end of capitalism rather than at the input end. Instead of organizing as workers over issues related to the control of production, people are organizing as citizens and consumers around issues related to their social roles in reproducing themselves outside work. This is more than a "displaced class struggle" (Harvey, 1978), since the shift from organizing around production issues to organizing around reproduction issues no longer pits a working class directly against a capitalist class, but may pit the working class and the professional class against each other, or unite them; it may separate the poor and the working class. This urban organizing has, in Manuel Castells's (1977) terms, a "'pluri-class' nature."

Localized social movements centered in urban neighborhoods, which are often struggling for control of land, provision of services, and community autonomy, are a classic case of this new social movement form. Cedar-Riversiders were once told by a New Town supporter that "this land is too valuable to have *you people* living on it." When land is commodified, when service provision is dependent on local and national economic circumstances, and when community autonomy requires economic self-sufficiency, the dynamics of capitalism are intimately involved in the struggle. Thus, *community* becomes the new site of class resistance—of resistance to the commodification of neighborhoods—even though community citizens do not express their struggle in class terms.

These new social movements have become located not in classes, then, but in class-structured communities. African Americans, women, students, and especially neighborhoods may be located in particular places in the class structure. These groups, however, mobilize not on behalf of a class consciousness but on behalf of a community consciousness. That was especially true in the case of Cedar-Riverside. As the community formed around a variety of radical theories, including Marxism, residents organized with a highly developed critique of capitalism—not as workers, but as neighborhood residents who were seeing their housing and community services threatened by a capitalist developer working with the endorsement and financial backing of the state. On the foundation of these radical theories the residents built a vibrant alternative culture. And they happened to be located on land that both capital and the state considered crucial for purposes other than community building.

Cedar-Riverside: Background

Cedar-Riverside, named after the two main avenues that intersect in the neighborhood, is situated on top of some of the most valuable real estate in Minneapolis. The neighborhood lies just across the freeway from the city's central business district. It is also adjacent to the University of Minnesota's "West Bank" campus, on the west side of the Mississippi River across from the "main" campus, leading many residents to refer to the area as the "West Bank."[1]

Cedar-Riverside was increasingly cut off from the rest of the city through the 1950s and 1960s by the construction of the Interstate 94 freeway along its southern border and the Interstate 35W freeway along its western border. The Mississippi River completed the neighborhood's isolation, intersecting with I-35W at the northern tip of the neighborhood and with I-94 at the eastern tip. Cedar-Riverside was one of the most clearly demarcated neighborhoods in the Twin Cities.

Within that tightly bounded three-hundred-acre triangle are four distinct residential areas. In the north end of the neighborhood is Seven Corners, named after its main intersection—until the late 1980s a severely underdesigned octopus emptying three thoroughfares into Cedar-Riverside. It is the "compromise" section of the neighborhood, where activists allowed a high-rise hotel and medium-density apartments to be constructed in order to save the rest of the neighborhood and create tax-increment funds for its rehabilitation. Seven Corners is set off from the rest of the neighborhood by the West Bank of the University of Minnesota on its southern side.

To the south of Seven Corners, in the southwest section of the neighborhood, rise the concrete towers of Cedar Square West, later renamed Riverside Plaza. An eleven-building complex looming as high as thirty-nine stories over the neighborhood, Cedar Square West was the development around which the battle for the neighborhood erupted. The bare concrete towers, punctured only by windows and randomly scattered, weather worn blue, red, and yellow panels, rise above this neighborhood of single-family and duplex housing like a mad architect's vision of the ultimate in college dormitory life. But Riverside Plaza is no dormitory. In fact, it was only the first stage of what was to be a ten-stage "New Town in Town" urban renewal project that would stuff thirty thousand people into a three-hundred-acre space. With an urban renewal plan created by city government, the project was to be implemented by a private developer supported by local capital and the federal Department of Housing and Urban Development (HUD). Riverside Plaza is all that remains of those grand plans. But even so, the complex houses about half the neighborhood's approximately 7,800 residents.

One block south of Riverside Plaza are the senior citizens' high rises, which continue the theme of high-density residential living. This complex began as public housing for senior citizens, but it gradually became transformed into public housing for the mentally ill population as well, leading to increasing conflicts. The young residents organized cultural, educational, and social services for the residents of the complex, but this segment of the neighborhood remained relatively separated from the political storms that raged on the West Bank.

Commercial activity radiates out from the intersection of Cedar and Riverside avenues, where Riverside Plaza, Seven Corners, the University of Minnesota, and the "old neighborhood" come together. This intersection is also the location of the New Riverside Cafe, the early center of militancy in the neighborhood.

The "old neighborhood," made up of predominantly single-family and duplex housing beginning across Cedar Avenue from Riverside Plaza and stretching east, was saved from the bulldozer and rehabilitated by the residents. The old neighborhood is divided into two sections. Cedar East is directly across the street from Cedar Square West and is bordered by the University of Minnesota on the north.

Riverside Park is isolated on the extreme eastern corner of the neighborhood, cut off by Augsburg College and St. Mary's and Riverside hospitals. It is the "suburbs" of the West Bank, separated from the bar traffic, congestion, and crime that spread out from the business district on the west side of the neighborhood.

Overall, the Cedar-Riverside neighborhood is a unique place. In the 1960s many of the residents were hippies, beatniks, and student activists, breaking away from the working-class and middle-class roots of their parents. The "Haight-Ashbury of the Midwest," Cedar-Riverside was a national center for the counter culture. But in contrast to many other counter cultural centers that withered away or turned into upscale boutique neighborhoods, Cedar-Riverside institutionalized much of its alternative character. The activists of the 1960s stayed on in the neighborhood and brought a mature community into the 1990s. It is also an urban community that exerts significant influence over its fate and continually strives to provide an alternative local culture and even a local economy.

In the 1990s you can still find the 1960s in Cedar-Riverside. When you walk north along Cedar Avenue, you may stop at the West Bank Co-op Grocery,[2] buy jewelry from a street vendor, take in the sounds of a street musician, or browse in one of the shops selling exotic clothing. At the corner of Cedar and Riverside avenues is the New Riverside Cafe, where you can feast on vegetarian meals prepared by a self-proclaimed anarchist collective. Next door is KFAI "Fresh Air" radio, Minneapolis's only alternative radio station. If you continue down Riverside Avenue a couple of blocks, you come to an intersection occupied by the People's Center, the Meridel Le Sueur Center for Peace and Justice, and St. Martin's Table, all of which are committed to various forms of alternative community services and political activism. Farther down Riverside is yet another co-op grocery, North Country Food Co-op, which is worker-controlled (as opposed to the West Bank Co-op, which is consumer-controlled) and emphasizes organic foods.

If you turn into the neighborhood residential areas, you pass through blocks of single-family homes, duplexes, and townhouses that appear brand new. Many of these buildings are not new, however, but have been rebuilt from top to bottom and inside out, often with the frame and the woodwork the only original equipment. And all the homes are superinsulated against the harsh Minnesota winters.

In Seven Corners and the old neighborhood the residents controlled the planning of rehabilitation and replacement of some 555 units of housing, more than half of which were single-family, duplex, or townhouse buildings, involving nearly $13 million in funds. This redevelopment was conducted with a rigid "no-displacement" policy and an eye toward affordability which preserved half the units for low-income residents, including 103 federally subsidized "Section 8" units. All the units are controlled by the neighborhood through leasehold cooperative or management cooperative housing contracts, providing secure and affordable housing for nearly two thousand neighborhood residents (Brighton Development Corporation, 1990).

Capital and Community: A Contradiction in Urban Renewal

In attempting to understand how the people of Cedar-Riverside could so dramatically influence the course of urban redevelopment in their neighborhood, this book provides a much needed integration of two veins of research: the new urban sociology and the sociology of social movements.[3] The new urban sociology literature gives us a perspective on urban dynamics that focuses on the role of powerful economic actors and economic structures that were sorely neglected by previous urban theories. New urban sociologists are centrally concerned with the character of power and inequality in the city: how the capitalist accumulation process and its accompanying crisis tendencies and capital-labor struggles shape the city, the interaction between capital and the state in arranging urban space, and the role of structure and agency in effecting urban social change (Zukin, 1980; Gottdeiner and Feagin, 1988). The social movements literature forces us to recognize the tasks involved in organizing citizens to attain power, asking questions about how social movements form and organize, how they recruit members, how they choose and use tactics, and what determines whether they succeed or fail.

Until now, attempts to study urban neighborhood mobilization have emphasized one or the other of these perspectives. The recent research on neighborhood movements in the new urban sociology tradition (N. Fainstein and S. Fainstein, 1974; Lowe, 1986; Davis, 1991) has emphasized urban structures and power brokers in attempting to explain urban insurgency, building diverse theories of urban social movements almost without a reference to the two decades of social movement theory that has developed. Social movement theory, on the other hand, has dealt with every movement, local or national, large or small, right wing or left wing, as if somehow the same explanatory framework is adequate.

In this book I show that neither perspective can explain why sometimes capital wins in struggles for the control of urban turf and why at other times communities persevere. Consequently, I steer an integrated course between those two perspectives, arguing, like Manuel Castells (1977, 1978, 1983), that the city is formed from struggle that is shaped, but not determined, by the class structure. It is also not dominated by economic elites, but neither is it a fair fight, since power is not as easily accessible to less class-privileged actors, even when they are organized.

We must integrate the new urban sociology and social movements theory primarily because neither can, by itself, explain the events of Cedar-Riverside. With a history spanning nearly three decades, the story of Cedar-Riverside shows how communities can fall victim to urban redevelopment that is planned from the top down and that displaces existing communities to produce profit rather than to serve community needs. A redevelopment plan sponsored by the City of Minneapolis designated the neighborhood an Urban Renewal District and specified that the existing neighborhood would be demolished and replaced by high-density housing to be constructed by a private developer. When Keith Heller entered the scene with the New Town plan, the Cedar-Riverside community lost four blocks of housing to Cedar Square West.

The history of Cedar-Riverside also shows, however, how communities can organize to resist urban redevelopment imposed from without. There were nine more Cedar Square Wests planned for the neighborhood, but none survived the neighborhood resistance. Neighborhood activists developed innovative strategies and tactics that used environmental law to obtain a court injunction against further construction, undermining the economic and political support for the New Town plan. And the history finally shows how a neighborhood with a will to survive and an alternative vision can conduct urban redevelopment that is affordable, prevents displacement, is democratically planned, and supports the community. Once the New Town plan had been defeated, residents set about the hard work of doing their own redevelopment planning, securing as much capital and state cooperation as possible to finance the rehabilitation, and overseeing the development itself. But this late history also shows that capital still imposes limits on what communities can do. Residents increasingly found that they had to trade community control for adequate financing: the more they relied on capital and government funding sources, the less control they could exert over the redevelopment.

The conflict between capital and community is described by the new urban sociologists (Logan and Molotch, 1987; Feagin and Parker, 1990; Castells, 1983; Lowe, 1986) as a conflict between use values and exchange values. Following the basic Marxist distinction between use values as the production of goods and services for one's own use and exchange values as the production of goods and services to exchange with others, these researchers show how capitalists and their supporters view the city in terms of its worth in an exchange relationship, while city residents view it in terms of its usefulness in providing services, sustenance, and quality of life. Thus, capitalists support urban development that will increase the chances of further commodifying urban land and infrastructure toward making a profit, while citizens press for urban development that preserves urban land and infrastructure for their use and supports their community (Mollenkopf, 1981; Cox, 1981). A city park, for example, offers use values for its citizens—provided for all and available for all. But that park cannot generate profit unless it is privately owned and its land exchanged for rent or sale to those who can afford the price. Thus, every time that a use value is transformed into an exchange value, the community becomes deprived of that resource.[4]

The conflict between capitalist exchange values and community use values is most obviously expressed in disputes over urban redevelopment. This type of conflict centers on the distinction between top-down, capital-conscious urban redevelopment and democratic, community-based urban redevelopment. In order to transform use values into exchange values, community objections must be effectively silenced. As a result, urban redevelopment in the city is typically planned from the top down by the minions of corporate and government leaders. Even though they may not represent the interests of a particular capitalist developer, they are carefully *conscious* of capital's profit requirements and the city's dependence on capital for fiscal health, jobs, and overall stability. These redevelopment plans are then imposed on community citizens with only token opportunities for review. Often the redevelopment displaces communities by bulldozing them or, more insidiously, by hastening community deterioration through diverting funds away from urban neighborhoods. The alternative to top-down, capital-conscious urban redevelopment is redevelopment whose plans are generated by the residents of those neighborhood communities through their direct participation in a democratic planning process based in their neighborhood. Of course, these two forms of urban redevelopment produce very different projects. Top-down, capital-conscious urban redevelopment produces immense, high-density, capital-intensive projects based on the hope for massive profits. Democratic, community-based urban redevelopment produces smaller, human-scale development that is much less able to generate high profits. In Cedar-Riverside the choice was between a developer's plan for housing thirty thousand residents in a three-hundred-acre space, or the community's housing and commercial rehabilitation plan to serve the four thousand or so residents who lived in the single-family homes and duplexes at the time.

To grasp fully the course of the struggle between capital and community, between exchange values and use values, and between top-down, capital-conscious development and democratic, community-based development, we must understand three concepts: the growth coalition, the community-based social movement, and the context in which the struggle takes place—the political opportunity structure.

Capital in the City and the Growth Coalition

Capital, the organized economic power of capitalists, built the great cities of the modern age. Whether labeled great industrialists or notorious robber barons, there is no disputing that it was those who controlled capital who designed and built the enormous steel mills, gleaming skyscrapers, massive feats of transportation technology and engineering, museums, universities, sports complexes, and everything else about which we marvel in the city. Capitalists have defined the shape and the quality of the city through modern history, deciding which neighborhoods would prosper and which would be destroyed, which workers would work and which would not, and what the city would become. And often they did this against the interests and sometimes the open rebellions of the citizens of those cities.

Little changed after World War II with the advent of the federal urban renewal programs to remove blighted neighborhoods long starved of capital. Since the start of federally sponsored urban renewal in the 1950s, capital has been its overwhelming beneficiary. From its beginnings in New Haven, Connecticut, where predominantly African-American housing was demolished for highway expansion and downtown retail development (N. Fainstein and S. Fainstein, 1986b; Domhoff, 1983), to today, when redevelopment dollars go to build mostly vacant office towers rather than housing for the homeless, urban renewal has directly or indirectly undermined urban communities. Urban planning has historically reflected a strong consciousness of the needs of capital and has created projects reflecting those needs—either directly through wiping out neighborhoods to build profit-based or tax-supported institutions, indirectly through wiping out neighborhoods to build infrastructure such as freeways, or in consequence through directing government dollars into urban redevelopment projects to benefit capitalists in downtowns rather than residents in neighborhoods. Urban capital's exchange-value orientation demands high-density, high-profit, and centrally controlled urban renewal. And though this often means that urban capitalists are directly involved in both the planning and the carrying out of urban renewal, that is not always the case. In fact, they can exert nearly as much influence indirectly as directly, because government is so "capital conscious," that is, aware of its dependence on capital and aware of capitalists' ability to move to the best "business climate" (Molotch, 1979; Logan and Molotch, 1987; Friedland and Palmer, 1984; Feagin and Parker, 1990). Thus, government, particularly local government, often acts as a capital-conscious agent in planning urban redevelopment that will retain and attract capital even if capital itself is not involved in the planning (Logan and Molotch, 1987; Friedland, 1983).

One of the strongest forms of capital control of urban redevelopment is the "growth coalition."[5] Portraying the city as a "growth machine," John Logan and Harvey Molotch (1987; also see Molotch, 1976) discuss the role of a variety of actors in the city who come together as a growth coalition to support urban growth, whether by providing services and other favorable investment conditions or by promoting the city's image. The main goal, for capitalists, is to increase the exchange value of land by intensifying land use and creating population growth (Domhoff, 1983; Lyon et al., 1981). Realtors, city institutions, corporations, media, and a variety of other capital actors also benefit immensely from urban growth (Logan and Molotch, 1987). In the process of forming a growth coalition, capitalists are able to achieve strategic access to local political parties and local government to promote their agenda outside the normal democratic process (Friedland, 1980). And politicians acquiesce, even though the increased costs in expanded city services, infrastructure repair and updating, and loss of tax revenue through tax abatement and other concessions made to corporations to produce growth often result in a net loss in city fiscal health. Labor unions also support top-down, capital-conscious urban renewal, falling victim to promises of jobs for their members—promises that are typically inflated and jobs that are often temporary. In fact, it appears that growth benefits everyone involved in the city except its residents, who have to suffer the pollution, social disruption, community displacement, competition for jobs, and pressure on infrastructure that come with growth.

The degree of power of a growth coalition to pursue its growth agenda and externalize the costs of growth on disenfranchised communities is variable. According to Roger Friedland (1980), capitalists have three possible sources of power on the urban stage. They have power through participation in local politics as interest groups, institutionalized influence in city government on boards and committees, and leverage over policy through their control of the local economy. When a growth coalition brings all three of these sources of power together to dominate the agenda of local government, it creates an "urban regime"—"an informal yet relatively stable group with access to institutional resources that enable it to have a sustained role in making governing decisions" (Stone, 1989:5). Growth-oriented regimes are difficult to oppose because they achieve the status of a governing force based on the enormous resources of economic wealth gathered by their corporate members and their control over local investment activity. Regimes can also be populist or progressive and thereby respond more to citizen interests. But this regime type is difficult to sustain without unified support from citizens through a system of patronage, strong ideological commitment, or a widespread and tightly organized network of community-based organizations (Stone, 1987).

Growth coalitions are not always able to achieve the status of a stable urban regime, however. Although we do not know a great deal about why growth coalitions can fail,[6] capital faces two problems in pursuing its growth agenda. The first problem is maintaining the local state's membership in, or support for, the growth coalition. The local state is a central capital-conscious player in holding the growth coalition together, if only because the planning process must be approved by various local government offices. Often, however, local government also has to go out and take the heat for the costs the development will impose on citizens. Essentially, the local state is caught between supporting capital accumulation and maintaining political legitimation through also providing "social reproduction" or "collective consumption" services—food, clothing, shelter, care—for citizens. The local state must maintain some semblance of democracy, and to cave in too quickly undermines the authority of local representatives. As the volume and power of community-based groups increase, it becomes more and more difficult for local government blatantly to support a progrowth project that is clearly anticommunity. Thus, the local state is not completely free to support capital's growth agenda unconditionally while ignoring the citizenry (Lauria, 1986; Stone, 1989; Stoecker and Schmidbauer, 1991; Elkin, 1987).[7] But it is even less able to support citizen communities against capital's growth agenda, since the mobility of individual capitalists allows them to hold the city's economic vitality hostage and enforce capital-consciousness on city hall. Capitalists can simply threaten to move out of the city, taking with them the jobs and tax base the local government is dependent on, unless their growth agenda prevails as public policy. Aside from mass citizen mobilization, about all that can block this influence are accumulation crises, in which capitalists overproduce, workers are laid off, the city coffers dry up, city services are cut, and citizens revolt (Harvey, 1978, 1985).

The other important problem faced by growth coalitions is that they are composed of actors whose individual interests are always potentially in conflict. It is often difficult for capitalists to agree on just what will facilitate growth. For example, the local rentier class, living off real estate investments and normally in favor of development, may oppose particular forms of growth fostered by large corporations (Molotch and Logan, 1984). And with limited markets, any increase in one market comes at the potential contraction of another. Capitalists are in a competitive relationship with regard to one another. Although they often call a truce for the purposes of attempting to expand markets overall, such agreements last only as long as all actors in the coalition define continued cooperation as in their individual self-interest. Thus, the growth coalition is prone to factioning, as individual capitalists may have different interests or may change their definition of what is in their self-interest (Domhoff, 1983; Feagin and Parker, 1990; Jenkins and Brents, 1989).

The divisions among capitalist members of the growth coalition are numerous, cross-cutting, and unpredictable. Early in the formulation of the growth-coalition concept, Molotch (1979) seemed to argue that multinational corporations were not as involved in growth coalitions as local capital, especially rentier capital. But other research disputes this notion (Morlock, 1974; Friedland, 1980), and some analysts hypothesize that big capital with local headquarters and locally residing professionals and executives is more likely to become interested in growth coalitions (Friedland and Palmer, 1984; Berger et al., 1992). To the extent that big capital does get involved in promoting growth, it may run up against opposition from rentier capital. Growth supported by big capital takes over or overruns small local firms without producing the spin-off growth most beneficial to rentiers (Molotch and Logan, 1984). Banks may also be difficult growth-coalition partners, since they do not necessarily concentrate their loans on local growth-coalition projects but instead focus on lending to other big capital that may not produce local benefits (Ratcliff, 1980). There are also distinct divisions within local capital: industrial, finance, merchant, and property capital (Fleischmann and Feagin, 1987), with property capital perhaps divided into development capital and construction capital (Feagin and Parker, 1990). Such divisions, though not inherently antagonistic, represent the possible sources of growth-coalition tensions.

Understanding the role of these two qualities of the growth coalition—the potentially democratic character of government, and capital fractions in the growth coalition—helps us work toward knowledge of how growth coalitions may succeed or fail. But we cannot achieve that knowledge by studying the growth coalition by itself. We must also explore the role played by the organized resistance of communities in the growth machine's path. For it is that developing resistance that has the capacity to attack the growth coalition's structural weaknesses. Understanding how communities might attack those structural weaknesses requires understanding the character of "community."

Community in the City

Against the growth coalition stands the community. The attempts to convince citizens that top-down, capital-conscious redevelopment is good for everyone are numerous and well funded. But those who stand in the path of urban renewal, who will lose their homes, their neighbors, and literally their communities—who have to pay the "externalities" of such redevelopment—are often not swayed by the glossy propaganda.

What is the community we are so concerned about displacing? Larry Lyon (1987) sees community as having three basic structural elements: a geographic area, common ties among members, and interaction among members. These are necessary but not sufficient conditions. In all the classic definitions of community, theorists and philosophers have emphasized the presence of common values and emotions—what Harry Boyte (1984) refers to as "communal ties" centered on values of cooperation, mutual aid, "closeness," and a shared culture that is exclusive to the community. Lyon's structural characteristics and Boyte's cultural characteristics provide the underpinning for the six factors that Logan and Molotch (1987) find in strong neighborhood communities: "a focal point in which one's daily needs are satisfied"; the availability of informal support networks; "a sense of physical and psychic security"; an identity; "agglomeration benefits," unique services provided because enough demand has concentrated in the neighborhood; and a shared ethnicity. I emphasize the importance of the qualities of community along with the location of that community in a specific geographic space. Space plays a significant role in struggles between growth coalitions and the neighborhood communities in their paths and, as we will see, affects the dynamics of the conflict in important ways (Čapek and Gilderbloom, 1992).

Community has been an issue of study for social researchers ever since the industrial revolution and the beginnings of sociology. As capitalism and industrialization destroyed rural community life and forced citizens into cities for survival, many analysts feared that the bonds that made social life predictable and orderly would disintegrate. Ferdinand Töennies (1963 [1887]) described the transition as a shift from "gemeinschaft"—in which the individual was one with the community, identifying with its traditions, customs, and values without question—to "gesellschaft"—in which the individual separated from the community and managed relationships from a perspective of rationality, disregarding traditional norms and morality. For Emile Durkheim (1964 [1893]), traditional life was based on "mechanical" solidarity, in which the members of the community were not distinguished by separate roles and practiced a strict conformity to cultural values. Industrialization created "organic" solidarity, in which the diversity of individuals occupying distinct roles and adopting divergent values was held together only by the interdependence of their roles.

It was the city where the fears of a gesellschaft lifestyle allowing only organic solidarity were concentrated. For Georg Simmel (1950 [1905]), it was in the city that all relationships were reduced to rational monetary relationships and individuals became emotionally cut off from one another. By the 1930s in the United States, Louis Wirth (1938) was echoing Simmel's concern, arguing that as city populations became larger, more dense, and more heterogeneous, the emphasis on individualism and the destruction of community ties increased.

The fear of the disintegration of community in the city continued into the 1950s with "community power" studies (Hunter, 1953; Dahl, 1961) that were concerned not so much with community as traditional bonds but with community as the web of power relationships and governing structures across the entire city. "Community" had become synonymous with "the city" and was no longer connected to the gemeinschaft quality of community life. Gemeinschaft community had become, analysis argued, "eclipsed" in the city (Stein, 1960), with a concomitant loss of cultural unity and "little sense of belonging, or feeling of identification, or intimate association with others" (Ross, 1955:4).

These analysts, along with many others, decried the existence of "subcultures" that, for them, were both cause and consequence of the loss of the city as a community. Convinced of the practicability of the melting-pot mythology, these researchers saw the persistence of independent, neighborhood-based communities as a tragedy. And in some ways, their evaluation was correct. As some urban neighborhoods, through either their class power or their race power, concentrated their efforts on preventing other neighborhood-based communities from gaining access to resources, or preventing "outsiders" from living or working within the neighborhood's boundaries, racism and class oppression was reinforced.

Other researchers, however, noticed that community was absent only at the most superficial level of analysis. At a deeper level of study of the city, one could find vibrant ethnic neighborhoods of tight community networks, stable traditions, and emotional security. Classic works by Herbert Gans (1982 [1962]), William Whyte (1943), Carol Stack (1974), and numerous others explored how poor people, ethnic groups, impoverished women, and traditional communities survived in the city in spite of forces that attempted to erode their bonds. Even in the most oppressed and exploited neighborhoods, the strong bonds of community were evident, as Stack (1974) showed. The sharing of members' resources, the cooperative work that generated community resources, and the mutual emotional and physical support provided by members, though invisible to the outside world, was a necessity for survival in the community that Stack studied. The invisibility of neighborhood-based communities, as well as their lack of legitimacy from the perspective of the melting-pot mythology, are what makes community studies of neighborhoods so important. And increasingly, those studies are of communities of resistance which recognize neighborhoods as the site of both community and political action in the city

(Henig, 1982; Fisher, 1984; Wylie, 1989; Davis, 1991; Saltman, 1¢

While capital builds cities through building exchange values,
zens build neighborhood communities through building use val
But like capitalists, who require a profit, or "surplus," to invest in ᴜᵢᵗy
building, citizens also require a form of "surplus" to succeed in community building. True communities take responsibility for providing
use values for their members: community services, celebrations, care
for the sick, support for those in crisis, and resources for the needy
all must come from a surplus that other members of the community
are able to provide through their wages or volunteer labor (Stoecker,
1992; Laslett, 1981). Thus, when communities attempt to influence
urban planning, it is to bring small shop owners back into their neighborhood commercial district, rehabilitate their housing, and support
community-based services to build the community surplus. But none
of this redevelopment generates the substantial profits attractive to
capitalists, and it in fact stands as a barrier to the unfettered expansion of capital because it prevents the transformation of community
resources into exchange values.

The conflict between capital and community is not only over material resources, however. It is a conflict between fundamental values
of urban cultural diversity, political participation, and the satisfaction of collective consumption needs (Castells, 1983). Capital requires
a growth consensus managed by centralized authority that emphasizes state support for the production of profit. Communities attempt
to maintain autonomous urban subcultures, struggle for political decentralization to allow for political self-management, and strive for
sustainable community services and an urban infrastructure that supports community life. The struggle between capital and community
is rooted not simply in a material contradiction, then, but also in definitions over what is right, what is good, what is humane, and what is
just. The struggle over high-density versus low-density living is not
just about material costs and profits, but about the ability to maintain
community under each condition. The debate over top-down versus
community-based planning is about fundamental values of democracy and respect for diversity: not just the material turf of urban
neighborhoods, but its cultural soul.

Community as Social Movement

Although culture may be the central defining quality of a strong
community, culture is not enough in and of itself to allow communities to win in struggles over urban redevelopment. To defend them-

selves against the pressures of top-down, capital-conscious urban re-development, communities must mobilize as social movements. That means they must be able to recruit participants for research, demonstrations, negotiations, planning, and a variety of other tasks related to fighting outside threats. They must also be able to organize those participants into a structure that will make the most efficient and effective use of their resources. And finally, they must be able to employ tactics that will allow them to achieve their goals. Research in social movements offers many, often contradictory, answers to the question of how to provide these three ingredients. Ultimately, each one poses a dilemma for social movements, since it appears to require the movement to choose from contradictory alternatives.

Recruiting members to a movement requires both getting people involved and keeping them involved. Movement recruiters often "frame" the movement's issues to appeal to the potential member's values and world view (Snow et al., 1986) and then provide an individual incentive to join up. As demonstrated in the "free rider" problem (Olson, 1965), it is not in any individual's self-interest to contribute to the provision of a collective good such as a clean environment, peace, or a saved neighborhood. Instead, potential members must receive an individual reward for becoming involved. But individual incentives maintain commitment only until the member receives the reward (Bailis, 1974; Piven and Cloward, 1979) and may fail to maintain commitment to "high-risk activism" (McAdam, 1986; Wandersman et al., 1987).[8]

A potential resolution to this dilemma is to employ "solidary incentives" (Wilson, 1973), which maintain commitment to the people in the movement rather than to the movement itself, essentially creating a movement community. When groups, rather than individuals, are recruited to a movement, the social relationships that maintain the group also can maintain involvement in the movement (Oberschall, 1973; Snow, Zurcher, and Ekland-Olson, 1980; Fine and Stoecker, 1985). Creating community, then, may be the best way to increase recruitment and commitment, and can hold a movement together even when it is in "abeyance" (Taylor, 1989). In a true neighborhood community that provides a focal point, support network, security, identity, agglomeration benefits, and a shared culture (Logan and Molotch, 1987), these solidary incentives already exist. Building community, then, builds solidary incentives.

The dilemma of organizing members is problematic both for the overall social movement and for individual social movement organizations. Organizing at either level can be centralized or decentralized. At the social movement level, Luther Gerlach and Virginia Hine (1970; Gerlach, 1976, 1983) argue that social movements typically adopt a movement structure of many leaders (decentralization) and many organizations (segmentation) with overlapping communication networks (reticulation).[9] This "DSR" structure is said to limit the effects of repression and failure of any movement segment, maximize diversity of strategies and tactics, and create rivalries between movement segments which increase the effort of each segment. This structure restricts coordination of the entire movement, however (Dwyer, 1983; McAdam, 1982:186). William Gamson (1975), in contrast, advocates a centralized and bureaucratic movement structure, centered on a single movement organization. He argues that this structure produces greater movement efficiency and coordination and reduces movement factioning.

The same dilemma occurs at the level of the social movement organization. Centralization increases efficiency (Gamson, 1975:89; Breines, 1980; Staggenborg, 1989b) and provides the added advantage of maintaining relations with establishment groups and funders (Jenkins, 1985; Staggenborg, 1988). Centralized organizations are subject to oligarchy and goal displacement, however, as the leaders become more concerned with maintaining their own power than with meeting the original movement goals (Michels, 1962 [1915]; Katovich, Weiland, and Couch, 1981). Decentralized organizations, by providing for greater involvement of members, better mobilize membership (Zald and Ash, 1966), increase strategic and tactical innovation and flexibility (Staggenborg, 1988, 1989b), and better develop member talents (Yates, 1973:79). But decentralized organizations can also become oligarchical if they are not formally structured (Staggenborg, 1989b; Rothschild-Whitt, 1979; Freeman, 1972–73), and they are less able to respond quickly to new crises and opportunities (Breines, 1980).

As with managing the recruitment dilemma, managing the organizing dilemma necessitates addressing the issue of community. The profession of community organizing is, essentially, about creating community. Saul Alinsky (1971) said that there is no such thing as a "disorganized community." Thus, the community is already organized, and if it has the characteristics of a true community, it is neither very centralized nor very bureaucratized, and the imposition of a rigid hierarchical structure on top of that community structure may create power struggles within the community. But not creating more formalized movement organizations may inhibit the community's ability to confront outside threats. An organized movement must be built from an organized community—connected, yet distinct, as we will see.

The tactical dilemma that all social movements face is fairly straightforward. Movements need both favorable policy decisions and resources from the outside world, including the news media, the public, and antagonists (Barkan, 1979). The impoverished rarely have resources to withhold or negotiate with, and bargaining is dependent on having something to bargain with (Turner, 1970). Disruptive tactics, including actions such as rent strikes for localized movements, do produce victories and sometimes are the only means of doing so (Shlay and Faulkner, 1984; N. Fainstein and S. Fainstein, 1974; Gamson, 1975; Lamb, 1975; Steedly and Foley, 1979). But the fear of repression makes militant tactics difficult to organize (Lowe, 1986), and such practices risk alienating moderate allies, who may then cut off resources to the movement (Schumacher, 1978; Barkan, 1986). Moderate tactics, such as informational pickets, negotiation, or lobbying, will not alienate moderate allies but may have little or no effect in slowing down the movement's target (Piven and Cloward, 1977).

A strong community may be better able to control members' fears and reduce the need for outside resources. The more that community members feel protected by the community, know their children will be cared for if the demonstration lands them in jail, and are supported and joined in militant action by others in the community, the more likely they may engage in those militant actions. The willingness of large numbers of Clamshell Alliance members to go to jail for their blockade of the Seabrook nuclear power plant, for example, was achieved with the community created by small "affinity groups," whose memberships remained stable and served as an immediate support group throughout the struggle against Seabrook (Barkan, 1979).

Capital, Community, and the Political Opportunity Structure

The struggle between capital and community plays itself out on the urban stage amid a variety of other characters. We can refer to this stage as the *political opportunity structure*. First coined by Peter Eisinger (1973) to help explain the outcomes of urban social movements, then picked up and elaborated by Sidney Tarrow (1983), this concept is useful for setting the stage. Briefly, the political opportunity structure refers to the openness or closure of political institutions, the stability of political alignments, and the availability of allies for ıflicting actors.

The government, or "state," plays a central role in the political opportunity structure. Some analysts define the political opportunity structure as synonymous with the state (Kitschelt, 1986). It is the state that directly affects how much access various groups have to the overall political process and determines what kinds of political alliances are available. And it is the state where political stability or instability ultimately expresses itself. In urban redevelopment it is the state that must adjudicate between the competing interests of capital and community.

Ultimately, however, the political opportunity structure is broader than the state, since political access is also determined by access to political parties or access to groups that themselves have obtained access to the political process. Though the state is the target of political pressure, it does not by itself control access to the political process. Capital-community struggles over urban redevelopment, then, are struggles to gain allies for one's cause, to obtain access to political institutions, and to align the political process in one's favor. The political opportunity structure is not necessarily a neutral stage, however, and it often provides more support for capital than for neighborhood-based communities. Growth coalitions, particularly when they include important actors in local government, bias the political opportunity structure in capital's favor. With media, major institutions, government, and even some citizen groups such as labor unions signed onto the growth coalition, community-based groups may find political institutions inaccessible and political alignments arrayed against them. When the inaccessibility and antagonistic alliances are cemented in a stable political environment, there is little room for discussion of alternatives to top-down, capital-conscious redevelopment.

The only chance for communities to resist top-down, capital-conscious urban redevelopment and implement democratic community-based redevelopment is for them to achieve access to the political opportunity structure in such a way as to gain resources to use in organizing as a social movement and disrupting the growth coalition. It was this task that Cedar-Riverside activists were able to accomplish.

Cedar-Riverside as a Case Study: Data and Methods

What can we learn from a single, unique neighborhood about the general struggle over urban renewal between communities and capital?

n fact, the unique situations that are best suited for theoretical
ration, because this is where we can best see these "theoreti-
processes occurring (Mitchell, 1983). My purpose is to show the
fic causal connections between the varying degrees of success
of a neighborhood movement's attempts to resist top-down, capital-
conscious urban redevelopment, and the political opportunity structure in which it operates. It is in tracing these causal connections that
the case study works best, because cause and effect can be directly
observed, rather than being inferred from commonality of occurrence
across cases (Stoecker, 1991a; Sayer, 1984). Thus, the specific cause-
effect relationships of the interaction of the political opportunity
structure and the movement become clear.

Tracing the path of the Cedar-Riverside neighborhood movement
as a single case history also provides the advantage of not needing to
address the "noise" introduced by comparing entirely different movements, each of which has at least partly unique political opportunity
structures. The history of the neighborhood movement provides for a
careful comparison between a changing social movement form and a
changing political opportunity structure. In Cedar-Riverside, the local
organized support within the political opportunity structure for top-
down, capital-conscious urban renewal went from tightly organized,
to disorganized, and finally to partly reorganized in support of democratic, community-based development as neighborhood activism expanded and developed. Thus, I can show the process and causes of
change in both the movement and the political opportunity structure.

Cedar-Riverside is an ideal-type neighborhood movement. Its complete history as a neighborhood defense movement and then a
neighborhood-based development movement exemplifies the transition in neighborhood movements from community organizing to
community-based redevelopment across the country. Because of its
uniqueness, Cedar-Riverside deserves to be studied as a model by critics of top-down, capital-conscious urban redevelopment and by advocates of democratic, community-based urban redevelopment. Two decades of successes and mistakes leave much to be emulated and much
to be improved on. The story of Cedar-Riverside allows one to study
those successes and mistakes through multiple movement stages. The
unique feature of this movement, which makes it most relevant as
a complete example of neighborhood organizing, is that it not only
halted urban redevelopment, but also created urban redevelopment.

In following the historical trajectory of community activism in
Cedar-Riverside, I used the multiple-method, case-study research

strategy widely advocated for community studies (Castells, 1983; Henig, 1982; Luxton, 1980). My task was made easier by the wealth of data that has accumulated from the earliest moments of the movement. In my six years of research, I met and interviewed central activists, more peripheral residents, and government officials. I read through reams of written material in the establishment press, the neighborhood newspaper *Snoose News*,[10] articles, books, and government documents and correspondence. I attended four years of monthly meetings of the Cedar-Riverside Project Area Committee, many of the monthly meetings of the West Bank Community Development Corporation, and numerous other ad hoc and regular meetings of other groups. And I lived in the neighborhood for five years, taking in the sights, sounds, smells, tastes, and textures of the West Bank. Every trip out my front door began a unique data-gathering experience.

Beginning this research, however, was initially easier said than done. Although I had some legitimacy simply because I lived in the neighborhood, I was not involved in the earlier neighborhood mobilizations and thus was "just a student" when I began learning about my new surroundings in 1984. When I first went to the neighborhood Project Area Committee office, I was confronted by Tim Mungavan, who put his feet up on his desk, leaned back, gave me a skeptical look, and explained to me, "We have students and reporters coming through all the time, asking neighborhood people to give their time and answer their questions. And we don't get so much as a copy of a paper from them. If I agree to talk with you, then I want you to agree that you'll give us a copy of the paper you write" (Mungavan interview, 1984).[11] Tim did not know what kind of trouble he was getting himself into. I took him seriously and began reading literature on interactive research (Laslett and Rapoport, 1975), praxis research (Lather, 1986), and participatory research (Brown and Tandon, 1983)—all of which emphasized bringing the community being studied into the research process itself (see Stoecker and Beckwith, 1992). Ultimately, at least six activists in the neighborhood regularly read and critiqued drafts of the numerous papers I wrote on the neighborhood and, eventually, of this book. They became my mentors as much as did the academic experts in the field.

The results of their labor appears in the following pages: the story of a vibrant community struggling against the odds to prevent its own destruction, and of a community coming of age to preserve the core of its alternative culture while adapting to the pressures of the outside world that threatened to undermine it. It is a story of dead chickens nailed to doors, air horns positioned in the neighborhood to warn of encroaching bulldozers, flat tires on police paddy wagons, and numerous other shenanigans. The history is fun drama. But the historical lessons are as important as the drama is fun, because Cedar-Riverside shows the power of community against overwhelming odds, as well as the limits of community in the face of capital. The residents did not get everything they wanted, and they lost more than they planned on. The housing is not always as affordable as they had hoped, and the restrictions imposed on its use by funders is greater than they were prepared for. But the residents also succeeded more than they expected and realized their alternative vision—which transformed a neighborhood held hostage by absentee capital into a neighborhood controlled by the community—more than anyone would have predicted.

Welcome to Cedar-Riverside. I hope you enjoy the story.

CHAPTER 2

Capital Invades
Cedar-Riverside

> It is somewhat ironic that the most striking, most tangible projects
> in which our local governments have engaged—projects that have
> been most loudly and confidently justified as being for the common
> good—have presented some of the severest threats to the neigh-
> borhoods and individuals unfortunate enough to have been in
> their paths.
>
> —*Jeffrey R. Henig*, Neighborhood Mobilization

THE URBAN redevelopment that mushroomed after World War II provides an extraordinary account of the destruction of urban communities, affordable housing, and community services. Blighted, poverty-stricken slums were targeted for grand schemes controlled by powerful central governments, institutions, and corporations. A flurry of concrete freeways, hospitals, corporate headquarters, and high-rise condominiums began replacing inner-city neighborhoods, which were politically—and literally—bulldozed. It seemed as if the neighborhood communities at risk from top-down, capital-conscious urban renewal stood little chance against the onslaught of urban re-newal dollars.

In the 1960s the Cedar-Riverside neighborhood was targeted for the same type of urban renewal that was destroying neighborhoods across the country. The City of Minneapolis's new official Urban Renewal Plan specified clearance of a primarily Scandinavian, working-class neighborhood. A neighborhood of single-family homes and duplexes was to be replaced by a high-density, high-rise living environment. Local developer Keith Heller stepped in with his "New Town in Town" plan and began buying up the neighborhood property.

The Context: History, Economy, and Politics of the Twin Cities

The "Twin Cities" Metropolitan Area, built around the two cities of Minneapolis and St. Paul, is the sixteenth largest metropolitan area in the country, encompassing a population of two million. Built on the historical rivalry between Minneapolis and St. Paul, which once, it is told, tried to beat each other out in census totals by counting headstones and barbershop customers as residents, Minneapolis eventually took the lead in both population and commerce, leaving St. Paul the center of state government. Dominating the upper Midwest economy, culture, and politics, Twin Citians have prided themselves on their quality of life. There has been a relatively small difference between metropolitan area and central city incomes, and the overall metropolitan economy has been more or less stable (Abler and Adams, 1976). In the "Land of 10,000 Lakes," at least twelve lakes are within or next to the city limits of the two center cities, and many others lie within the metropolitan area. The Twin Cities have, since the 1960s, developed thriving arts and theater communities with national reputations.

The failure of lumber and milling around the turn of the century, on which the Twin Cities rose to early prominence, provided the necessary capital and economic need to invest in new industries. "Enterprising" bankers, particularly in Minneapolis, began concentrating their capital into huge financial institutions. As a result, by the early 1900s Minneapolis was developing a fairly diversified economy (Workers of the Writers' Program, 1944). With its large amount of space, needed for distribution industries to locate conveniently and economically, Minneapolis was in a much better position to diversify than St. Paul, which was more limited and congested (Baldinger, 1971). St. Paul, more of an ethnic, working-class, and Catholic city than Minneapolis, was also more conservative, while Minneapolis was more "progressive" in altering its landscape to serve capital (Baldinger, 1971).

At the same time that the old economy was failing, some "high technology" firms were gaining a footing in the area—including Minnesota Mining and Manufacturing (3M) and Electric Thermostat Company (Honeywell)—as well as such companies as Super-Valu, Northern States Power, Land O'Lakes, American Hoist and Derrick, Dayton's, Northwest Bank Corporation, and First Bank System, which provided for a "fully diversified economic infrastructure" (Galaskiewicz,

1985:8). Minneapolis in particular was building its industries during the "golden age of invention" and was able to exploit new technologies without having to dismantle old plants (Workers of the Writers' Program, 1944).

The computer industry was founded in 1944 at Harvard University, and only two years later it started up in the Twin Cities with the incorporation of the navy-linked Engineering Research Associates (ERA), one of only three computer research organizations at the time (Draheim, Howell, and Shapero, 1966). In 1966 Draheim and his colleagues cited the conditions they believed, apparently correctly, would produce growth in the Twin Cities high-tech military business in particular and in computer production in general. First, there would have to be a high number of dollars going to military research and development, a large number of contractors receiving research and development dollars, and lack of domination by a single corporation. The Twin Cities ranked third in the nation for all three of these conditions. A second important factor is the breadth and depth of abilities in the area, that is, being able to provide materials and support services locally. The Twin Cities was ranked with Boston and Los Angeles, the two leaders at the time. Finally, the capacity to provide education in the home region was seen as important, and again the Twin Cities were perceived as equal to the task with the University of Minnesota technical programs. The William Hood Dunwoody Industrial Institute in Minneapolis was cited as the only endowed institution of industrial and mechanical training in the upper Midwest, 30 percent of whose graduates went to work in computers (Northern States Power Co. et al., 1959).

Thus, the Twin Cities avoided becoming saddled with heavy industry and the economic problems that befell manufacturing centers and were instead able to build a modern, diversified industrial base. In fact, since 1900 only 25 to 30 percent of the labor force has been in manufacturing (Draheim, Howell, and Shapero, 1966), well below the national averages early in the century of over 50 percent (Browning and Singlemann, 1978). Instead, Minneapolis has become a corporate and professional capital. Noyelle and Stanback (1984) describe Minneapolis as a diversified service center for corporate complex activities, distributive services, and government and nonprofit activities. In terms of a snowbelt city, however, Minneapolis stands apart in Noyelle and Stanback's statistics as one of only three northern cities to gain a significant number of Fortune 500 headquarters from 1959 to 1976.

The Twin Cities, and Minnesota, have an interesting political history. In this historically liberal state, the Democratic Party is referred to as the DFL, or Democratic Farmer Labor Party, after a merger of the Democratic Party and the leftwing populist Farmer Labor Party in 1944 (Valelly, 1989). Minnesota is also the home of Eugene McCarthy, whose 1968 bid for the Democratic presidential nomination on a strong antiwar platform helped split the Democratic Party between McCarthy and Hubert Humphrey, a fellow Minnesotan. The state has seen a radical governor vaulted into office through the Farmer Labor Party in the 1930s (Valelly, 1989) and has retained a sense of maintaining government responsibility to provide for the good of the citizen, even on occasion against capital. And local capitalists have generally been cooperative, recognized as national trendsetters for their sense of noblesse oblige and level of corporate philanthropy (Galaskiewicz, 1985).

But not all was rosy in the Twin Cities, particularly Minneapolis. Calling itself the "Minne-apple" because of its self-perception of a New York City sophistication and atmosphere in a small-town community, Minneapolis suffered from a latent inferiority complex. The loss of the Minneapolis Lakers basketball team to Los Angeles in 1960 (Hollander, 1979); the lack of a major-league baseball, football, or basketball franchise until 1961, when the Washington Senators baseball team moved to Minnesota and the Minnesota Vikings football franchise formed as an expansion team (Bjarkman, 1991; Bennett et al., 1977); and the lack of national attention contributed to the sense of inferiority. The city's tremendous wealth and resources were going unrecognized.

Minneapolis was not immune to the problems of all major northern cities after World War II. The population decreased by 28.9 percent in Minneapolis and by 13.1 percent in St. Paul between 1950 and 1980 (Galaskiewicz, 1985). The downtowns deteriorated; the infrastructure was in disrepair. But Minneapolis, especially, had talent and wealth and began in the 1950s and 1960s to take advantage of federal urban renewal program money that emphasized the construction of freeways, educational and medical institutions, and downtowns (Mollenkopf, 1983). The city's urban redevelopment projects included the I-35W and I-94 freeways, which would sever the Cedar-Riverside neighborhood from the rest of the city. In 1972 construction was completed on the city's downtown jewel, the fifty-seven-story IDS center (Smith, 1988), in whose enclosed courtyard Mary Tyler Moore gleefully flings her hat in the air. Amidst this flurry of urban renewal the

University of Minnesota expanded across the Mississippi River into Cedar-Riverside.

It was in this context of a city with an increasing reputation for cutting-edge technology, culture, political liberalism, and a vague inferiority complex that the New Town in Town came to the drawing table. The New Town in Town was an innovative idea never before tried in the United States, and it brought together a new high-rise housing technology, sophisticated social planning, and liberal notions of economic integration of housing. The image problems of a slum neighborhood next to the state's flagship university and across the freeway from downtown led city officials to target Cedar-Riverside for the New Town.

The Local State: An Urban Renewal Plan for Cedar-Riverside

In the early, or "directive," period of urban renewal in the United States, local state officials took the lead in obtaining federal money for local urban renewal. Although this form of state-directed urban renewal was on the decline nationally by the mid-1960s (S. Fainstein and N. Fainstein, 1986), in Minneapolis the local state exerted a strong role in planning urban renewal up to the early 1970s. But the city was ahead of the trends in another sense. Rather than the local state attempting to access large federal subsidies and implement urban renewal itself, city government looked toward private developers both to find the funding and to implement plans for local state goals, a redevelopment pattern not popularized nationally until the 1980s (Levine, 1989; Berger et al., 1992).[1]

Minneapolis government was well suited for urban renewal dominated by private developers and motivated by growth interests. Weak mayor governmental systems in which mayors do not have veto, budgeting, or planning power did not allow for the vigorous leadership exhibited by strong mayors in promoting renewal in such cities as Pittsburgh (Sbragia, 1989) or New Haven (N. Fainstein and S. Fainstein, 1986b). Minneapolis, at the time, provided the mayor with veto power but strictly limited his budgetary and planning powers. Minneapolis City Hall was also a partly "reformed" local state, where elections were held on off-years between national elections with nonpartisan primary ballots.[2] These characteristics of the local state make it difficult for citizens, and especially minority interests, to be strongly represented (Lineberry and Fowler, 1971; Alford and Lee, 1971; Clark,

1971). Minneapolis did have a thirteen-member city council elected by wards, which tempered the reform effects and provided the possibility of greater representation of citizen and minority interests (Schultze, 1974; Banfield and Wilson, 1963; Karnig, 1975; Engstrom and McDonald, 1981). But the alienation of the Democratic (DFL) Party by the takeover of the sixth ward DFL club by student radicals (Lebedoff, 1972) and the domination of the ward, which included Cedar-Riverside, by Republican alderman Jens Christensen did not bode well for the representation of the substantial number of citizens who opposed the urban renewal plan that was eventually passed.

It was in this context of a partly closed and relatively stable political opportunity structure that the Minneapolis City Planning Commission undertook an extensive study of the Cedar-Riverside neighborhood in the middle 1960s. The University of Minnesota, heretofore located across the Mississippi River, had recently expanded to the West Bank and thus found itself in the middle of the most deteriorated neighborhood in the city. Less than 15 percent of the housing units were owner-occupied. Rents were $41 to $60 per month, compared to a city average of $67 per month. Half the neighborhood homes were built before the turn of the century. Mobility in and out of the neighborhood was high. Neighborhood unemployment was 10 percent, compared to a city average of 5 percent, and there was an "extremely low level of income." The proportion of "dilapidated" housing (the worst census category) was five times the city average (Minneapolis City Planning Commission, 1965–66).

With the expansion of the university to the West Bank and the presence of two hospitals and a small college, Cedar-Riverside was being redefined. What had been an ethnic enclave of primarily poor and working-class Scandinavians (Armitage et al., 1973) was reconceived as an educational and medical housing and service center for the university, Fairview and St. Mary's hospitals, and Augsburg College. The Planning Commission (1965–66) estimated that the number of students living "in or near" Cedar-Riverside would increase from 1,935 in 1960 to 9,200 in 1980—all in a neighborhood of 6,920 residents in 1960. The emphasis, in this early planning stage, was on housing for students. The Planning Commission's preliminary plan report (1966:9–10) asserted that the neighborhood would need a dramatic increase in housing density to provide living space for the huge influx of students anticipated.

The redefinition of Cedar-Riverside from an impoverished, low-density neighborhood to a high-density student housing complex was conducted with the participation of at least some sympathetic members of the community. The Planning Commission's 1966 report emphasizes that its conclusions were based on extensive neighborhood discussion and exhaustive analysis. The Cedar-Riverside Area Council (CRAC), dominated by representatives from area institutions (Martin, 1978), was formed in 1965 to begin discussing the direction redevelopment should take. Then, "five committees, that included local residents and businessmen who were not delegates of the organizations forming CRAC, were named to examine the future needs of the Neighborhood and to express their ideas for the development of Riverside" (Minneapolis City Planning Commission, 1966:14). The redevelopment goals adopted by CRAC for the 1966 commission plan (based on a supposed "broad consensus") emphasized a "heterogeneous population" and "densities compatible with the future character of Riverside" (p. 14), among other things. Whether the more specific operationalization of these goals, which provided for enormously high densities and pointedly stated that there should be no single-family detached housing, was also based on a "broad consensus" is unclear. Even with all this high-density concrete, the 1966 Planning Commission report nonetheless emphasized, "It is imperative that Riverside be developed as a neighborhood that clearly expresses humanistic values" (p. 71).

The 1966 report did ultimately allow for a greater variety of types and prices of housing for a variety of residents, not just students, but the focus was clearly on adapting the neighborhood to institutional needs. According to the commission's 1965–66 report, the goal was to "develop a unique, coherent and prestigious image" (p. 125). The 1966 report emphasized that "the neighborhood is becoming the site where one of Minnesota's most economically, as well as socially, important products—trained minds—will be developed, and the environment should reflect the importance of this function to the State and to the Metropolitan area, as well as to individuals" (p. 71). Apparently, however, there was some dispute over the desirability of making the neighborhood an arm of the institutions, though the commission was not budging:

> The expansion of the institutions, which is being forced by continuing population growth and by increasing need for education and health care, has been feared and resented by many in the past. However, this expansion is not only economically and socially necessary, it has also provided the basis for the increase in the selling

price of all property in the neighborhood, most of which would otherwise find few buyers.   (p. 29)

The 1965–66 and 1966 commission reports set the stage for what was to come. Both focused on serving the medical and educational institutions and their clients. Both emphasized that private, not public, renewal was the direction to pursue. The 1965–66 commission report saw in Cedar-Riverside "the best opportunity for large-scale private renewal that will occur in Minneapolis in the foreseeable future" (p. 127). The 1966 report saw the need for a "total improvement program" (p. 20) to help obtain financing of as much as $100 million for private profit or nonprofit developers. This was to be no piecemeal redevelopment of three-story "walk-up" apartments. The plan was to increase the population nearly fourfold to twenty-five thousand, three to four times the density of even the most populous neighborhoods in Minneapolis at the time. Walk-ups would accommodate only fifteen thousand at most.

The urban renewal plan that was developing for Cedar-Riverside was typical of the federal urban renewal programs of the time. Founded in the 1949 Housing Act, federal urban renewal policy emphasized clearance of blighted neighborhoods rather than rehabilitation, a policy referred to by critics as "urban removal" or "negro removal" (Kleniewski, 1984). The primary mechanism for planning such redevelopment was a local agency, and the primary form of renewal was private development, not public housing (Greer, 1965). The federal government's role was to provide for land clearance and some construction subsidies (Levine, 1989), as well as to approve all plans. Consequently, the possible renewal projects were limited to those from which private developers believed they could extract profit (Levine, 1989). Amendments to the Housing Act in 1954 and 1961 made affordable housing an even less central goal of the program (Greer, 1965). So devastating were the results that, by 1965, Greer (1965:3) concluded, "At a cost of more than three billion dollars the Urban Renewal Agency . . . has succeeded in materially reducing the supply of low-cost housing in American cities." The Cedar-Riverside Urban Renewal Plan, by specifying very high densities, made the area much more attractive to private developers. After buying up single-family homes, a developer could construct high-rise, high-profit residential towers. With government safety nets reducing the risk, there was little reason for private developers to be either fiscally cautious or socially conscious.

The Cedar-Riverside Urban Renewal Plan was also ahead of its time as an adaptation and expansion of the "public-private partnership" concept, which would come to dominate urban redevelopment through the 1980s (Squires, 1989a; Levine, 1989). Unlike most public-private partnerships, urban renewal planning in Cedar-Riverside was focused not solely on downtown, but also on the needs of medical and institutional expansion as well as housing for downtown workers. This planning effort was also not spearheaded by an entrepreneurial mayor. But two other characteristics of public-private partnerships stand out in urban renewal planning in Cedar-Riverside: federal leveraging of resources and the role of the autonomous redevelopment authority. The federal government, through the Housing and Urban Development agency, would become heavily involved in providing loan guarantees in Cedar-Riverside.

Minneapolis city government at the time is probably best characterized as an "activist regime." According to Clarence Stone's (1989:188) analysis,

> Maintenance of traditional services needs only minimal effort and adherence to a set of conventions or norms that reinforce passivity. . . . An activist regime confronts a more substantial task. In order to pursue a program such as redevelopment, a governing coalition must be able to sustain efforts by a variety of actors and to ensure that the high level of coordination needed for complicated projects is achieved, sometimes in the face of controversy.

Helping along university expansion, freeway construction, downtown development, and the construction of four towers of public housing for senior citizens in Cedar-Riverside in the 1960s, Minneapolis City Hall was clearly in an activist mode.

In order to manage the tension between supporting capital accumulation and maintaining political legitimation, a tension always threatening to disrupt top-down, capital-conscious redevelopment, Minneapolis adopted a model followed by many cities of the time. Cities faced with the need to support growth-oriented development projects created special economic development agencies insulated from political accountability, concurrently establishing other more accessible sectors of government devoted to shoring up political legitimation (Fleischmann and Feagin, 1987). Thus, the primary responsibility for making the Cedar-Riverside plan into public policy fell on the Minneapolis Housing and Redevelopment Authority, or MHRA. Redevelopment authorities were designed to, and effectively able to, insulate urban planning from democratic accountability. Typically appointed rather than elected, and having sometimes vast powers, redevelopment authorities provided growth coalitions with both technical resources and political cover (Squires, 1989a; Levine, 1989; N. Fainstein and S. Fainstein, 1986b).

In early 1968 an MHRA plan operationalized the Planning Commission's recommendations. The plan called for mass demolition, with the subsequent creation of an "intensively developed major educational, research, and health complex with supporting residential and commercial uses" (Minneapolis Housing and Redevelopment Authority, 1968:4). Only one hundred acres of the neighborhood were not slated for institutional expansion. "Permitted" land uses on those one hundred acres were multiple family buildings (three or more units), colleges, universities, educational and cultural institutions (including hospitals), offices, recreation areas and parks, religious institutions, and public housing. Walk-up apartments were not permitted. And the MHRA plan did not propose "to acquire any real property for purposes of rehabilitation and conservation in this project" (p. 19).

The reaction from neighborhood residents to the announcement of this plan was the first indication that perhaps there had not been as much citizen participation as the Planning Commission had asserted. One resident threatened a lawsuit on the basis that the plan would require property owners to move in two years, which would lower property values and drive away renters. Seventy residents, including many students and elderly people, opposed the plan at a public meeting and charged that it neglected neighborhood aesthetics and low-income housing. Another forty residents and merchants later protested that the City Council was rubber-stamping the plan and not protecting property owners from receiving artificially low payments when the city acquired their land through eminent domain.

On August 15, 1968, the *Minneapolis Tribune* reported that "400 angry residents," many of them "young and given to mustaches or sideburns," turned out to oppose the MHRA urban renewal plan. The hearing was moderated by the neighborhood's Republican alderman, Jens Christensen, and led by the president of the University Development Corporation, John S. Pillsbury. Representatives from Augsburg College, the University of Minnesota, and Fairview and St. Mary's hospitals—all located in the neighborhood—voiced their support. Residents again emphasized the lack of citizen participation in planning and the lack of affordable, low-income housing in the plan. Although one-third of seven thousand new units were to be low-income, residents charged that the rents would be nowhere near the low rents they were then paying. According to William Betzler, who had been a campaign worker for Christensen, the alderman thoroughly backed the plan and argued that students and renters did not care about the neighborhood. City officials perceived no "organized" resident groups but noticed significant opposition from individuals.

> The City Council had two public hearings. And the first one was at Augsburg College and started at seven o'clock and lasted until about one in the morning. And because of the large number of people that turned out and the fact that there wasn't enough time to listen to everybody's comments, City Council held another public hearing several weeks later at City Council chambers that lasted from about seven in the evening until five in the morning. There was a lot of controversy. . . . Most of the people who were concerned about it, it seemed at the time, were people that lived there and felt that they would be displaced by this renewal action—both individuals, families, and businessmen. (Robert Drew interview, 1978)

The residents did not end up with much, however. The final draft of the MHRA plan allowed for a one-year hold on property acquisition and provided for open space requirements, but it also gave the MHRA wide latitude in adjusting those requirements. The MHRA certified "that there is no deficit in the housing supply for low-rent public-housing, private rental accommodations, or housing offered for sale" (MHRA, 1968:24), and the Urban Renewal Plan was passed as law in 1968.

The creation of the 1968 Urban Renewal Plan illustrates the top-down, capital-conscious qualities of 1960s urban redevelopment planning. The dramatic high densities demanded by the plan were designed specifically to serve the local educational institutions, hospitals, and downtown employers. Even more important, but unspoken, were the enormous profits that would accrue at such high population densities. The explicit goal of serving the employees of the major local employers is consistent with capital consciousness: increasing population density is part of the overall growth-coalition strategy for economic expansion (Logan and Molotch, 1987; Lyon et al., 1981). The planning process itself was well insulated by being centralized in the MHRA, and what neighborhood opposition there may have been in the early planning stages was effectively ignored by the neighborhood's conservative alderman. Intriguingly, this plan was created without the direct and overt influence of capital. A growth coalition was not yet well organized; the city would have to wait for one to form to implement the plan.

Capital Takes Over: Keith Heller, Cedar-Riverside Associates, and the New Town in Town

In 1963, even before the Minneapolis City Planning Commission's studies of Cedar-Riverside, Keith Heller and Gloria Segal made their first purchase of land in Cedar-Riverside. One year earlier Heller, a lecturer in the University of Minnesota's School of Business Administration, had entered into a partnership with Martin and Gloria Segal. Martin Segal was a silent partner and professor at the University of Minnesota School of Medicine; Gloria, his wife and a student, was to become centrally involved in the redevelopment scheme (CRA, 1972; Martin, 1978). She was given the title of "do-good den mother" by some Cedar-Riverside activists. Although other speculators had been buying land in the neighborhood, Keith Heller soon became the central figure in landholding and development planning.

Apparently, Heller and Segal happened onto Cedar-Riverside without any initial plans for the neighborhood. According to Ralph Rapson, head of the University of Minnesota School of Architecture and eventually "project architect" for Heller, Heller-Segal's first plan for Cedar-Riverside was to build a "demonstration project" before building across the Mississippi River nearer to the main campus of the university, where they had already acquired land. After their initial acquisitions in Cedar-Riverside, Rapson continued to urge Heller-Segal to acquire enough land for the demonstration project.

As Heller-Segal bought West Bank land from the older residents who lived there or their landlords, they rented the properties at relatively low rates. There is some evidence that the cheap rents were used to create a tax shelter. Many activists argued, and were supported by a Heller-Segal employee, William Betzler, that the housing was allowed to depreciate, creating tax shelters, while land consolidation drove up land values. Thus current holdings could be mortgaged and remortgaged as prices rose, allowing the purchase of more land with little real capital.

There are also charges that the cheap rents were used to attract "undesirable" tenants who would frighten the remaining older residents into selling out of the neighborhood—"blockbusting" (Armitage et al., 1973; Snoose News, November 1987:8)—though Keith Heller says he instructed his agents not to use intimidation. One story has it that buyers would go door to door, telling the old residents that "those hippies are gonna bomb your house if you don't move out." In any case, beatniks, hippies, and radical students continued to move into the area, and their presence attracted yet more, until by 1973 the old residents made up only 25 percent of the West Bank population. Gloria Segal helped this process along by recruiting artists and theaters to the area (Martin, 1978), although their attraction to the counterculture ambience of the area would have likely brought them to the West Bank anyway.

It is unclear whether Heller and Segal had any impact on the Cedar-Riverside Urban Renewal Plan created at City Hall. Robert Drew, from the MHRA, noticed that Heller and Segal owned much of the land in Cedar-Riverside at the time and "had many conversations with them" but asserts that they had no impact on MHRA plans. Once those plans were in place, however, Heller and Segal went to great lengths to lobby for approval of the New Town plan to fulfill the Urban Renewal Plan objectives. Charlie Warner, a HUD staffperson at the time, described a "luncheon extravaganza" at which "the table was groaning with food." Plans lined the walls of the room for officials to see as they filled and emptied their plates. "HUD employees weren't supposed to take gratuities, and gratuities include free food, but we all chowed down that day."

As the MHRA plan went to the City Planning Commission and the City Council, and the resultant Urban Renewal Plan was accepted in 1968, Heller and Segal formed Cedar-Riverside Associates (CRA, pronounced "C-R-A") with Henry T. McKnight, the son of a local lumber baron with experience and contacts made as a state senator (Martin, 1978). The Heller-Segal-McKnight partnership enlisted various local supporters, including a University of Minnesota sociologist to do social planning, a former assistant executive director of the MHRA and city coordinator, a senior partner in a major law firm, a former vice-president of Northwestern National Bank and chair of the Minneapolis Urban Coalition, and a former real estate executive and commissioner of the Minnesota Department of Economic Development (CRA, 1972).

McKnight was particularly important because of his national-level connections. McKnight's influence is described by former CRA employee William Betzler: "He brought in his capital, and he brought in his political contacts. . . . He was the first and the foremost and he was their darling. And when things went wrong, Henry McKnight could be called upon to take a trip to Washington to shake down what was going on." Word spread quickly through the neighborhood that McKnight was a friend of George Romney, secretary of the federal office of Housing and Urban Development (HUD) (Charles Warner interview, 1978). Betzler believes that this connection allowed CRA to circumvent local and regional administrations to get project support directly from the top in Washington, D.C. This conclusion is indirectly supported by Tom Feeney, from the local HUD office, who had reservations about the project; by Charlie Warner, local HUD employee who witnessed memos of concern about the project which were ignored by Washington; and by Robert Drew, from the MHRA, who emphasized that the MHRA was not involved with CRA and that CRA contracted directly with HUD.

Cedar-Riverside Associates developed a formidable growth coalition, with connections to local capital, the MHRA, and ultimately the very top of the HUD hierarchy. CRA itself became an enormously complex corporation with multiple subcorporations, millions of dollars in real estate holdings, and snakelike financial maneuvering that slithered through banks, limited partnership investors, and $24 million in federal loan guarantees (Martin, 1978). CRA had to compete with as many as twenty other power brokers or investors for control of the neighborhood turf, and the rivalry between real estate speculators was perceived by Keith Heller as more important than any resident opposition.

By 1968 Heller and his associates owned eighty-five of the one hundred acres available for redevelopment, and their plans had expanded, eventually embracing the "New Town in Town" concept. Essentially, the New Town in Town idea proposed a leveling of all West Bank housing, to be replaced by a "planned community" of high-rise apartments and condominiums which would increase the population from a bit under four thousand in 1970 to thirty thousand when the project was finished. In a 340-acre neighborhood, one-third of it residential, ten stages of high-rise housing were to be constructed in two-year intervals (CRA, 1972).

Underlying the New Town plan was a provision of the federal Demonstration Cities Act of 1966, otherwise known as "Model Cities." This "new communities" provision supported the construction of "New Towns"—communities planned from scratch, away from existing settlements (and protestors), whose design was supposed to create a self-sufficient community protected from problems of transportation, crime, and gesellschaft alienation. Drawn from European models, but with far less government involvement, the bill committed the federal government basically to providing loan guarantees to the developers, with little oversight. With further supporting legislation passed in 1968, the New Town concept spread like wildfire until there were more than 130 New Towns into the early 1970s (Clapp, 1971). It was this legislation that brought the New Town to Cedar-Riverside. But in Cedar-Riverside there was a twist. For the first time, the New Town would be "in town" rather than outside the city (Martin, 1978).

Keith Heller saw the MHRA Urban Renewal Plan, apparently correctly, as a "mandate" for high-density housing. With the adoption of federal Title IV in 1969 and Title VII in 1970, both oriented toward the creation of "New Towns," the office of New Community Development of HUD "asked" CRA to apply for Title IV and Title VII assistance, and by mid-1970 CRA had received conditional approval. By the end of 1971, CRA had received $24 million in land loan guarantees from HUD through the New Communities Project Agreement (CRA, 1972). The contacts made by McKnight were again important here, as he had already secured financing for the Jonathan New Town Project in Chaska, Minnesota (Betzler interview, 1978).

The New Town in Town was the perfect solution to accomplish the growth-machine tasks of providing services, upgrading the area's image, increasing population, and raising land values (Domhoff, 1983; Molotch, 1976). With the redevelopment of the nearby downtown and the expansion of the University of Minnesota to the West Bank, would-be developers had a clear interest in both upgrading Cedar-Riverside's image and speculating on its land. The New Town in Town would rationalize Cedar-Riverside's land, remove blighted housing and blighted residents, and bring a seven-fold increase in neighborhood population. As a result, consumption would be bolstered and land values increased. Minneapolis, along with all large cities of the 1960s, was rapidly losing population to the suburbs, and there was an increasing need for City Hall and capitalists to bolster a sagging tax base for the city coffers and a consumption base for downtown.

The New Town plan was touted as solving those problems and more. The New Town in Town was not just a housing complex, but an innovation in urban planning to make Minneapolis a leader in urban renewal. The New Town would also integrate socioeconomic groups, and half the housing was targeted for low-/*and* middle-income persons.[3] And the theoretical emphasis was on creating a *town*, a self-sustaining community with its own shopping, its own services, and its own web of social relationships. Social planning was to be an integral part of the New Town development. The concept was so highly touted that when Mary, in television's 1970's "Mary Tyler Moore Show," moved from her quaint little apartment in the house by the lake in Minneapolis into a high-rise apartment building, it was widely held that she moved into Cedar Square West.[4]

The fractured liberalism of Cedar-Riverside Associates was also reflected in their treatment of neighborhood residents. CRA was still intent on serving the community it was about to displace. After negotiations with neighborhood residents, CRA agreed to relocate the residents displaced by Stage I of the New Town in Town *within* the neighborhood. Early in 1972 CRA obtained a $20,000 grant from the National Endowment for the Arts to the Minnesota Arts Council to hire an arts advocate planner (CRA, 1972). Gloria Segal continued to strive to bring artists to the neighborhood (Martin, 1978). On the other hand, Dave Raymond, a professional employed by CRA, says that the group held open houses to elicit comments on the development plans, but as soon as the comments from residents became "uncomplimentary," the efforts dwindled. And residents charged that the level of deterioration in CRA-owned houses was unconscionable, with leaky roofs; "central heat" provided by a single, large, gas space heater in the center of the house or duplex unit; inside walls that glazed over with frost in the winter; and cracks in walls and windows through which the winter wind whistled.

By the end of 1970 all the bank loans were in place, and four square blocks of housing west of Cedar Avenue was agonizingly shredded, ripped, and cleared by bulldozers. In the dust of destruction rose the concrete towers of Cedar Square West, the first stage of the New Town in Town.

Urban Renewal and a Stacked Deck

Early in the struggle against the New Town plan threatening to level their neighborhood, Cedar-Riverside residents were told by a sympathetic political official that the New Town project was "already bought and paid for in Washington" (Ralph Wittcoff interview, 1978). Why was it so easy to implement an urban redevelopment plan so antithetical to the Cedar-Riverside community? The answer can be found by understanding the power of the political opportunity structure in the city and the level of organization of different political actors. These two influences are not equal in power. The political opportunity structure determines the extent to which different politi-

cal actors in different structural positions can gain access to poli
institutions and political support. Actors must effectively orga
to gain that access, however. And different political actors pract
the same sophisticated level of organizing capacity may reap vastly
different results.

Since the local state stands at the center of the local political opportunity structure, it becomes the first prize in the struggle between
capital and community. At the most general level, the struggle between capital and community is over the use of the local state to
support exchange values or use values. Are local state resources to be
used to facilitate the capitalist production process through tax abatements for job creation or land clearance for capital investment, or to
maintain communities by providing social services such as medical
care, education, or housing? In the city the local state is the "court of
first resort" for balancing those contradictory interests and adjudicat-
ing the conflict they generate (Schulz, 1979; Markusen, 1978).

The growth coalition formed through Cedar-Riverside Associates
achieved easy access to the political opportunity structure through
the local state; at the same time, the local state was relatively insulated from citizens. With a redevelopment authority separated from
political accountability, the technology and expertise of urban planning centralized behind a protective city government bureaucracy,
and the neighborhood's representative on the City Council turning a
deaf ear to the residents, it was quite clear that the political opportunity structure was not open to citizens. Few allies were available to
neighborhood residents; no other neighborhood was threatened the
way Cedar-Riverside was, and after all, it was just a bunch of hippies.
The New Town proposal could appeal to interest groups across the
metropolitan area. It was promoted as a way to reverse the declining
Minneapolis tax base, provide construction jobs, and generate development spin-offs in a slum. It would also provide housing that was
supposed to, by its very design, reduce class segregation. The public
relations of the project made it difficult to oppose unless, of course,
you happened to be in its way.

Although the political opportunity structure was closed to residents, capital was invited to participate. The city Urban Renewal Plan
specified that capital, and not City Hall, should actually implement
urban renewal in Cedar-Riverside. This intent was accomplished with
the blessing and support of the federal government. Part of the bias
of the local state derives from its relation to higher levels of the state.
Cynthia Cockburn (1977) coined the term *local state* to emphasize

the dependence of local government policy on higher tiers of the state. With federal urban renewal laws that supported slum clearance, centralized planning, and capital-intensive development, Minneapolis City Hall was in a much better position to support high-density, high-concrete urban renewal than it was to provide for maintenance of existing communities. With the support and encouragement of all state levels, a very strong growth coalition led by Cedar-Riverside Associates formed, which co-opted the hearts and imaginations of local financiers, local state managers, and even the federal office of Housing and Urban Development.

Community power is ultimately dependent on gaining access to the resources of the political opportunity structure. In many cases that means finding ways to change that structure so it can provide more resources to neighborhood-based communities. In some cases it might mean exploiting the local state's dependence on the national state (Frug, 1980; Clark and Dear, 1984), as the civil rights movement did to help abolish poll taxes, literacy tests, and segregated public facilities maintained by local states in the southern United States. In other cases it may mean removing strategic targets from the growth coalition, thus destabilizing political alignments, as occurred in Boston, San Francisco (Mollenkopf, 1983), and Chicago (Bennett, 1989; Giloth and Mier, 1989) when neighborhood-based voting blocks elected mayors less sympathetic to unaccountable, top-down, capital-conscious redevelopment. In 1969 Pittsburgh, Pennsylvania, residents elected Peter Flaherty, an unendorsed Democrat who championed the rights of neighborhoods, to the mayor's office (Sbragia, 1989). Mayor Richard Lee's New Haven, Connecticut, growth coalition was torn apart by rebellion from black citizens in the late 1960s (N. Fainstein and S. Fainstein, 1986b). Other city governments, such as Milwaukee, Wisconsin, grudgingly swung their support behind low-income housing as housing protests destroyed the business-as-usual practices of previous urban renewal programs (Norman, 1989). Often these concessions even received the support of local capital hoping new housing programs would calm the turmoil making the cities of the 1960s "ungovernable" (S. Fainstein and N. Fainstein, 1986; Norman, 1989). But it is only in creating advantageous changes in the political opportunity structure and then maximizing the resources made accessible by those changes that communities can hope to gain power.

Gaining access to the resources of the political opportunity structure was problematic from the beginning for Cedar-Riverside residents. Not only was the political opportunity structure relatively closed to residents and dominated by opposing interests, but there was also a dramatic difference in the organizing capacity of neighborhood residents compared to the growth coalition that allowed urban renewal planning to proceed so resiliently against community needs. In this earliest period of the struggle for control of the neighborhood the residents were not organized. There were strong student activists and a growing collection of hippies, but tensions existed between those two groups and especially between those groups and the remaining old residents. Until 1970 there were no organizations in Cedar-Riverside that could effectively represent and mobilize the growing resistance in the neighborhood. That lack of organizing was further hindered by lack of access to the political opportunity structure, and thus to information on the Urban Renewal Plan and the New Town plan, and to expertise on the process by which those plans were created and could be fought. Cedar-Riverside Associates, on the other hand, was solidly connected to the most powerful capital and government actors in the city and nationally, with access to vast amounts of expertise and technical information.

Most important, there was also not yet a stable new community in place in Cedar-Riverside; the six conditions of community were not yet formed, making organizing difficult. Neighborhood services had not yet developed either agglomeration benefits or a focal point. The neighborhood's identity and culture was still in flux as Scandinavian working-class residents moved out and counterculture students moved in. And consequently, the support networks and sense of security that depend on the other characteristics were also not yet developed, and neighborhood political factions divided even the new residents. Thus, what political resistance the residents did provide was not built on a strong community base. And Cedar Square West, the first stage of the New Town in Town, began to rise from the dust on the west side of the neighborhood. It was almost enough to prevent a new community from ever developing in Cedar-Riverside. But CRA made some strategic mistakes.

Setting the Stage for Struggle: Hidden Fissures in the Growth Coalition

Perhaps a more important question than why capital was able to have such a favorable Urban Renewal Plan dropped in its lap is why it ultimately failed to go beyond the first stage of the New Town. Both the federal government and local government eventually fell into line with the growth coalition, with the federal government providing millions of dollars in loan guarantees. Powerful local capital actors had signed on to the project. And residents were effectively isolated from participation in the planning process. But even in the very earliest days of planning the New Town there were fissures in the growth coalition. Those fissures lay along the two main theoretical fault lines for growth coalitions: the need for the local state to preserve legitimacy and the problem of maintaining a coalition of self-interested capital actors.

The local state in Minneapolis was organized around a district council, and redistricting in the 1970s made the City Council much more politicized and accessible to neighborhood residents than before. The HUD guidelines specified that there be a resident review board in all Urban Renewal Plan districts, and the Environmental Policy Act of 1970 required that all federally funded projects submit extensive and detailed environmental impact statements, allowing residents more input than in the early urban renewal planning process. At both the local and national levels there were significant concerns about the project. Staff members in the HUD regional office in Chicago were worried about the New Town financial structure, which had virtually no real capital supporting it; the marketability of particularly the high-income units in the complex; and the adequacy of high-rise housing for families with children (Thomas Feeney interview, 1978; Charles Warner interview, 1978).

The New Town plan was built on a financial foundation of sand, which could not tolerate even the most innocent wrong move or delay. With the entire project's financial health contingent on continually increasing land values, which required constant construction, unrealistically projected low interest rates, and the speculative mortgaging and remortgaging of CRA-owned properties to create the appearance of greater capital, investors had much to worry about. New Town investors were significantly more concerned about their profit margins than Keith Heller appeared to be, and there were struggles over how to cut costs and raise revenues within the growth coalition (David Raymond interview, 1978).

In addition, the growth coalition organized to support the New Town was constructed from potentially conflictual fractions of capital. The five categories of redevelopment decision makers identified by Feagin and Parker (1990) provided the source of the fractures. One category—industrial and commercial location decision makers—did not have a strong role in the development except in the general sense

of providing support for the planning of a shopping mall th
never built. The other four groups were important, however. Th
struction decision makers—architect, engineers, builders, and
contractors—created internal conflicts over the design of the
plex. To meet various regulations and financing constraints, son
the most attractive design features were altered, such as reducing outdoor patios to tiny ledges barely wide enough for a narrow kitchen
chair (Martin, 1978). Financial decision makers such as the First
National Bank of St. Paul, which became a major backer of the project,
were increasingly important as CRA ran into financial difficulties.
Support decision makers, such as the Chamber of Commerce, the
Greater Minneapolis Metropolitan Housing Corporation, and others
also became significant as CRA needed financial propping up. These
decision makers all had to be regularly wooed to maintain their involvement in the growth coalition by the fifth category of decision
maker—the developer, Cedar-Riverside Associates.[5]

It is along these lines that cleavages can develop in the growth
coalition. The more that representatives holding power in each area
can be brought on board the growth coalition, the greater the chances
for success of the development project. But the cleavages do not go
away, and the solidarity of the coalition is dependent on development
decisions that attract capital, can provide riches to others, and will
be able to pay the bills and repay loans. As soon as any member of
the coalition no longer believes his or her investment will be profit-
able, the struggle within begins. That was not a problem initially for
Keith Heller and Cedar-Riverside Associates, as they assembled a formidable growth coalition with representation from all these decision
areas. Once problems began for the project—problems created by the
developing opposition in the neighborhood—these lines of cleavage
became the undoing of the New Town growth coalition.

Finally, the centralized accumulation of neighborhood housing in
the hands of Cedar-Riverside Associates, and its liberal intentions
toward existing and future tenants, created the conditions for community. The Marxist concept of class consciousness, which is thought to
develop as capitalists bring workers together on the shop floor and the
workers then have an opportunity to become aware of their collective
exploitation—the core contradiction leading to class struggle—also
applies to communities. Although the initial urban renewal planning
and CRA land acquisition disrupted community life, displaced the
old residents, and led to conflicts between resident factions within
the neighborhood, in the long run it displaced a traditional commu-

nity of old, working-class immigrants with an activist community of young radicals. They were all brought together and given a common landlord, who also became a common threat. And rather than demolishing the neighborhood all at once, which was so effective in eliminating the resistance of Poletown residents to the construction of a General Motors Cadillac plant on the ground of an ethnic Detroit neighborhood (Wylie, 1989), Cedar-Riverside Associates demolished only the housing standing in the way of Cedar Square West, relocating a group of angry residents across the street.

CRA's mistakes mounted in the future as the residents organized more effectively and the political opportunity structure changed. But before that happened, the new residents of Cedar-Riverside had to build a community and taste their first defeat.

CHAPTER 3

A New Community Forms
Against the New Town

So, faced with an overpowered labour movement, an omnipresent
one-way communication system indifferent to cultural identities,
an all-powerful centralized state loosely governed by unreliable
political parties, a structural economic crisis, cultural uncertainty,
and the likelihood of nuclear war, people go home. Most withdraw
individually, but the crucial, active minority, anxious to retaliate,
organize themselves on their local turf.
                    —*Manuel Castells*, The City and the Grassroots

B Y 1970, when the first community organization formed to oppose the New Town in Town, the national social movements
that had sustained the new residents of Cedar-Riverside—the civil
rights movement, student movement, and antiwar movement—had
already peaked. As those movements waned, the people of Cedar-
Riverside turned toward building an alternative community, one that
would be insulated from the insidious influence of capitalism, bureaucracy, and conformity. What began to form in Cedar-Riverside in the
late 1960s was a new community, founded on the counterculture that
the new residents had adopted and the use-values orientation that this
culture emphasized. A variety of community institutions was springing up. Residents directed some of these institutions toward themselves and some toward the development plans that threatened them.
The Community Union, New Riverside Cafe, People's Center, People's
Pantry, and Project Area Committee (PAC; pronounced "pak") all developed out of the increasing sense of "community" the new residents
were experiencing and, in turn, reinforced that community experience.

How does a community develop and transform itself into a social movement? In this chapter I explore the development of the early community-building institutions in Cedar-Riverside and the residents' initial attempts to mobilize as a social movement.

The Development of an Alternative Community and Its Institutions

The Cedar-Riverside neighborhood movement was embedded in an intriguing blend of the community organizing movement and the countercultural left in the United States in the 1960s. The struggle against the New Town plan began on the heels of what Fisher (1984:91) identifies as "the neighborhood organizing 'revolution' of the 1960's." This revolution was the first period of open revolt against entrenched power since the Great Depression. Before this time, during the period of top-down, capital-conscious urban renewal, "a cry of 'We won't move' was, for the most part, in most places, unthinkable" (Worthy, 1976:29). But in the 1960s, two developments came together to remake neighborhood organizing for the next decade or more: the SNCC and SDS organizing projects and the 1964 War on Poverty.

SNCC (pronounced "snik"), the Student Nonviolent Coordinating Committee, was a southern civil rights movement organization formed in the wake of the famous student lunch-counter sit-ins to force southern businesses to desegregate eating facilities (Piven and Cloward, 1977; Morris, 1984; Bloom, 1987). SNCC saw its role as organizing African-American communities to resist and eliminate racism across the South. Voter registration drives, local protests against segregation, and coalition organizing were its forte. SNCC's organizing strategy of identifying indigenous leaders, developing personal relationships, maintaining a loose organizing structure, and developing community "free spaces"—overall very similar to Saul Alinsky's (1969, 1971) model—directed community organizing into the 1980s (Fisher, 1984).

SDS, Students for a Democratic Society, built on this model through the Economic Research Action Project (ERAP) community organizing program. SDS, though mainly an organization of white middle-/ and upper-class college students, was heir to both the resources of the institutionalized socialist and union movements and the vision and tactics of the civil rights movement. The primary focus of SDS was the college campus, but the ERAP program also moved the organization into poor communities and focused its energies squarely on community-based economic issues. SDS brought more to the struggle than a commitment to end poverty. For Wini Breines (1989:xiv), the greatest contribution of the New Left, of which SDS was a part, was an emphasis on "prefigurative politics": "The effort to build community, to create and prefigure in lived action and behavior the desired society, the emphasis on means and not ends, the spontaneous and utopian experiments that developed in the midst of action while working toward the ultimate goal of a free and democratic society." The struggle of the New Left was not just for rights or equality, or freedom, but for *community*. Here was a movement that wanted to find the gemeinschaft qualities of emotional connectedness and mutual support in an atmosphere of maximum personal freedom.

This gathering of the alienated resulted in the 1960s counterculture, whose members formed communities inside and outside cities. These communities were developed not out of blind obedience to tradition but out of a conscious effort to create a community of freedom and connectedness. The most extreme manifestation of the movement was the rural commune, in which people attempted to return to the land and to operate relationships on the basis of sharing and mutuality, emphasizing use values against exchange values. These groups, while trying to pursue a more cooperative, emotionally connected lifestyle typical of classic gemeinschaft communities, did not in most cases enforce a rigid tradition (Zablocki, 1971; Melville, 1972; Gardner, 1973). Within the cities, communal neighborhoods also formed, probably none more famous than San Francisco's Haight-Ashbury. The closeness of such communities to mainstream society made it difficult for these urban centers of gemeinschaft to maintain themselves (Fraser, 1988), but they provided the springboard for much of the resistance to top-down, capital-conscious urban renewal.

Although separations existed between hippies and New Left political activists, there were also strong connections between the two movements, each of which sought the ultimate goal of community (Fraser, 1988; Breines, 1989). In Cedar-Riverside the cultural splits between the New Left and the counterculture made initial organizing against the New Town and its supporting Urban Renewal Plan difficult. By 1968 New Left student activists from the West Bank had succeeded in taking over the DFL 6th Ward Club and were leading the attempt to bring Eugene McCarthy the 1968 Democratic presidential nomination (Lebedoff, 1972). But activists and politicians agree that the majority of the community never became really active in the

DFL. During the 1968 McCarthy campaign, for example, one resident explained that, because of the residents' clothing and hairstyles, it "was almost impossible to find someone who could be seen outside the West Bank" to gather support for the candidate. Activists cite separate sets of names of those they describe as DFL activists and neighborhood activists, with antiwar activists yet a third group. There were certainly overlaps, but the groups themselves focused on their own issues. Early defeats of McCarthy and a DFL senatorial campaign may have soured many residents on heavy electoral involvement, and others were skeptical of mainstream politics on ideological grounds.

The first large demonstration to come from the counterculture faction of the new community was directed at City Hall. In 1968 the City Council voted not to renew the dance license of Dania Hall, a historic neighborhood building where the neighborhood "youth" held dances. The council charged that the dance hall was a center for drug dealing. In July two hundred demonstrators took to the street but were persuaded by a sympathetic police officer to confine the demonstration to a parking lot. A news article on the first mass protest erupting from the closing of Dania Hall in 1968 brings out the community's playful counterculture spirit: "When the 'confrontation' ended, the police left with flowers in their lapels, 'Save Cedar-Riverside' buttons in their hats—and an empty paddy wagon" (Minneapolis Tribune, July 4, 1968:24).

By the time the New Town plan was established in Cedar-Riverside, the 1960s counterculture youth had settled in. Their values were antimaterialistic, participatory-democratic, and activist; they practiced a radical emphasis on the creation of use values against exchange values, reflected in the community institutions they would create. They lived on very little, with fewer than half the residents working fulltime and many working only half time. The new residents played music, made and sold art and crafts, sold drugs, worked at neighborhood bars and cafes, and shared their wealth. At least a third to a half of them were living communally, sharing childcare, housework, and incomes (Ralph Wittcoff interview, 1988; Dorothy Jacobs interview, 1988). And the isolation created through residents' participation in the illegal drug and draft-resistance undergrounds cemented community bonds. The new residents of Cedar-Riverside were establishing an alternative community, based in three very important community institutions: the Community Union, the Cedar-Riverside People's Center, and the New Riverside Cafe. The initial community organizing also led to the creation of a Cedar-Riverside Project Committee—the only organization focused specifically on the New Town and its supporting urban renewal plan—but its impact was much less gratifying.

The Community Union

Early in 1970 the Cedar-Riverside Community Union emerged to advocate self-determination and neighborhood control of redevelopment (Armitage et al., 1973). This organization, which led the charge against the New Town and university encroachment on the neighborhood, was formed from a variety of interests. Bill Teska, an Episcopal minister from the University Episcopal Center, was a central figure involved as both a spiritual activist and a resident. Steve Parliament and Joyce Yu, who worked on Eugene McCarthy's bid for the 1968 Democratic presidential nomination (a movement that began in Cedar-Riverside) and in an unsuccessful attempt to unseat conservative alderman Christensen, were also central figures. Jack Cann, the only person not yet living in the neighborhood, became involved through the Minnesota Tenants' Union, which was working on the problems that "urban renewal" neighborhoods were experiencing. Ralph Wittcoff, who had lost money through an unsatisfying agreement with CRA to rehabilitate his own rental house in exchange for what became a miniscule rent rebate, and who was angry at learning the neighborhood was to be demolished, became involved through Bill Teska. Many others were involved, but these individuals depict the range from Democratic Party politics, to university activists, to angry residents.

The initial organizing of the Community Union was founded on little hope and multiple issues. Indeed, it was this multiple-issue focus that led to a "Community Union" rather than a "Tenants' Union," as residents had first discussed (Joyce Yu interview, 1978). There was some sentiment among members of the group that they had already lost, but they did not give up: "In 1970 we called a general meeting of the neighborhood. We put out posters and plastered the whole neighborhood and had everybody come to a large meeting. . . . We called ourselves the Community Union and divided ourselves up into geographic groups—block groups" (Steve Parliament interview, 1978). Many people came to the first meeting out of self-interest, expecting relocation money when they were forced to move out to make way for the New Town, but others came because of their interest in radical politics. And perhaps as many as one-third of those attending were the remaining older residents facing condemnation by the university or eviction by CRA. All told, between 125 and 200 people showed up in the heart of a Minnesota winter.[1]

The first meeting established a steering committee of about a dozen people to set agendas, organized about twenty block groups, and focused on the issues of university expansion, relocation benefits, community services, and citizen participation.

> Then we had those people at the first meeting go out and work the area that they came from. They went back out and worked and went door to door and invited everybody in that area to the next Community Union meeting. So the next one was bigger, and it had better representation from all over the neighborhood. And then at the second meeting we actually founded the Union. (Parliament interview, 1978)

The Community Union was christened with a steering committee formed from representatives from each block group. The only requirement for membership was residence in the neighborhood. Decisions were made by a basic consensus. In fact, too much structure and especially hierarchical structure was always eschewed by residents.

The young residents' rejection of structure alienated the older residents and created strains in the organization itself. The strains between younger and older residents, particularly those older residents who were homeowners, resurfaced at critical points later in the struggle for the neighborhood. In the beginning, though, the new residents struggled among themselves over how formally organized the Community Union should be.

> So there was another group of people who got together and started talking about how to prevent the Union from becoming too structured. It was very important to keep it very loose, very grass roots— without too many representative layers on top of it. That was an important thing for the more anarchistic elements in the neighborhood—keep it democratic. And that theme just pervaded every other organization that we've set up on the West Bank to prevent any kind of hierarchy from forming in organizations. (Parliament interview, 1978)

Meetings varied, depending on the development of crises in the neighborhood; sometimes they occurred weekly and sometimes the Community Union stood idle as other organizations took over the tasks the Union set. The Community Union became the neighborhood's general purpose organization and was used when no other organization was available to meet the task. In most cases the Union called meetings to deal with a neighborhood crisis and then created a specific separate organization to address the crisis.

The Community Union arose out of more than the need to defend the neighborhood from the immediate New Town and university threats: "The Community Union was a combination of people who were interested in forming the People's Center, a co-op grocery store, and . . . some kind of citizen participation group organized to represent the neighborhood at the housing authority when decisions were made on what was gonna happen to the neighborhood" (Parliament interview, 1978). Consequently, the Community Union's first activities were to establish two neighborhood service organizations: the New Riverside Cafe and the Cedar-Riverside People's Center.

The New Riverside Cafe

The New Riverside Cafe was founded as an alternative to the Cafe Extempore. Bill Teska was on the Cafe Extempore board and left when he discovered the board was controlled by CRA and its supporters. Community-controlled services were an important issue in the Community Union, and Teska organized church funds and a group of five to ten residents. The New Riverside Cafe opened in September 1970 after the members themselves rehabilitated the space, and its staff quickly grew and reorganized itself into a horizontal collective. The radical residents' sense of fate and hope is reflected in the debate over what to call the organization.

> The day before we were scheduled to open, we were going to call it the "Last Stand Cafe"—short for "The Genuine Original Old Time Bohemian and Leftover Beatnik Last Stand Cafe"—Teska's idea— but people didn't like "leftover last stand." We preferred "new beginning." An SDSer said, "Why not just call it the Riverside Cafe?" I said that would be nice except there already was a Riverside Cafe that was redeveloped out, so it became the New Riverside Cafe. (Wittcoff interview, 1978)

Cafe members lived communally, eventually buying a house in the neighborhood. The cafe quickly established itself as Cedar-Riverside's "living room," where residents could get whole vegetarian food, learn the latest on the resistance struggle, and participate in that resistance. The Community Union met at the cafe, and the cafe "catered" neighborhood events.

The cafe collective, composed of self-described anarchists, was the most militant organization in the neighborhood, taking responsibility for paint attacks on CRA's offices and dead chickens nailed to its office door: "Going into it from the beginning with the idea we had already lost, no tactic was too gross" (Wittcoff interview, 1978). The militant culture of the Cafe also provided the movement with a symbol and a slogan. Zack Zniewski, a cafe collective member and graphic artist, as the story is told, came up with the idea one inspired evening. The symbol he drew was a black cat with back arched and eyes piercing, accompanied by the slogan, "We Never Forget—We Never Sleep": "It was an energizing symbol, one that reminded us that small creatures can have a big impact on large creatures. Few people can have a black cat cross their paths, even today, without thinking for a moment about bad luck" (Ralph Wittcoff quoted in the *West Bank Newsletter*, March 1986).[2] The "watchcat," as it came to be called, appeared across the neighborhood over the next two decades. Neighborhood flyers, banners, and even garbage cans proudly displayed the symbol.

The Cedar-Riverside People's Center

The other community-controlled service established through the Community Union was the Cedar-Riverside People's Center, a community-controlled, full-service medical center for people and their companion animals. Both the young and old residents of Cedar-Riverside at the time were very poor, and neither could afford adequate health care. The new residents in particular were dissatisfied with the services CRA was establishing in the neighborhood.

> What we saw was a lot of little social services being set up on the West Bank—the Free Store, drug information stuff, YES [an organization], all sorts of stuff. And people were saying, "God, you got all these little things; we should have one place that we control, that Heller-Segal doesn't control," because Heller-Segal had a hook in every other agency in the West Bank. . . . And so those agencies were not able to oppose Heller-Segal as a community force and they were frequently paraded in front of the public or HRA or HUD or whoever Heller-Segal was trying to get money from, as being a grass-roots organization that supported them. And we wanted a grass-roots organization that didn't support them. (Yu interview, 1978)

The only source of health care in Cedar-Riverside was "Dr. Judy," who operated a free clinic in the neighborhood on twenty thousand annual dollars from the county's General Hospital, and she was retiring. So the Community Union, in conjunction with medical students from the university, organized and incorporated the People's Center to provide free health care for the neighborhood. A board was established by names drawn from a hat. Medical students from the university, social workers, birth control counselors, patient advocates, and veterinary students volunteered their time; foundations and corporations contributed money; and a local church rented a building to the organization for minimal cost. The Community Union was able to get Dr. Judy's budget transferred to the People's Center: "We felt it was a right that we had this money. It was not a favor that the honchos were giving us, that communities had a right to tax dollars located in their communities—so that was our whole idea: community-based medicine, not hospital-based medicine" (Yu interview, 1978).

The lobby of the People's Center also provided a new home for People's Pantry, an early version of a buyers' club allowing residents to obtain bulk organic foods at low cost, which had been operated from one resident's porch. People's Pantry gained increasing popularity in its new location and eventually grew into the worker-controlled North Country Co-op with its own building. North Country became not only another pillar of the neighborhood's alternative community, but another front in the battle over the neighborhood when Augsburg College threatened to displace the co-op through expansion. The New Riverside Cafe, People's Center, and People's Pantry functioned as "free spaces" in the neighborhood. Sara Evans and Harry Boyte (1986:17) define "free spaces" as voluntary associations that bring community members together to "act with dignity, independence, and vision." It is these community institutions that are the source of community maintenance: they provide the space where the community preserves and develops its particular subcultural values and practices. Whether the corner drugstore, the feminist bookstore, the neighborhood church, or the community center, these free spaces provide the hub for both geographically focused communities and geographically dispersed communities. In Cedar-Riverside it was the community-controlled services that defined and expressed the alternative culture of the new residents.

These organizations themselves were not highly structured. Suzanne Staggenborg (1989b) expands on Jo Freeman's (1972–73) work to make a crucial distinction between the degree of centralization and the degree of formalization of a movement organization. In her model it is possible to have anything from a formally decentralized organization, with strict rules to maintain that decentralization, to an informally centralized organization, whose lack of rules allows a few to centralize power. In Cedar-Riverside, residents attempted as much as possible to maintain informal decentralization. Business was conducted "on a joint and a handshake." The New Riverside Cafe operated for a time without prices, requiring only that patrons "eat what you need and pay what you can." People's Pantry was run by anyone who had the time to volunteer. And although the Community Union did have a board composed of representatives from all the organized blocks in the neighborhood, it met irregularly, and everyone who came participated in consensus-building. The People's Center Board was organized a bit more formally but still attempted to limit any differentiation.

> The policy board of the People's Center . . . was selected by drawing their names out of a hat, who were nominated. You didn't have a popularity contest and that was the whole idea: that everyone was equally qualified. If you want to do it, and you want to put your name in the hat, you won't feel bad if you don't get it. And so no one became alienated from the organization.   (Yu interview, 1978)

Normally, the risk from this form of informal decentralization is inefficiency (Zald and Ash, 1966; Breines, 1980). The neighborhood was quite adept at responding quickly and massively to crises within the community that could be handled through the community-building institutions, however. And the crises were common and diverse, such as one day when a full truckload of organic figs unexpectedly arrived at the warehouse for the Twin Cities grocery co-ops: "There wasn't even a forklift. The driver was really pissed; he thought he'd never make his next stop. The call went out to the Cafe and the co-ops. Fifty hippies converged in old pickup trucks and unloaded the trailer in half an hour, and the amazed driver was on his way" (Wittcoff interview, 1988).

The third main organization created in the neighborhood was directed outward at the threat facing the community from the New Town. Initially, however, it was less useful to the residents because it was outside their control.

The Cedar-Riverside Project Area Committee

The Community Union's tentacles spread into citywide political activity when the Union joined a coalition of neighborhood organizations in Minneapolis to push for greater citizen participation in urban redevelopment. Here neighborhood activists could find some support at the federal level. Along with the 1954 amendment to the Housing Act (Greer, 1965) was the "Workable Program for Community Development," which required those planning urban renewal to "enlist the finest leadership of every sphere of community life and action" with "special emphasis . . . placed on minority group participation" (U.S. Housing and Home Finance Agency, in Bellush and Hausknecht, 1967:276). This citizen-participation requirement was largely ignored or only minimally observed (Dahl, 1961). Moreover, the Economic Opportunity Act of 1965 required the "maximum feasible participation" of inner-city minorities. As resentment toward top-down, capital-conscious urban redevelopment grew, neighborhood activists made the most of the citizen-participation requirement to appeal their demands over the heads of local officials directly to the federal government (N. Fainstein and S. Fainstein, 1986a).

When neighborhood activists discovered that HUD regulations required that citizen-participation groups, or Project Area Committees (PACs), be established in Urban Renewal Plan districts, the Community Union sent a letter to the MHRA asking it to recognize the Community Union as the Cedar-Riverside PAC. The MHRA refused, arguing among other things that Cedar-Riverside was a "clearance neighborhood" and therefore did not require a PAC.

> When the Union applied for recognition as a PAC, the Housing Authority turned us down, basically. So the Community Union and a number of other neighborhood groups from all over the city got together and filed an administrative appeal of the city's workable program. And the workable program is a report that goes to the federal government on how well the city is doing in all kinds of housing performance areas. And if it doesn't live up to certain standards, then the federal government can't give federal money to the city for urban renewal. So one of those standards was citizen participation. . . . And there wasn't any in Cedar-Riverside and a number of other neighborhoods. . . . And HUD issued a directive to the city that it had to set up a Project Area Committee in Cedar-Riverside. (Parliament interview, 1978)

In the meantime HUD held up millions of dollars in urban renewal money from the City of Minneapolis, until the MHRA funded PACs in both the Cedar-Riverside and Nicollet Island neighborhoods.

Establishing a PAC was one battle. Establishing a PAC that represented neighborhood residents was yet another battle. Joyce Yu notes that neighborhood activists had been ambivalent from the beginning about whether a PAC could be more than a distraction. "We went through a lot of agony about whether we wanted to form a PAC or whether we just wanted to be the Community Union on the fringes pressuring and confronting HRA." The residents' suspicions were grounded in the other reason MHRA had refused to recognize the Community Union as the PAC: developers could not be members of the Community Union. "So the Housing Authority staff came in and held public meetings and wrote essentially their own idea of what a PAC ought to be. And it included all the developers and institutions and business interests and social service agencies, and an election of delegates from the neighborhood" (Parliament interview, 1978).

The MHRA initially established a PAC in which only half the members were residents. The other half consisted of institutions in the neighborhood, developers, and absentee landlords. Neighborhood activists drove to Chicago to meet with HUD officials and persuaded them to force the MHRA to limit developer representation on the PAC. CRA officials flew to Chicago and persuaded HUD to allow developers and institutions to vote on the PAC. The result of all this travel was that HUD limited nonresident representation to one-third of the total PAC seats but allowed nonresidents to vote on the PAC. The early PAC elections resulted in a PAC made up of about half Community Union members and one-third developers and institutions; the remainder consisted of old homeowners who tended to side with CRA and were described as mostly involved to ensure a good selling price for their homes.

Initially, Cedar-Riverside residents were thoroughly disappointed in the PAC. The PAC

> had no power at all. The only power it had was the power of information, of requesting hearings of the Housing Authority, of hassling the Housing Authority. It was not any inherent power that the PAC had; it couldn't actually stop anything. But as a legitimate advisory board from the city, the city had to pay attention to it—the Housing Authority was obligated to listen to it. . . . So just because of that it gave you a slight tactical advantage to occasionally delay things long enough so that you could understand what it was that was going on.   (Parliament interview, 1978)

With time, however, the PAC became a central and crucial organization for neighborhood activists.

The formation of these four organizations was the beginning of

neighborhood activism, and, with the exception of the PAC, neighborhood activism was very much directed toward community building.
Around the time the Community Union was formed, small groups
of residents began turning vacant lots into parks, painting murals
on buildings, and organizing to petition Heller-Segal to improve the
electrical system in "The Whale," a leather-goods store, so that the
businessperson/tenant could operate shoe-repair equipment (Armitage et al., 1973). And the "beer boogie" was beginning to achieve
the status of an institution, as neighborhood bands played at benefits
for the community organizations forming in the neighborhood. Developing in the neighborhood was a radical emphasis on use values.
Adapting the language of the times, Cedar-Riverside was claimed as
the "people's neighborhood." Signs sprouted in vacant lots declar-
ing them "people's parks"; the free clinic was the "People's Center"; People's Pantry provided food. The Electric Fetus record store
achieved notoriety, and lost its lease, by holding a "naked sale," giving
albums away to anyone coming in naked (Armitage et al., 1973). The
New Riverside Cafe survived for a time without setting prices on its
food. Residents shared drugs, sex, and rock 'n' roll. The new neighborhood community was living an explicit rejection of exchange-values
culture.

From Community to Social Movement:
Social Movement Dilemmas, Political Opportunity
Structure, and the Problem of "Fit"

Early in the 1970s the citizens of Cedar-Riverside had succeeded in
establishing a strong community. The underpinnings of community—
geographic boundedness, common ties, interaction (Lyon, 1987), communal ties, and an exclusive culture (Boyte, 1984)—could not have
been more pronounced. The Mississippi River and freeways thoroughly delineated the neighborhood, and the community's alternative culture thoroughly isolated it. Consequently, the community was
off the scale on the measures of community proposed by Logan and
Molotch (1987). Neighborhood community service organizations became focal points in the neighborhood; support networks were created through the "strong ties" of communal living as opposed to the
"weak ties" (Granovetter, 1973) that are more often characteristics of
urban neighborhoods (Fischer, 1982). Residents joked that they had
the safest neighborhood in the city because "all the criminals lived
here," and the drug use and draft-resistance activities that made them

criminal required careful mutual vigilance against authorities. The identity of the neighborhood was the most intense of any in the city and was developed through late-night discussions about communism, anarchism, and a variety of other philosophies. The agglomeration benefits that came from this radical culture—free medical and veterinary services, vegetarian food, drugs, music, and a myriad of other alternative services—expanded as time wore on. The only characteristic of community that was not prevalent in the neighborhood was a shared ethnicity. But the richness of the neighborhood culture more than made up for this lack.

The strong ties of the Cedar-Riverside community became the base for the social movement that formed from it. Steve Buechler (1990) discusses the concept of a "social movement community." Less formally organized than a social movement organization, a social movement community is a community whose members identify with a social movement and work toward the realization of the movement's goals. For Buechler, the community does not have to be geographically bounded, but his definition does not exclude geographically bounded communities such as neighborhoods. The new residents of Cedar-Riverside already identified with or participated in the civil rights, student, and antiwar movements, making the neighborhood a generic movement community. As the threats to the neighborhood and the community from both the University of Minnesota and the New Town compounded, the movement community became increasingly focused on the single cause of defending the neighborhood.

> At that particular time, the university's plans were the most pressing, because they had just decided to acquire a number of blocks in the neighborhood: the block that the People's Center is on, the block the church is on—the Catholic church—and the next block, and then the block that is now primarily a parking lot. And also, they had acquisition plans for the area the law school is now on. At the same time, CRA was talking about beginning Stage I and displacing all the people that lived in the four or five blocks that Cedar Square West is now on.   (Jack Cann interview, 1978)

The citizens of Cedar-Riverside needed more than their own community services when threats arose from both the University of Minnesota—which laid claim to the buildings providing homes to the New Riverside Cafe and the People's Center—and Cedar-Riverside Associates, whose New Town plans were marching on. They needed to transform their community into a social movement. As Cedar-

Riverside mobilized as a social movement, it had to confront the same dilemmas confronting any social movement: how to recruit members, how to organize them, and which tactics to choose in confronting its antagonists. The movement's choices also had to "fit" the political opportunity structure. That is, the forms of recruitment, organizing, and tactical strategy had to gain access to the greatest amount of resources from the political opportunity structure while providing maximum defense against its threats.

Recruitment to the Community: Defending the Social Reproduction Base Against University Expansion

The early community organizing that resulted in the creation of the New Riverside Cafe and People's Center also created a base for mobilization that defended those two organizations against university expansion. In this initial period people were recruited to the community more than to the movement. The new residents developed strong "place meanings" (Rivlin, 1980) with Cedar-Riverside as countercultural community activities encompassed more of their lives. These activities were organized not around protest, however, but around "social reproduction"—meeting basic needs of food, clothing, shelter, and care for residents and their intimates and dependents, to reproduce themselves on a daily basis (Markusen, 1980; Stoecker, 1992). The countercultural organization of social reproduction in the neighborhood created more "biographical availability" (McAdam, 1986) for movement activities. Communal living allowed residents to spend less time in wage work to accumulate the "family surplus" (Laslett, 1981) required to care for children, who could not contribute to the economic resources of the commune. Collectivized childcare and domestic work also reduced the time burden on individuals. Even "traditional couples" traded off working full time so that only one person worked at a time. The New Riverside Cafe's "take what you need, pay what you can" policy reduced residents' reproductive costs. Cafe collective members themselves had to work only three shifts per week. The People's Center's free health care, the general low cost of living of the time, and the neighborhood's informal economy that made art and recreational drugs a means of income also reduced individuals' need to engage in traditional wage work (Wittcoff interview, 1988; Jacobs interview, 1988).

The commitment to the community was an ideological one. Residents argued regularly among themselves from the writings of Marx, Mao, Kropotkin, Trotsky, Castro, Guevara, Goldman, and many others.

Probably no recruitment incentive is stronger than the "purposive" or ideological incentive, even in neighborhood movements (Oliver, 1983). When members are heavily involved in the community and there are multiple strands of relationships and strong ties, extensive and densely knit communication networks, and relative isolation of members through solidary activities, neighborhood mobilization for both routine and emergency matters is increased (Wellman and Leighton, 1979; Crenson, 1974). The way in which Cedar-Riverside organized its social reproduction activities created just this kind of community.

Thus, when the social reproduction services that helped to sustain the community were threatened, the crisis was direct and immediate. In 1971 the cafe, the People's Center, and People's Pantry were settling in just when the university was about to expand on the land granted to it by the MHRA Urban Renewal Plan. This expansion threatened both the People's Center and the New Riverside Cafe, which were located on the land to be acquired by the university. With both a clear target to defend and existing organizations to act through, it was relatively easy to recruit residents to protest these immediate threats to the community's social reproduction base.

> The first real action involved the university expansion. What we did was get a lawyer and put together a case challenging whether or not the taking was for a public purpose. The university had planned to acquire stuff that spring and clear it that summer and put in athletic fields. The legal challenge, which was totally unexpected, delayed their plans through that summer, and a series of demonstrations and so on got the university to sit down and talk with us. (Cann interview, 1978)

The New Riverside Cafe building was slated for demolition for a university parking lot, and it looked for a time as if the neighborhood would lose its living room, since the New Riverside block contained the only commercial buildings not already owned by CRA.

> The university did in fact condemn the building and told the cafe that they were gonna have to move by June first of 1971. . . . And some of the West Bank campus ministers and some of the cafe members told the university . . . "If we're not provided with suitable relocation within the neighborhood, we just won't go. We'll stay there until the 'heliocopters' [sic] come." So at that point the university became very interested in helping the cafe relocate. Where previously CRA had already refused up and down, they owned

the only property in the neighborhood, now the university applied some pressure, and because of that pressure we were grudgingly awarded the present location at the corner of Cedar and Riverside. (Wittcoff interview, 1978)

After lengthy resident-university negotiations and university-CRA negotiations, CRA agreed to provide space at reasonable cost one block down, where the cafe members again rehabbed their own space and reestablished the New Riverside Cafe, which remains to this day.

Both the cafe and the People's Center benefited from the militant demonstrations across the Mississippi River by the East Bank University campus, where students were protesting over a "Red Barn" fast-food restaurant franchise. The People's Center made explicit connections to that struggle when they discovered their building, which had been acquired by the university, was going to be used for office space. When university officials met with the People's Center board, they confronted a room packed with Cedar-Riverside residents and their own medical students.

> We had this huge meeting, and we invited the community to come. [The university] thought they were gonna meet with six people. And there were fifty or a hundred people there. And all the medical students came. . . . People in the community stood up to say, "You think ten thousand fighting . . . the Red Barn over a little hairdresser and bookstore [is bad], and you're talking about closing down a free medical clinic. You think ten thousand people in front of that Red Barn is something, wait till you see what we do here." . . . And the university just backed down. That was the beginning of the university realizing that they had a force to contend with at the People's Center. (Yu interview, 1978)

The university allowed the People's Center to remain.

Defending Against the New Town: The Problem of Movement Organization and a Closed Political Opportunity Structure

The community was far more successful in saving the community-based institutions than in mobilizing against Cedar Square West initially. The difference in outcomes can be related to the fit between social movement strategy and the two different political opportunity structures the neighborhood confronted.

The political opportunity structure in which the struggle against the New Town was embedded was relatively closed and tightly stabilized, and it provided few allies to the movement, as we have seen. The struggle against university expansion, however, took place within a much more volatile political opportunity structure with more allies. In contrast to the city bureaucracy, about which the residents knew very little, and the HUD bureaucracy, from which they were almost completely insulated, the university bureaucracy was quite familiar to the residents and they could thus gain access to it more easily. They knew who to demand meetings from and how to confront them. The university political opportunity structure was also much less stable; Minnesota, like campuses across the country (Fraser, 1968), was being shaken by student demonstrations and polarized within as students, faculty, and administrators chose sides. No member of the growth coalition—the city, HUD, or CRA—faced the same desta-bilizing revolts. Finally, the residents had access to much stronger allies in the struggle against the university. The University Episcopal Center, supporting both the People's Center and the organizing at the New Riverside Cafe, carried greater weight with the university than it did with the city or HUD or CRA. The medical students who came out in force were also an important ally, making the People's Center an educational issue: "The medical students stood up and said, 'This is the most important educational experience of my career. This clinic is doing more for us than anything I've ever experienced' " (Yu interview, 1978). Since the People's Center was being financially sup-ported by foundations, corporations, and Dr. Judy's General Hospital budget, it was also much less isolated than the residential houses that CRA demolished for Cedar Square West.

It is clear, then, that the New Town political opportunity structure was antagonistic to resident interests and exerted a profound influ-ence over the movement's inability to stop Cedar Square West. But the neighborhood movement was also not organized to take advantage of the few opportunities to attack the fissures in the growth coalition.

Demolition for Stage I of the New Town in Town began in the fall of 1970, when the housing east of Cedar Avenue was leveled. The Com-munity Union was able to achieve relocation rights and benefits, and many tenants were relocated to the west side of Cedar Avenue (Martin, 1978). Not yet ready to bow to defeat, the residents discovered the newly created National Environmental Policy Act, which required that developers file an environmental impact statement (EIS). The EIS was supposed to include an analysis of development options and en-vironmental impacts and was to be approved through public hearings (Pascal and Parliament, 1977). Steve Parliament and Jack Cann came across a case at the Minnesota Tenants' Union about residents who brought suit against a developer and forced the developer to file an EIS. "Jack and I read that, and we said to ourselves, 'What the hell is an EIS? We never heard of one of those before. And it sounds like we should know.'"

Parliament and Cann first stopped at the Minnesota Public Interest Research Group (MPIRG) offices, where they got HUD handbooks that discussed this new environmental law. Then they went to a lawyer in town who discovered that an EIS had been filed for Cedar-Riverside in the summer of 1971. Steve Parliament went to CRA and got a copy of what he was told was an "in-house environmental statement." After finally getting the HUD-approved EIS, Parliament and Cann compared it to the CRA "in-house" document and found that it was "95 percent identical . . . except for some cover bureaucratese."

The PAC, in the spring of 1972, wrote a letter to the Council on Environmental Quality raising the objections that Cedar-Riverside Associates' EIS did not discuss options and impacts and was not approved through a public hearing process. The council referred them to HUD, which said that the community should wait until the next stage, when the EIS would be reviewed again. The PAC also proposed to CRA to send a joint PAC-CRA request to HUD not to continue Stage I until a new EIS could be drafted, an idea that CRA of course rejected (Cann interview, 1978). The concrete towers of Stage I rose from the rubble of demolished homes.

Activists had identified crucial targets in the New Town political opportunity structure. But they lacked an organizational structure that could make the most of those opportunities. This early movement structure is best characterized as a "group movement" (Fine and Stoecker, 1985), composed of at least semiautonomous groups, similar to Gerlach and Hine's (1970) decentralized, segmented, and reticulate movement structure. The differences are that there is no necessary overlap or coordination between movement cells. This model accurately describes the community structure of the early period, as residents of the neighborhood were organized into various independent communes, or separate organizations. When the People's Center and the cafe were threatened, each organization mobilized its own resistance. But because their primary goal was not political, these early groups did not often coordinate their activities against the New Town. And with the PAC out of activists' control, the early political mobilization against the New Town was centralized in the Community Union.

The movement structure, then, with only one outwardly directed political organization, lost a great deal of flexibility. The Community Union somehow had to respond to the multiple actors in the New Town growth coalition all by itself. There were no organizations whose purpose was specifically to organize residents, to study environmental law, to play politics at City Hall, or to raise money. In contrast to the community-building side of the movement, where there was a specialized health care organization, two specialized food-provision organizations, and numerous independent service activities, the political side of the movement was not well developed. Thus, recruitment to political activities was limited as well. Although Community Union organizers could bring neighborhood citizens out to meetings with the selective incentive of learning how to receive relocation benefits, visibly activating large numbers to become involved in a mass strategy was difficult unless there was a "hot issue." Consequently, the neighborhood movement was viewed as a small group by the media and New Town proponents (Martin, 1978; *Minneapolis Star*, September 11, 1973:1). This restriction on the movement's tactical options propelled the community to an explosion of militancy in 1972.

Limitations on Tactics and the Turn to Disruption: The Dedication Ceremony Uprising

The frustration of being stymied in the battle over Stage I, the struggles with the university, and the escalation of the war in Southeast Asia were all taking their toll in the neighborhood. The split between the neighborhood activists and antiwar activists was about to close.

On May 9, 1972, the front page of the *Minneapolis Star* reported President Nixon's announcement of the mining of Haiphong Harbor. Also a few days into May, Cedar-Riverside activists heard from their contacts in CRA that the secretary of HUD, George Romney, was scheduled to appear at the dedication of Cedar Square West, Stage I of the New Town, an eleven-building complex containing 1,299 housing units. The dedication would become the ultimate "hot issue." CRA had been sprucing up the neighborhood for the May 9 dedication, but it was clear that the cleanup was only cosmetic.

> During the week or two before Romney was coming, Heller-Segal started painting the whole neighborhood. They would paint just the front of a house. So we knew which path Romney was gonna take

through the neighborhood, because they would plant geraniums on every corner where he had to make a turn and then put little picket fences along 5th and 19th. (Yu interview, 1978)

On the night of May 8, residents used both their well-established crisis-communication networks and their leafletting skills to organize a meeting for the next morning. Much of this was done by word of mouth, since the new community had become very tight. Across the river, antiwar movement leader Marv Davidov and a large contingent of antiwar activists were gearing up to demonstrate against the Haiphong Harbor mining. And at a regular meeting of the New Riverside Cafe collective, where they had just paid their bills and everyone had five dollars left, the collective began discussing how it should get involved in the Cedar Square West dedication the next day.

> Everyone was sitting with their five-dollar bill in their hand, drinking beer and chatting, and somebody said. . . "Maybe we should get involved with this." And we said, "Well, what should we do?" "Well, we could stencil a slogan all over the neighborhood Romney couldn't miss when he came there." . . . And everybody dutifully threw their five dollars back into the pot and bought some poster board and an X-acto knife and Zack made a stencil and we went to an all-night Seven-Eleven and bought a bunch of cans of spray paint and ran around stenciling the neighborhood all over. (Wittcoff interview, 1978)

Collective members stenciled the neighborhood until well into the early morning. The stencils, cut out of large pieces of cardboard, read: "THIS NEIGHBORHOOD IS BEING 'REDEVELOPED' WITH NO CONCERN FOR THE RESIDENTS OR THE ENVIRONMENT." The action became a comical competition, as CRA sympathizers witnessed the cafe collective's nocturnal mission and contacted CRA, which sent a work crew to attempt to paint over the political redecorating before morning:

> Heller-Segal had a lot of what we called spies living on the West Bank—secretaries and people who worked for him who lived on the West Bank in cheap housing. They saw this happening, so they called "the crew." The crew came out, very characteristically at that time, with gray paint. We called the West Bank at that time "Graytown." So, literally, Ralph [Wittcoff] would spray this white sign. Two minutes later, the crew would come running up and paint it gray. Ralph would come around the block, when it would dry, and

spray over this nice background. The crew would come back, and paint it over. This lasted all night.   (Yu interview, 1978)

At about eight the next morning two hundred people met at the People's Center. Antiwar movement leader Marv Davidov was there to inform the neighborhood of the antiwar demonstration across the river. The neighborhood activists, working with Davidov, had made up flyers inviting antiwar activists to the dedication ceremony demonstration and arranged to have a Cedar-Riverside speaker at the antiwar demonstration to personalize the invitation. At ten o'clock about forty people representing various housing projects in the city joined the meeting (Yu interview, 1978). The most important issue of the meeting focused on tactics: "We had a big philosophical argument about whether to throw marshmallows, eggs, or rocks—that was a highly philosophic discussion that was going on then. And we had decided that marshmallows and eggs were appropriate and we weren't gonna throw rocks" (Parliament interview, 1978).

The entire group of two hundred or more made its way over to Cedar Square West, where the project had been fenced off. Down Cedar Avenue came the Minneapolis Police Tactical Squad, and down Riverside came five hundred or more antiwar demonstrators. The tactical squad lined up on the Cedar Square West side of the fence, and the demonstrators were on the other side.

> The Tac Squad sergeant with a big bullhorn was saying, "All right, men; X, Y, 5," and all the Tac Squad men would go into this little maneuver on the other side of the fence. On our side of the fence, Dean Zimmerman, one of the prime organizers in the area, was there with a big orange bullhorn that said "PEOPLE'S BULLHORN" on the side, and he would say, "All right, men; Z, A, 7," and all the Tac Squad men would jump around and look puzzled.   (Wittcoff interview, 1978)

Meanwhile, according to Joyce Yu, neighborhood activists had heard from a CRA secretary that Romney, having been told that his safety could not be guaranteed, was not going to set foot in Cedar-Riverside and had decided to fly over instead. Not to be outdone, two demonstrators got to the top of one of the neighborhood business buildings. In big, helicopter-size letters they painted: "END THE WAR— REHAB NOW."

On the ground, demonstrators began pelting the Tac Squad with marshmallows, and the New Riverside Cafe brought a case of eggs.

It is unclear what happened next. Some charge that the Tac squad began macing protestors, provoking a barrage of rocks. Ultimately, however, the crowd did escalate to using rocks, and the Tac Squad charged over the fence. Mace and rocks and billy clubs "raged up and down Cedar Avenue for a couple of hours" (Wittcoff interview, 1978). The demonstrators moved on to block traffic and engage in isolated acts of violence that resulted in seventeen arrests and a number of injuries.[3]

The police reaction was important. Up until this time, relations with police had ebbed and flowed, with increasingly frequent drug raids (Martin, 1978). The killing of one resident by an undercover agent led to a tenuous cooperation in 1971 and a relatively friendly relationship with the neighborhood "beat cops."[4] But after the dedication ceremony demonstration it was difficult for the community to have mixed feelings about the police. As one resident described it, "You suddenly knew which side they were on." In later years the West Bank PAC office proudly displayed a collection of photos on the wall entitled "The Battle of the West Bank" in memory of the occasion.

The switch to militancy was a result of the restricted organizational flexibility of the movement. There were no multiple political organizations that could allow the movement to practice greater tactical flexibility. Neighborhood activists attempted to negotiate for a new environmental impact statement process, and got nothing. They attempted to negotiate for a PAC, and got a PAC that was controlled by CRA and its allies. It became increasingly clear that negotiation would have little impact. Electoral tactics, which could have unseated the conservative council member and turned over control of the PAC to the neighborhood, did not mobilize enough residents to succeed. Alienation from the mainstream political process, the inability of anti-war activists to see the relevance of neighborhood issues, and a lack of belief that it could work inhibited the development of this tactic. Cedar-Riverside had few "resources" in the traditional sense and consequently, in relation to the outside world, had no bargaining position. Often the only strategy available to groups with few resources and few allies is disruption (Piven and Cloward, 1977; Schumacher, 1978). By the time of the dedication ceremony uprising, disruption was a "nothing left to lose" strategy. If the activists lost the fight, they would lose their homes and their community anyway, so there was literally nothing left to lose. As a result, the tactics of the early phase of the movement increasingly emphasized the threat of disruption.

There were indications of a more sophisticated tactical approach, however, during this early period. In the struggle to establish a PAC in Cedar-Riverside, the multineighborhood coalition that the neighborhood joined exploited the lack of autonomy of local states from higher-level states (Clark and Dear, 1984; Frug, 1980). Neighborhood activists discovered that they could use millions of dollars of HUD money as leverage to force the city to establish PACs in the Cedar-Riverside and Nicollet Island neighborhoods. The neighborhood movement was attempting to disrupt the growth-machine coalition and play factions against one another. Although this early attempt established a PAC that was out of neighborhood control, the tactic became the central source of success in the middle period of the movement. Activists expanded on this tactic once Cedar Square West was up and running. CRA had big bills to pay, and it soon became clear that the project could not support itself. When the towers of Cedar Square West "were going up we were kind of glad because it proved to the city that they were ugly and that all of Gloria Segal's public relations about New Town in Town, the center of living, was not what it was cracked up to be. So we were very glad, in some respects, to see those towers go up" (Yu interview, 1978). Transforming the community into a movement that could effectively oppose capital and fracture the New Town growth coalition, however, required a much more sophisticated approach to solving the recruitment, organizing, and tactical dilemmas. Building on the strong community base already established, community activists proceeded to develop just such an approach.

Building on Community:
Organizing the Resistance

We were real pleased. We were pleased because it showed that
we were serious and that, just because those buildings had gone
up, the battle was not over, and that we were gonna use every tool
and every cause that could join us to do it.
>   —*Joyce Yu, on the Cedar Square West demonstration*

T HE NEIGHBORHOOD movement lost the first battle. But members now recognized that it was only the first battle. Their hope-
lessness and fatalism was replaced by outrage and the strength of a
threatened community. The dedication ceremony uprising was not in
vain. The residents had established a solid community base and felt
a new sense of empowerment. They had not been able to stop Cedar
Square West, but they had been able to create a dramatic disruption
that turned the project's dedication ceremony into chaos. On the other
hand, residents were no longer certain that "ending up in prison or
the hospital would help the neighborhood." The early rabble-rousing
was thus followed by strategies that pinpointed the hidden fissures
in the growth coalition and transformed the movement community
into a community movement. The residents established the Cedar-
Riverside Environmental Defense Fund (CREDF), which successfully
filed a lawsuit to stop the New Town in Town; organized a Tenants
Union; and took over the PAC by organizing the neighborhood vote.
Community control of the PAC gave the residents the ability to print
Snoose News, the neighborhood newspaper. And the residents created an alternative Community Development Corporation (CDC).

In many ways part of the cause of the movement's early failure was
the reason for its success in the second period. The inward-focused

movement of the first period, which insisted on building a strong community first and resistance to the New Town second, created both a collective will to continue the struggle and a physical neighborhood to struggle for. The presence of social reproduction organizations—the New Riverside Cafe, the People's Center, and North Country Co-op (formerly People's Pantry)—provided for residents' basic needs in alternative ways. With the necessities of life managed by these collective organizations, residents could spend their social surplus fighting the New Town.

In contrast to Piven and Cloward's (1977) argument that organizations *deplete* movement resources, the developing organizational base on the West Bank actually *created* resources. Activists could receive low-cost, community-controlled services and salaries through the PAC, People's Center, Community Union, Tenants Union, New Riverside Cafe, North Country Co-op, West Bank Grocery Co-op, CDC, Free School, two hardware co-ops, a bicycle co-op, various theater companies, recreational drug sales, and art and music activities. Residents could obtain and disperse knowledge efficiently through the New Riverside Cafe and *Snoose News*. Consequently, a unified, solid neighborhood movement developed in Cedar-Riverside. The tenant transience that often undermines tenant organizing (Shlay and Faulkner, 1984), and the members' attachment to outside institutions that often strains their loyalties (Crenson, 1974), were prevented in Cedar-Riverside, allowing the community to provide a stable, unified attack. A PAC survey in 1977 found that residents in the old neighborhood had been there an average of 6.1 years, longer than for most other areas of the city. And the organizations with which people were involved, and their work, were generally in the neighborhood.

This community stability created the precondition for a neighborhood-based social movement. Michael Smith and Richard Tardanico (1989), using an analysis of third world community mobilizations, argue that there are four features of third world cities that promote those mobilizations. First, because of dependent urbanization that inhibits industrial development, organizing around labor issues is especially difficult. Second, the institutionalized political system is relatively inaccessible and unresponsive to citizens. Third, "resource pooling networks" based in neighborhoods provide the greatest source of cohesion. And fourth, the problems of urban neighborhoods overcome normal class cleavages. These conditions were also present in Cedar-Riverside. Having opted out of the traditional laboring culture and networks, West Bankers were not pulled toward labor organizing. They had been shut out of decision making at City Hall. They had organized their social reproduction needs around collective activities centered in the neighborhood for resource pooling and community building. And there was no need to overcome much internal diversity, since the culture and class standing of the residents had become relatively homogeneous.

In this chapter I explore the development of a social movement structure that built on, and depended on, that community strength. Essentially, Cedar-Riverside activists innovated a powerful social movement structure that increasingly shifted the community's focus away from the challenges within to the threats from without.

The Importance of Social Movement Structure

Of the three social movement dilemmas—recruiting members, organizing the movement, and employing tactics—the most important is organizing the movement. Members are recruited to a movement, and a movement must be organized before anyone can be recruited to it. Often the movement structure stays in place even when members are lacking. Organizations are the means by which grievances are transformed into protest (Pickvance, 1977). Leila Rupp and Verta Taylor (1987; see also Taylor, 1989) have shown how a "movement in abeyance," such as the women's movement, is sustained by an organizational network during periods of repression and backlash. And tactical strategy can be carried out only by an organized movement, a distinction that separates a movement from a mob. One of the primary contributions of researchers working in the resource mobilization tradition was the evidence they compiled that social movements were far more organized than mobs and could not be just lumped in with crowd actions, as collective behavior theory had done up to that time (Traugott, 1978; Jenkins, 1983; Hannigan, 1985).

As we have seen, there are two basic models of social movement structure. First is the model asserting that social movements are and should be structured with many leaders (decentralization), many organizations (segmentation), and overlapping communication networks (reticulation)—a DSR structure (Gerlach and Hine, 1970:63; Gerlach, 1983, 1976). This structure is believed to maximize movement flexibility and diversity, but it inhibits coordination of various movement constituencies, and its characteristic interorganizational competition reduces efficiency (Dwyer, 1983; McAdam, 1982:186; Henig, 1982:171). The contrasting model advocates a centralized-bureaucratic movement structure. This structure creates greater efficiency and coordination, along with reducing factioning (Gamson, 1975), but it lacks flexibility (Gerlach, 1983; Weissman, 1981).

Both these structures create problems for localized social movements, however. Both require considerable resources to implement, and the resources available from the political opportunity structure of localized movements, as opposed to geographically more dispersed movements, are limited. A relative shortage of movement members and other resources, organizational exclusivity, ideological differences, and a lack of overlapping memberships and interorganizational interlocks—all typical problems of localized social movements —increase the chances for intramovement conflict for any social movement (Zald and McCarthy, 1980). To employ the DSR model effectively, a social movement must have access to a wide range of resources and members. But localized movements have a strictly limited potential membership base, restrictions on other resources such as money and knowledge, and few issues available to them. The centralized-bureaucratic model—as we saw in Chapter 3 where protest mobilization against the New Town was concentrated in the Community Union—fares no better. The lack of flexibility of a centralized movement does not fit the multiple tasks or manage the internal conflicts endemic to neighborhood-based social movements.

To overcome the limitations of both the DSR and centralized-bureaucratic movement structures, localized movements composed of multiple organizations often adopt a type of umbrella structure (Henig, 1982:171; Morris, 1984; Lawson, 1983). Saul Alinsky's Citizens Action Program united single-issue groups in Chicago to attack the city government with a unified and broad-based front (Reitzes and Reitzes, 1987:83). Other Alinsky-style federated organizations have been used to defend urban neighborhoods and provide community services (Lancourt, 1979:114). "Local movement centers" of the civil rights movement, such as the Montgomery Improvement Association, organized the heterogeneous populations and multiple organizations of local African-American communities to facilitate mass protest (Morris, 1984:40). Decentralization and segmentation at the grass-roots level was coordinated through more centralized, higher-level organizations in the New York City tenants' movement (Lawson, 1983). But even this umbrella structure lasts only so long as the localized movement groups that make it up are able to maintain a sense of common interest (Lancourt, 1979). And that task is particularly challenging for localized movements, which often must compete for severely limited resources and where ideological disputes quickly become personal.

The citizens of Cedar-Riverside overcame the limitations of all these options by innovating an entirely new social movement structure. That structure was composed of three new organizations—the Cedar-Riverside Environmental Defense Fund, the Tenants Union, and the West Bank Community Development Corporation—along with the transformation of the Project Area Committee into a resident-controlled organization, and the existing base of the Community Union and the social reproduction organizations. Each organization had a unique origin that derived from the political needs of the neighborhood at the time the organization formed. And each organization, as a result, was appointed an exclusive mission.

The Cedar-Riverside Environmental Defense Fund

Activists joke about how "we never could come up with an acronym that sounded good," and CREDF (pronounced "kredif") is probably the best example of that problem. But the acronym was the only fault with CREDF, as it achieved the greatest success of any of the neighborhood organizations.

In the wake of the Cedar Square West demonstration, the activists won a PAC vote to authorize representatives to seek legal advice on the environmental impact statement issue. These representatives returned to the PAC in the fall of 1972 recommending that the organization authorize filing a suit. Neighborhood activists and sympathetic community members packed the meeting in an attempt to bring pressure on the PAC to approve a lawsuit, but the suit was voted down nineteen to thirteen. "And we lost that vote . . . so the whole community stood up and walked out of the PAC meeting that night. It was really a dramatic scene with all these residents walking out. We went over to the New Riverside Cafe and reconstituted the Community Union" (Steve Parliament interview, 1978). The Community Union decided to act outside the PAC and hired a lawyer from the law firm the PAC representatives had originally approached. He advised the residents to form a nonprofit organization that could raise funds to allow the community to file its own lawsuit. On the basis of this advice, in late 1972 the Community Union founded the Cedar-Riverside Environmental Defense Fund.

CREDF first attempted to negotiate with CRA's lawyers, but early in 1973 it became clear that CRA would not budge. At that point CREDF prepared to file suit and spent until the fall of 1973 researching and raising money. Along with foundation grants and "beer boogie" funds, CREDF organized "small, intimate dinners" for potential funders from all over the state. Steve Parliament recalls, "People thought we were crazy radicals bent on destroying capitalism," and although many activists held that sentiment, the dinners were intended to get beyond that stereotype to make the case about the environmental problems that would derive from the New Town.

These problems included increased traffic and its accompanying air pollution, pressures on the local infrastructure imposed by significantly increased population densities, and the problems that would be faced by families with children in a high-rise living environment. This last environmental critique was interesting. Here was a "bunch of hippies" organizing their lives far outside the mainstream, protesting an urban redevelopment plan partly on the basis that it would not support traditional family values. But it was not a cynical pragmatic position. Residents were becoming parents in the neighborhood, and though many were raising their children communally, they realized the value of green space, easy access to the outdoors, and the ability to supervise children outside that detached, single-family housing afforded. In time this position would come back to haunt the neighborhood. But for now it was a heartfelt and powerful moral ground from which the New Town could be attacked.

In late 1973 the Community Union elected a board of directors for CREDF, and it was incorporated as a tax-exempt, nonprofit organization. Even with a board of directors, however, CREDF was run much like other neighborhood-controlled organizations. Some procedural decisions were made by the attorney or by a small group of board members, but settlement offers were always brought to mass community meetings of fifty to one hundred people struggling toward consensus.

By this time CRA had already completed plans for Stage II, which would create two more towers of housing, stuffing 1,200 more units into the neighborhood, and had received preliminary approval from the MHRA. CRA was also working on plans for the "Centrum," which would replace much of the neighborhood's business district, as well as four blocks of housing, with a mall-type shopping structure (Martin, 1978; *Minneapolis Star*, October 4, 1974:A16).

Aware that there was little time to lose, CREDF filed suit against HUD, CRA, and the MHRA in federal district court in late 1973, challenging the adequacy of the Stage II environmental impact statement. Judge Miles Lord, infamous in Minnesota for his outspoken populist politics, which included a strong judgment against the Reserve Mining Co. for polluting Lake Superior, a light sentence for two peace activists who destroyed military computer hardware being manufactured at the Sperry Company, and a public scolding of the manufacturers of the Dalkon Shield intrauterine birth control device (Serrill, 1984; *Business Week*, 1984; Berkowitz, 1985), heard the case. "We figured our chances were pretty good, that we did in fact have a real solid case. However, we weren't very confident that the courts would see it our way. . . . I think if we had gotten any other judge, for instance, it would've been a lot harder to win. We lucked out with Miles Lord" (Ralph Wittcoff interview, 1978). CREDF succeeded in obtaining an injunction against further construction pending resolution of the suit (Armitage et al., 1973). This injunction marked the turning point of the conflict. Dependent on continued construction to pay its bills, Cedar-Riverside Associates could not afford court-imposed delays. And as its financial base was compromised, CRA also lost its political control over the neighborhood.

The Liberation of the PAC

Neighborhood activists achieved another victory in the spring 1974 PAC elections when they organized their vote and gained a voting majority on the PAC. "Finally, we looked around at the elected representatives, and figured, 'I think that the elected representatives have the votes to unseat the developers.' We said 'We don't want to have developers on this PAC.' And through a period of six to eight months, that in fact became a reality" (Wittcoff interview, 1978). With liberation[1] of the PAC and its budget, activists began publishing *Snoose News* in 1975, a monthly newspaper that dramatically expanded the community's access to information about the urban renewal plan and the struggle against it.[2]

The neighborhood's first successful foray into mainstream political action signaled an expansion of the kinds of tactics the residents were willing to use. Although CREDF allowed activists to achieve legitimate access to the legal system, the liberation of the PAC from CRA's control gave the residents a legitimate organization that had a right to full information on the New Town Plan and a right to have its voice heard about that plan. And residents made the most of these resources, as the PAC became the central source of resources to promote and facilitate democratic community-based redevelopment planning. The organization was restructured to represent neighborhood districts drawn so that the residents of the old neighborhood, who were most affected by redevelopment planning, were guaranteed a majority of the PAC votes. Eventually, the PAC organized neighborhood-based planning meetings, lobbied for those plans at City Hall, and oversaw their implementation in the neighborhood.

The use of the PAC as a proactive planning organization would have to wait, however, while the community struggled against the immediate threat of the New Town. But the neighborhood PAC takeover and the delays being caused by the CREDF suit were already hurting CRA, and its investors were increasingly concerned. The computer models for the New Town financing were based on a maximum of 6 percent inflation, and the reality was double-digit inflation (William Betzler interview, 1978). The subsidized units at Cedar Square West were renting well, but only half to three-quarters of the market-rate units and only a quarter of the luxury units were rented a year after opening (Martin, 1978). And the costs to acquire the remaining available land parcels in the neighborhood were skyrocketing (Ralph Rapson interview, 1978). CRA, having lost battles on two fronts, lashed out at the neighborhood with a huge rent hike, leading to the next neighborhood organization.

The Tenants Union

To increase the cash flow or to try to break the resistance movement (it is not certain which), CRA suddenly cranked rents up across the board in mid-1974. CRA officials told Dave Raymond to develop a plan for a rent increase. He came up with a plan of two months' notice, with an average 10 percent increase and a maximum 15 percent increase, to be implemented incrementally. Management vetoed that plan, however, and decided to institute a 50 percent rent hike with as little notice as possible, a policy that activists believe was chosen in hopes that the community would not have time to react. "The thing was carried out in such an incredibly heavy-handed manner, and arrogant. They just said 'Fuck you, we need the money and we're gonna increase the rents. We don't care who has to move out of the neighborhood as a result. We don't care what you all think.' So the logical response was a tenants union" (Jack Cann interview, 1978). Once more the Community Union sprang into action and called a meeting. One hundred to two hundred fifty people showed up and founded the West Bank Tenants Union. Old and new residents who did not want to give CRA more money and could not afford the rent hike joined. Activists estimated that community resistance to CRA tripled, and many of these new people soon became drawn into the struggle against the New Town.

The Tenants Union was another loosely run organization. It had a coordinating committee to organize an agenda, but decisions were typically made by one hundred to two hundred people trying to reach a consensus. People volunteered or were volunteered to be on negotiating committees. The Tenants Union would work out a platform of demands, a negotiating team would meet with CRA and bring back its response, and the Union would decide collectively whether to agree or not.

At the end of July Cedar-Riverside residents voted a rent strike after CRA had refused to freeze rents during negotiations and to recognize the Tenants Union as the exclusive bargaining agent for tenants. It was an immediate militant response, as residents were certain that beginning with moderate tactics and working up to a strike would fail. "The problem in this situation with going through that series of moves was that the rent increase was so drastic that large numbers of people simply could not afford to pay it and if we waited a month, even an extra month, people would simply be driven out of the neighborhood" (Cann interview, 1978). The plan was to turn rent money over to the Tenants Union to hold in escrow, begin listing code violations in their units, picket CRA offices, and flood the courts if CRA attempted evictions. It is uncertain how many people joined the strike—at least two hundred residents, and perhaps as many as two hundred *units*, went on strike. Not content just to withhold rent, one hundred fifty people also showed up for a rally at the CRA office in August. The New Riverside Cafe wanted to "strike 'em until they're dead."

After about three months the Tenants Union and University Community Properties Incorporated, or UCPI (the property management subcorporation of CRA, referred to by residents simply as "CRA" or as "uk-pee"), agreed to a 2 to 4 percent annual increase with a maximum increase of 26.7 percent—a clear victory. But the resolution of the first strike did not last, as both sides went on the offensive. The Tenants Union tried to pressure CRA on maintenance issues. Many units had only large gas space heaters for warmth in the Minnesota winter and were replete with code violations. The results here were mixed, as CRA agreed to fix minor problems but threatened to close buildings that had major defects and were slated for demolition.

The most contentious issue threatening the tentative and insecure peace between the Tenants Union and CRA was created when UCPI began raising rents for people who had moved into the neighborhood after the strike settlement, arguing that the agreement did not apply to new tenants. But the new residents, already organized by the Tenants Union, refused to pay the increase, prompting CRA to serve them with unlawful detainer eviction notices. Thirty-five Tenants Union members promptly marched over to CRA headquarters and sat-in. Fifteen were eventually arrested—all peacefully, except that someone punctured a tire on the paddy wagon.

In March 1975 the new-renter issue led to a second rent strike. By this time some Cedar Square West tenants had become disgruntled with high-density living and were also preparing to strike. The Cedar Square West Residents Association had formed in 1973 and had cooperative relations with Keith Heller and Gloria Segal. But activist organizing and the rent increases led to a Cedar Square West Tenants Union. The Cedar Square West union struck in June 1975 when 10 percent rent increases were to go into effect without CRA's providing the required audited justification.

This second strike dragged on for months. The expanded and renamed East-West Bank Tenants Union was in its fifth strike month in July 1975 and voted in the Cedar Square West Tenants Union as a local. The Union had succeeded in gaining thirty-day continuances on CRA's eviction attempts. One hundred tenants had been taken to court and requested jury trials, though some had been originally decided in favor of the Tenants Union, with Judge Peter Lindberg ruling that UCPI had violated the UCPI-Tenants Union agreement. He also referred the strike in the old neighborhood to the Minnesota Supreme Court to determine whether rent could be withheld to press for collective bargaining rights as well as to protest poor maintenance.

The fight between CRA and the Tenants Union escalated into 1976. The original Cedar Square West rent strikers, neither as well organized nor as militant as the old neighborhood residents, settled out of court. The Cedar Square West tenants in the project's federally subsidized Section 236 units, however, filed a class action lawsuit against UCPI (CRA), asking that rent increases be rolled back. CRA, having all but given up on its fractured liberalism, attempted to evict a social service agency from Cedar Square West for allowing tenant organizers to use its phone to collect tenant complaints. *Snoose News* turned up the heat by publicizing information from internal CRA and HUD correspondence on poor maintenance, above-market rents, CRA misappropriation of tenants' security deposits and laundry money, and general financial mismanagement of the complex (*Snoose News*, June

1976:1). *Snoose News* also obtained and divulged the results of an internal CRA survey of Cedar Square West, showing that the majority of tenants rated the project "poor" or "not so good" for families and children and rated neighboring and general satisfaction low (*Snoose News*, August 1976:4).

In June 1976, with the second rent strike still in the state supreme court and rent being paid out through Judge Lindberg to help CRA cover expenses and repairs, UCPI informed residents in the 370 units in the old neighborhood that they would receive an average 12 percent rent increase on July 1 and would have to sign a new lease. Anyone not signing the new lease, which contained the interesting provision that tenants would be liable for any legal costs involved in bringing tenant-landlord disputes to court, would be evicted at the end of the month. The Tenants Union threatened to go out on strike for a third time, refusing to sign the new leases and charging that UCPI had not upheld its end of the agreement with the Tenants Union requiring tenant participation in any decisions concerning rent increases. On June 11 a mass of tenants demonstrated in front of CRA offices and then at the home of CRA president Robert Jorvig. UCPI attempted to drive a wedge between residents by announcing that any negotiated settlement would apply to all tenants regardless of whether they were Union members, forcing the Union to announce that it was negotiating for members only.

This time Minnesota state officials and city officials stepped in. State Senator Allan Spear and State Representative Phyllis Kahn scolded CRA, and Speaker of the House Martin Sabo asked that the eviction notices be rescinded and urged negotiation. Three City Council members also "introduced a city resolution calling for negotiations between the Union and CRA as the proper way to settle the problems" (*Snoose News*, July 1976:6). For a change, a settlement was quickly reached on August 3, 1976, specifying a 6 percent rent increase, with another 2 percent contingent on signing a collective bargaining agreement. The agreement also settled the previous strike, except for the cases that went to the supreme court, and provided more acceptable leases.

The Tenants Union also took on the University of Minnesota in late 1975. The university was attempting to demolish its decayed houses in the neighborhood to increase parking space. One house in particular, on the People's Center block, sparked the debate. As negotiations between the PAC, the Tenants Union, and the university continued, the Tenants Union "installed an airhorn in the vicinity of the house to be activated at the first sign of the bulldozers and issued a leaflet urging all residents to come and physically prevent demolition at the sound of the horn" (*Snoose News*, November 1975:3). After Mayor Albert Hofstede and Aldermen Zollie Green and Tom Johnson applied pressure, the university agreed to delay demolition indefinitely and to make a community survey of all university houses.

The Tenants Union was the center of community-based resistance in the mid-1970s. While CREDF and the PAC provided the expert resources and access to the official power structure, it was the Tenants Union that kept the residents of the neighborhood from being driven out by rent increases or CRA's heavy-handedness. But the neighborhood required one more organization if the movement was to go from defending the neighborhood to developing an alternative to the top-down, capital-conscious New Town urban redevelopment plan.

The West Bank Community Development Corporation

The neighborhood movement also formalized its community development activities in the mid-1970s. The West Bank Community Development Corporation (CDC; pronounced "C-D-C") was founded on February 16, 1975, at a community convention where an "initial policy board" of seven people was elected under quite adverse conditions. "We decided the easiest way to form one was simply to call a community-wide convention—put out notices in the entire neighborhood, call a founding convention of the CDC. . . . There was a howling blizzard on the day of the convention, and I think the planes were delayed with the speakers coming in, and I think a handful of people showed up" (Parliament interview, 1991). The CDC was incorporated as a development body for implementing "democratic, residential-based redevelopment," with one part-time staff member working out of an office in North Country Co-op. Its first task was to begin developing plans, through a series of neighborhood meetings cosponsored by the PAC, for the "Riverbluff" section of the neighborhood on the site of CRA's stymied Stage II. The CDC planned three hundred to six hundred units of low-rise, cluster-type housing and submitted a funding proposal to the Greater Minneapolis Metropolitan Housing Corporation. In early 1976 the CDC received thirty thousand dollars in Community Development Block Grant (CDBG) funds to pay staff and plan the Riverbluff housing.

The CDC also focused on helping to expand the neighborhood's social reproduction base. With the CDC's assistance, the newly forming West Bank Co-op Grocery received forty thousand dollars in CDBG funds in early 1976 to rehab its space. It was in the planning for the West Bank Co-op Grocery that conflict over how to do community-based development first revealed the minefield that lay ahead for the neighborhood movement, showing the tension between practical financial necessities and alternative visions.

> There was a meeting called by the CDC, a community meeting to hash it out. . . . And it was packed. Everyone was out for blood. One faction was led by [an] ex-New Riverside Cafe member. . . . He was the motivating force behind "this is gonna be collective management, this is how we run everything else and we've been so successful at it and we're not gonna buy into the system with this" and that was that. On the other side was Jack, he was, "No, this is not gonna be any hippie bullshit. This is real money; this is real life now . . . and so this is gonna be traditional management right down the line." . . . And finally, Jack is so enraged. His face is bright red, his eyes are popping out of his head, his hands are clenched, screaming at the top of his lungs, "You fuckin' scippie humbag!" He was so wrought up he could not even get out the words "hippie scumbag," which was what he meant to say. . . . Right in the middle of the meeting, they go at it . . . so that's when I first started noticing cracks. (Wittcoff interview, 1978)

For the time being, however, those tensions would not have much opportunity to divide the movement. The threat of the New Town was too prominent, neighborhood unity too great, and other tasks too pressing. On the heels of a study being conducted by the PAC to determine the feasibility of rehabbing neighborhood housing, a task force of CDC and PAC members and other neighborhood residents, along with seventy residents from the old neighborhood, volunteered to participate "in an intensive grass roots planning effort" to design a housing rehabilitation project (Snoose News, January 1977:7).

But like the PAC, the CDC would have to wait for its proactive mission to come to fruition. That did not make these two organizations superfluous during the 1970s, however. As we see in the next chapter, the development of carefully detailed and thoroughly argued alternative redevelopment processes and plans helped to pull city officials and private investors out of the growth coalition as much as the financial and political disasters created for CRA by CREDF and the Tenants Union. It was the combination of these organizations built on the base of a solid community, rather than the isolated actions of any single organization, that gave Cedar-Riverside activists new advantages.

Strategic Innovation: The Federated
Frontstage Structure

Into 1976 the organizational base in the neighborhood was stronger than ever, with CREDF, PAC, the Tenants Union, the CDC, the New Riverside Cafe, North Country Co-op, the People's Center, a "free school" alternative high school, and the Tenants Union. And this organizational structure was taking its toll on CRA and the New Town plan. In Cedar-Riverside the community service organizations, and the political organizations built and maintained on them, provided a structure from which mobilization could be accomplished cheaply and efficiently. The resultant organizational structure is the most important innovation developed by the neighborhood movement and provided the conditions under which the movement could make an impact on the political opportunity structure.

The Cedar-Riverside neighborhood movement evolved an organizing structure similar to Gerlach and Hine's (1970) decentralized-segmented-reticulate model. But there was more to the movement than a DSR structure. Clearly, there were not enough thoroughly active residents to maintain so many organizations in a single neighborhood. Rather than each organization mobilizing a separate membership, however, many residents were involved in all or several of the organizations as formal or informal members.

> There's always been a lot of interplay between the PAC and the Tenants Union, and CREDF . . . and the Community Union, and the People's Center, and the cafe, North Country Co-op, and the West Bank Co-op Grocery. They're all interlocked—again, not in a really formal bureaucratic way, but through friendship linkages and through many of the same people serving—for instance, I worked at the cafe, was a volunteer at the Tenants Union, and a plaintiff in the CREDF lawsuit. On the other hand, except for that one year, I didn't have a whole lot to do with the PAC. That was other people I knew. Other people from the cafe were on the PAC, for instance. (Wittcoff interview, 1978)

This was a "federated frontstage structure" (Stoecker, 1993), allowing the community as a whole to engage in a variety of tactics on a variety of levels directed toward a variety of audiences. "Front organizations" are commonly thought of as organizations behind which an otherwise "illegitimate" group can operate, such as United States Communist Party front organizations in the early twentieth century or nuclear power industry front organizations in the contemporary period (Zald and Ash, 1966; Klehr, 1984; Useem and Zald, 1982).

The idea of the federated frontstage structure of the middle period of the Cedar-Riverside neighborhood movement expands on the front organizations concept. Rather than cover the identity of an illegitimate group, this structure allowed a single unified movement constituency to engage in separate bureaucratic and legal tasks through officially independent and specialized organizations without fear of threatening the legitimacy or funding of some organizations or of confusing goals. The structure allowed the same residents who were militantly occupying CRA offices as Tenants Union activists also to lobby city officials with alternative redevelopment plans as PAC officials, providing immense flexibility in neighborhood strategies and tactics. The structure allowed less active residents to become involved through a variety of organizations, providing multiple incentives for recruitment and commitment.

The federated frontstage structure is distinct from the DSR model in two basic ways: it is segmented only in the front stage, not the "back stage" (Goffman, 1959:106), and its membership is not reticulated or loosely networked but densely networked, since it is formed by a single constituency creating multiple organizations. When a new issue arose, activists literally created a new organization custom-designed to fill that niche, as in the dynamics of the pro-choice movement (Staggenborg, 1989a), though in a more planned manner and based in a unified movement membership. This movement structure preserved the advantages of the DSR structure and overcame its main disadvantage by providing much greater coordination of activities.

The neighborhood movement really had two structures, then: a frontstage structure and a backstage structure. Frontstage, the movement consisted of a collection of "federated" organizations with separate tasks. The backstage structure consisted of community "leaders" (some residents estimate that as many as one hundred people could be identified as leaders at various times), many organizers, and the mass of other residents who could be mobilized for "hot issues." The Cedar-Riverside neighborhood movement operated differently in its front region than it did backstage. Behind all those formally separated organizations was a single, cohesive community with a highly elaborated countercultural ideology and a base of collectivized social reproduction. Leadership was markedly decentralized and frequently rotated, and many residents were involved in all the organizations. Members of the New Riverside Cafe collective contributed to CREDF, were elected to PAC, belonged to the Tenants Union, and sat on the CDC board and People's Center board. Nearly everyone involved in any of these organizations was also an active member of the Tenants Union. All the staff members of the PAC, CDC, and Tenants Union came from the neighborhood and shared the same office for a while. There was no interorganizational competition, since the organizations were backed by a unified neighborhood membership, and each tapped different funding sources. Though there was not a complete overlap in organization memberships, the organizations rose out of the needs of a single cohesive group of neighborhood residents and not out of separate groups in the community. Organization members even actively discouraged outside groups from becoming involved in the neighborhood's struggle by publicly criticizing them and destroying fliers announcing their meetings.

The federated frontstage structure was an important improvement on the earlier movement structure, which centralized the neighborhood's political activities in the Community Union. In that earlier period, as a result of the lack of fit between the movement structure and the political opportunity structure, the movement was unable to resolve recruitment, organizing, and tactical dilemmas. In contrast, the federated frontstage structure was much more successful at managing all three movement dilemmas.

Organizing Democracy and Protecting Efficiency

The federated frontstage structure allowed the movement to manage the organizing dilemma by emphasizing efficiency in what Boyte (1980) calls "public interest groups," using research, disclosure, publicity, and litigation (the PAC, CDC, and CREDF); and by stressing democracy in the "direct organizing" groups, using pressure tactics and rallies (the Community Union, the New Riverside Cafe, and the Tenants Union). The formal, more hierarchical structures of the PAC, CDC, and CREDF helped the movement effectively meet court deadlines and, later, development deadlines. The apparently clear chain of command in the organizations also reassured outside officials, who demanded bureaucratic accountability before they would release development funds. The more loosely structured direct organizing groups, on the other hand, made the most of their apparent lack of accountability, confronting officials with unexpected demands or positions. The Community Union and Tenants Union in particular maximized the involvement of community members through their open membership structure and participatory democratic decision-making rules.

Each organization was individually structured to reflect its task. Underlying even the more formally structured organizations, however, was an emphasis on participatory decision making. As much as possible, residents attempted to structure their organizations as "collectivist" with no hierarchies, minimal rules, and egalitarian decision making (Rothschild-Whitt, 1979). The Community Union, the Tenants Union, and the New Riverside Cafe were loosely organized. Tenants Union organizer Tim Ogren lamented, only partially tongue-in-cheek, "I must have had two hundred bosses."

CREDF was, on its face, more formally organized. There was a board of directors, but any major decisions on settlement offers or legal strategies were made by any interested members of the neighborhood who showed up for the meeting. "It was very much like the Community Union in practice, although in theory there had to be a board of directors and so on because we were a nonprofit, tax-exempt corporation. But in practice, decisions were made on the basis of weekly meetings when something came up. Anybody who wanted to could come to the community meetings" (Cann interview, 1978). CREDF's only task was to raise money and provide legitimacy for the environmental impact statement suit. As a financial channel, CREDF needed to maintain enough legitimacy to be able to lobby elites and attract both political support and money for the EIS lawsuit.

The PAC was a different story. Restricted by city funding restrictions and HUD regulations, the PAC was the epitome of the formal organization. It had a chair, vice-chair, secretary, treasurer, and delegates elected from neighborhood districts. Meetings were run according to Robert's Rules of Order, and decisions were made by voice and sometimes hand votes. This organization could do the "legitimate" work of conducting planning workshops, organizing proposals for a new Urban Renewal Plan, and making decisions about new development in the neighborhood without having to overcome the stigma of militant activity attached to the Tenants Union and the cafe collective. With an operating budget that grew to more than $100,000,[3] the PAC enabled the neighborhood movement to move away from organizational maintenance tasks. The PAC could pay staff to organize meetings, hire architects and legal experts, and lobby at City Hall as the neighborhood's official voice.

The CDC was also formally structured with elected officers. As a nonprofit community development corporation, it had government-imposed constraints that specified a percentage of low-income board members. In contrast to the PAC, whose delegates were elected from districts, the CDC board was elected at annual town meetings with the only restriction being, initially, that voters worked or lived in the neighborhood. After beginning with one staff person paid $25 per week from donations from North Country Co-op, the CDC grew to become the wealthiest organization in the neighborhood, with as many as thirteen staff members and an annual operating budget of more than $300,000 at one point.[4] The CDC was the one organization in the neighborhood that was entirely focused on development.

The frontstage separation between the organizations was not always clearly maintained, particularly in the early years of the CDC, when there was no development work to do.

> We all had our offices in a small room at the People's Center, the CDC, and the Tenants Union. . . . There was the feeling that if a major thing happened with the Tenants Union, people put all their energy in. The PAC and the CDC, they poured in the resources for demonstrations and court appearances. And even doing their own work, they did Tenants Union work as part of it, so it was much more coordinating together.   (Tim Ogren interview, 1991)

Although the flexibility to ignore those formal separations served the movement well in the second period, it created problems later on.

Recruiting Members: Multiple Organizations and Multiple Incentives

The federated frontstage structure enhanced recruitment and commitment by using multiple incentives, as in the multiple organization substructure of the Baltimore black sit-ins, whose participants were recruited differently through "alienating" and "conformist" organizations (Von Eschen, Kirk, and Pinard, 1971). In Cedar-Riverside the Tenants Union recruited using immediate material incentives: rent hikes. Tenants Union organizers continually generated new issues, with the help of CRA's lack of cooperation, to maintain mobilization, and the Union became the movement's central recruitment organization. Many residents who had not responded to the countercultural goals of the early neighborhood movement reacted quickly to a 50 percent rent hike. As a result, the neighborhood movement could attract new members through the Tenants Union and then attempt to increase their commitment to alternative definitions of community and political power through involvement in other movement activities.

The other neighborhood movement organizations used the Tenants Union to recruit for other activities. Thus, the Tenants Union provided for "entry-level activism," and members who developed useful skills and knowledge were recruited into other movement roles. Residents who were not comfortable with militant activities could choose to be involved in the PAC, CDC, and community service organizations such as the People's Center and the co-ops. The goal of moving beyond selective incentives was enhanced through the PAC and its neighborhood newspaper, *Snoose News*. Local community presses are important for both information dispersal and community integration, helping local residents to adopt common definitions of local issues (Ward and Gaziano, 1976; Janowitz, 1967). *Snoose News* explained the functions and goals of the PAC, the CDC, the Tenant's Union, and CREDF and provided the residents with updates on earlier battles and information on new battles.

The commitment to the community that was created through the New Riverside Cafe, the People's Center, and then the other political organizations also helped to increase commitment to the movement to save the neighborhood. The movement drew heavily on its own residents to eke out support for the neighborhood organizations. Starting the CDC, for example, was very difficult, since the neighborhood was still tied up by the court injunction and no one could conduct any development work. But the community came to the rescue:

> And there's no development income, of course. So we had to
> get funding out of the community. So we had, for a period of a
> year there, easily twice a month, we had boogies. And musicians
> would donate their time, or play for cheap. We either had it at the
> People's Center gym or the Firehouse Theater. And we'd pull in
> huge amounts of people, sell amazing quantities of beer, and make
> enough money to keep the CDC goin' until the next one, and to
> pay salaries and organize neighborhood committees, and give Jack
> somethin' for what he was doin'. (Wittcoff interview, 1991)

Behind the federated frontstage structure, commitment to the neighborhood movement was enhanced through the adoption of a small group structure. Mancur Olson (1965), who argues that people are not likely to join a movement to procure a "collective good" when they will receive the good whether they participate or not, maintains that one of the most effective ways to overcome the "free rider" problem is to organize people into small groups. And as the movement began planning for democratic, community-based redevelopment, activists followed just such a strategy, organizing residents block by block to sit down and begin planning for the rehabilitation of the housing on their block.

> At that point it was a question: How are the people who live here going to decide what this place is gonna look like? And I took a page from Chairman Mao. Chairman Mao, when he was restructuring the society, had neighborhood committees. I said, "Well, let's have neighborhood committees." So we divided the neighborhood up into small groups—three or four blocks each—and we organized neighborhood committees in each of those blocks. We had meetings, got out pictures, maps, and wooden houses, and started moving 'em around.   (Wittcoff interview, 1991)

The multiple organizations of the federated frontstage structure were also able to generate responses to multiple issues, leading to the ability to mobilize around multiple "crisis events" (Freeman, 1983a). Two major crisis events came together in the spring of 1972 with the announcement of the mining of Haiphong Harbor and the dedication of Cedar Square West. With the establishment of a PAC, the residents' realization that the Stage I environmental impact statement had been filed before the PAC had been formed, and their further realization that the radical residents were a minority in the PAC, a new crisis event loomed with the impending start of Stage II of the New Town. Thus, residents organized CREDF and the EIS lawsuit. Another crisis event was created when CRA raised the rents. Jack Cann reflected on that particular event: "You could almost count on CRA to do the dumbest possible thing just when you needed it the most." Here was an issue that could mobilize people not only ideologically, but also on the basis of material incentives. Rent raises are one of the primary causes of tenants' unions (Lawson, 1983), and the drastic and sudden rent hike in Cedar-Riverside provided the impetus for a strong and militant tenants' union.

Multiple organizations also create the opportunity for multiple successes. CREDF succeeded quickly with the injunction, halting further construction of the New Town. And the Tenants Union organized an immediate and successful rent strike. There were now two major triumphs for the neighborhood movement. Success in early mobilizations profoundly influence commitment to later mobilizations (McCarthy and Zald, 1977), and neighborhood resident involvement

in the movement grew, particularly in the Tenants Union, throughout the 1970s. With CRA's continuing attempts to break the Tenants
Union, outmaneuver the environmental legal challenge, and gain further funding for the New Town, the movement was seldom without a
new grievance or a new crisis.

Diversifying Tactical Strategy

Curt Lamb's (1975) research on neighborhood protest strongly
supports the contention that the use of a wide range of tactics, including militant tactics, is crucial to the success of neighborhood
mobilization. As with recruitment strategy, the federated frontstage
structure allowed the movement to practice a wide diversity of tactics. The structure maximized tactical flexibility by allowing some
organizations to develop alliances with moderates while other organizations acted more militantly. The PAC, CDC, and CREDF were especially restricted in the tactics they could use because of their funding
structures and the necessity for maintaining a responsible profile for
negotiations. These organizations employed the mainstream symbols
of "family" and "children" in the CREDF lawsuit and the alternative
planning process in the same effective manner as in other community movements (Boyte, 1982; Strange, 1973). The PAC and the CDC's
workable urban renewal plans also helped residents appear "responsible," an effective tactic for enhancing a challenging group's negotiating position (Strange, 1973). These groups were bureaucratically
legitimate organizations, particularly the PAC, which was established
by HUD, and City Hall was forced to pay attention. The Community
Union, the New Riverside Cafe collective, and the Tenants Union did
not operate under these constraints and thus could engage in militant
tactics without having to worry about how they might affect funding
or legitimacy. The Tenants Union's disruptive tactics probably forced
negotiations where more moderate tactics would have failed. This
unique movement structure, built on the legacy of the Cedar Square
West dedication ceremony uprising in 1972, also led to a unique negotiating strategy: the threat to unleash the "uncontrollable elements."
"Whenever we were sitting across the table negotiating, we could
always remind them of the uncontrollable elements—that, if they
didn't negotiate with us, then there were these crazies in the neighborhood that we couldn't control. Of course, we were the uncontrollable
elements" (Ogren interview, 1987). The mystique and mythology of
the uncontrollable elements would serve the neighborhood well.

The most important tactic in the arsenal of this period of the movement, however, was a formal legalistic one: the environmental impact lawsuit. It is important to look briefly at this particular legal strategy, since it is filled with paradoxes. For one thing, the National Environmental Policy Act itself was ambiguous and the regulating agency it created was impotent (Handler, 1978), making it relatively ineffective (Logan and Molotch, 1987). The weakness and ambiguity of the statute would seem to make it a poor alternative for the movement, but the reverse is actually the case. It is the predictability of the rational legal form that facilitates capitalist accumulation (Trubek, 1977). This act was ambiguous enough to make predictability problematic and therefore to hinder efficiency. It allowed sympathetic lawyers and judges to fill the gaps and actually create tougher environmental protection than the statute was designed for (Handler, 1978). The neighborhood movement was fortunate in getting Judge Miles Lord to hear the case, though the special master Judge Lord appointed concurred, so this legal success was based on more than a single sympathetic judge.

The New Town was highly dependent on the efficient accumulation of capital in order to maintain financial solvency. Once the suit was filed and Judge Lord issued an injunction against further construction, a financial nightmare of construction delays began for CRA. As Logan and Molotch (1987) have argued, the most the opposition can normally hope for is delay. But as Joel Handler (1978) has shown, although it is difficult for social movements to win environmental litigation because it is long-term and complex, sometimes all that social movements need is publicity and delay. Social movements can use the judicial system for "extrajudicial" purposes. The combination of legally imposed delays and high inflation was to have the same impact on the New Town as it did on nuclear power plant construction. In both cases the National Environmental Policy Act prepared the ground for legal challenges that imposed direct delays and, in the case of nuclear power, also brought about delays by creating more regulatory hoops (Rosa and Freudenberg, 1984; Camilleri, 1984:91, 100). And in both cases social movements organized to use those new policies and bring legal challenges. The effect of recession and high inflation was crucial, as was timing. In the case of nuclear power, inflation and recession were so important that they all but nullified whatever boost nuclear power had received from the Arab oil embargo in 1973 (Camilleri, 1984:170–171). The New Town received no such boost to counter the devastation of the middle 1970s' economic collapse.

The danger was, however, that the neighborhood movement would wither away while awaiting a final decision on the case. By the time the case was appealed and perhaps decided in CRA's favor by a less sympathetic judge, a movement might not exist to take to the streets again. And even if the suit succeeded, what then? The movement needed to continue to defend itself from displacement through rent hikes and building condemnation and ultimately had to come up with its own plans to preserve the neighborhood.

The federated frontstage structure was the insurance against these risks, since it could channel the movement's energy into a variety of other movement tasks. In a movement structure of separate organization memberships, any single organization forced to wait out a court case could fold. But in Cedar-Riverside the community's attention could shift from the Tenants Union to CREDF to PAC or to CDC issues as they arose. While residents were waiting for a finding on the environmental suit, they could devote their energies to the rent strike.

The Tenants Union took the legal strategy one step farther, making it part of a repertoire of disruptive tactics. The fact that the Union was willing to withhold rent for legally questionable causes such as union recognition, and to escalate conflict by occupying CRA offices and refusing to give in to state supreme court decisions restricting its activity, served as a valuable negotiating tool. Rent withholding also had a disruptive economic impact on CRA.

Neighborhood residents were also learning the value of mainstream electoral tactics during this period. The legitimacy of the PAC and CDC came partly from the fact that they were democratically elected bodies, requiring the neighborhood to get out the vote. In the case of the PAC, electoral success meant the transference of tens of thousands of dollars to the movement and dramatically increased access to information and decision makers. As we see in the next chapter, the residents were able to expand dramatically on these electoral victories at the level of City Hall and even the mayor's office.

Conclusion: Transforming the Political Opportunity Structure

The Cedar-Riverside federated frontstage structure was specifically tailored to its political opportunity structure, allowing it actually to *create* a more open and volatile political opportunity structure. Although the Community Union treated CRA, City Hall, HUD, and the banks as a single target in the early period, the federated frontstage structure facilitated the use of Alinsky's (1971) "divide and conquer" strategy as the movement was able to *separate the targets* and destabilize political alignments. Interestingly, neither the organizations nor their activities were created with any grand plan. Activists made up organizations as they went along. Consequently, each organization played a specific role in disrupting the New Town growth coalition while preventing the movement itself from getting its own political wires crossed.

The New Riverside Cafe, the People's Center, North Country Co-op, the free school, alternative theaters, and the bicycle, hardware, and grocery co-ops that developed in the neighborhood provided for the social reproduction needs of the residents and reduced dependence on outside resources. Thus, outside resource holders were prevented from applying leverage against the neighborhood resistance. And with the exception of the New Riverside Cafe, these neighborhood organizations were not central actors in the resistance itself. The cafe would prove the wisdom of this division of labor, coming within a hair of losing its lease and being forced out of existence because of involvement in neighborhood rent strikes.

While the social reproduction organizations concentrated on keeping the outside world at arm's length, the other organizations focused on taking advantage of "target vulnerabilities" (Walsh, 1986). One of the New Town's greatest vulnerabilities lay in its financial needs, and CREDF and the Tenants Union were able to attack that vulnerability with enormous success. CREDF made the most of the relative autonomy of the state, achieving the court injunction that halted the New Town's accumulation of capital and threatened its financial base. CREDF's sole purpose was to attempt to stop the New Town through the legal process, but its effect was to undermine the project's financial integrity. That created anxiety among the other four decision makers in the growth coalition: bankers, builders, support resources including state officials locally and at HUD, and the corporate community, which would be asked to help shore up CRA's failing financial health. The Tenants Union made things worse for CRA, not only depriving it of increased rent revenues, but also preventing it from having any rent revenue at all for months on end while CRA–Tenants Union negotiations were held up in court.

The other vulnerability of the New Town growth coalition was its tottering political legitimacy. The fact that a group of hippies, through CREDF, could obtain such success on its initial injunction request called CRA's expertise into question. CREDF, through legitimate legal maneuvers, was able to make CRA and Cedar Square West look bad to the local financial community and the media, severing the corporation from potential backers. CRA's reactions—repeated eviction attempts, maintenance neglect, and refusal to honor past agreements—strained relations between CRA and city and state government.

Finally, the resident-controlled PAC and the CDC were slowly able to extract City Hall out of the growth coalition by developing a relationship with city officials. The PAC was busy nurturing an alliance with City Hall by sometimes using diplomacy and sometimes using levers. The CDC worked on getting support from City Hall, HUD, and private foundations to support democratic, community-based redevelopment, drawing support away from the New Town. Eventually, the PAC and CDC conducted alternative neighborhood planning sessions, developed detailed neighborhood redevelopment plans, and organized project budgets for those plans. They held joint workshops with the MHRA to review the 1968 Urban Renewal Plan and were able to obtain meetings with City Council members and even the mayor efficiently and regularly. While CREDF and the Tenants Union undermined CRA's legitimacy, then, the PAC and CDC activated in the local state the latent contradiction between "legitimation" and "capital accumulation." The PAC and CDC influenced the local state to attempt to shore up its legitimacy by responding to the neighborhood resistance rather than remaining tightly allied with an urban renewal agent whose own legitimacy was failing.

The result, as we see in the next chapter, was a dramatic shift in the political opportunity structure. First, the movement created more access where there had been little, opening doors to council members' offices and the mayor's office. Second, the movement began to scare away CRA's allies and gather allies of its own. And third, the result of this process was an increasingly unstable political opportunity structure, with all the actors—City Hall, HUD, the banks, the investors, and the neighborhood—eventually fighting for position against all the other actors. In the second half of the 1970s, then, the growth coalition was thrown into chaos and the political opportunity structure was thrown up for grabs.

CHAPTER 5

The Growth Coalition Falters

This power cannibalism of the Haves permits only temporary
truces, and only when equally confronted by a common enemy.
Even then there are regular breaks in the ranks, as individual units
attempt to exploit the general threat for their own special benefit.
Here is the vulnerable belly of the status quo.
                         —*Saul D. Alinsky*, Rules for Radicals

L ATE 1974 signaled the beginning of the end for the New Town
in Town. Financial backers started pulling out, and City Hall
began to review the Urban Renewal Plan. During one of the CREDF
fundraising dinners, neighborhood activist Steve Parliament learned
of the growing skepticism of the Minneapolis corporate elite when a
member of that elite remarked that the "financial community in Minneapolis felt that CRA was a house of cards" and an organization to
stay away from. The political opportunity structure, which had been
so well organized in CRA's favor, was shifting.

Through the second period the neighborhood movement's federated frontstage structure allowed the movement to practice a sophisticated "divide and conquer" strategy against the New Town growth
machine. Saul Alinsky (1971) understood this strategy well, noting
that elites are ultimately only self-interested and that any unity they
show occurs only because they temporarily see unity as in their self-
interest. As soon as they perceive greater advantage in breaking out
of the coalition, they will do so.

This self-interest is structurally based. Claus Offe (1985) notes that,
whereas labor exists in discrete individuals who must be organized
to exert collective power, capital can be organized by individual capi-

talists. Similarly, community can be obtained only through the collective organization of individual citizens, but capital can exist in an organized form in the hands of a single capitalist. In the case of a growth coalition, separate organized capitals are brought together, and the same problems that hinder community organizing—diversity of perspective, conflicting self-interests, and competing allegiances— also hinder growth coalitions.

The "relative autonomy" of the local state also creates problems for capital (Clavel and Kleniewski, 1990; Markusen, 1978; Clark and Dear, 1984). Because the state is structurally independent from individual fractions of capital, its support for any individual capitalist policy is always tentative. Caught between the necessity of supporting top-down, capital-conscious urban redevelopment to ensure the city's fiscal survival and maintaining legitimacy in the eyes of residents, the local state can be a fickle growth-coalition partner.

The divide-and-conquer strategy has an impact on the political opportunity structure by exploiting the structural independence of capital elites and the local state in the urban power structure, opening and destabilizing it. This strategy enhances the real structural divisions between capital and the state and between fractions of capital to weaken the power of the movement's target. In Cedar-Riverside the neighborhood movement's federated front-stage structure drove wedges in the growth coalition, attracted resources for the community, destabilized the political opportunity structure, and stopped the New Town. Consequently, political alignments destabilized, elites shifted position, and the barriers to the local state began to fall. The chaos in the political opportunity structure lasted through the end of the decade.

In this chapter I focus on the two main problems of growth coalitions: organizing fractions of capital and overcoming the relative autonomy of the local state. I explore how the talents of a small neighborhood were able to take advantage of these problems to halt the march of the New Town.

Cracks in the Growth Coalition

External Changes

In the 1970s four developments in the political opportunity structure, independent of the activism of West Bankers, reduced CRA's insularity from the neighborhood movement. The changes began in 1972 when Henry McKnight suddenly died. McKnight's unexpected death was a psychological, if not material, blow to the growth machine. His connections had helped to secure the initial financing for the New Town; his absence when new financial and political problems emerged made it more difficult for CRA to defend itself. "When he died, probably as much as anything else, Cedar-Riverside Associates lost the ability to weather the storm. They lost that contact with D.C. and their ability to circumvent local and regional level offices and just zoom to the head of the class" (William Betzler interview, 1978).

A less sudden but equally important change was the collapse of the economy and the rise in inflation and interest rates in the middle 1970s. As a result, construction costs went up, mortgage rates increased, and remaining neighborhood land was difficult to purchase (Martin, 1978). That worsened the effect of CRA's financial problems and shook the "house of cards" financing scheme of the New Town.

The structure and composition of the local state in Minneapolis also changed somewhat through the 1970s. The Republican-dominated City Council was recaptured by Democrats after the 1970 census reapportionment, and partisan primary elections were established. City Hall was slowly opened up to the neighborhoods. Cedar-Riverside was split into three districts, giving activists access to three council members.

Finally, and most important, Cedar Square West was built, creating economic vulnerability where it had not existed before. The project also became a political symbol. It was something opponents could point to, criticize, and struggle to define as evil. Its immensity— eleven buildings lifting as high as thirty-nine stories, containing 1,299 housing units (Martin, 1978)—was overwhelming. Cedar Square West served as such an overpowering symbol of insensitive urban planning that it tainted the very idea of centralized corporate or state planning for the neighborhood.

The neighborhood movement also obtained greater allies and resources. CREDF attracted money from the Stern Fund[1] and other private donors and was able to hire a lawyer who was willing to work for intermittent pay. The PAC budget provided money for organizers, architects, and legal experts for the neighborhood. The People's Center funded an organizer. And the growing CDC also brought money for experts.

With the fuel provided by these few small advantages, the CREDF,

Tenants Union, and PAC attacks lit the match, and the fire spread through the growth coalition and the city bureaucracy.

Exploiting Fissures in the Growth Coalition

The held-up second stage of the New Town in Town provided the obstacle over which the growth coalition would stumble during this period. One site of tension developed between the MHRA and City Hall, where the resident-controlled PAC had already begun to make inroads. The MHRA still backed the New Town in early 1974, giving preliminary approval to the Centrum shopping mall plans, including $12.35 million to build it, even though the PAC had voted nineteen to ten against the project. City Hall was more concerned about CRA's financial health and was discussing the formation of a development corporation to replace CRA, composed of representatives from the City Council, the mayor, residents, private investors, and the MHRA.

Members of capital also began backing away from the growth coalition, and new invitees to the coalition balked. About the same time as the city takeover plan developed, Dayton-Hudson Properties, a subsidiary of the retailing giant, withdrew as a consultant to CRA's Centrum project, since CRA had fallen behind on payments to Dayton-Hudson. This threatened withdrawal was the first public indication of the degree to which the Minneapolis business community was losing faith in CRA. The Greater Minneapolis Metropolitan Housing Corporation (GMMHC), a nonprofit group backed by fourteen local corporations, was next, in late 1974. Henry Porter, vice-president of General Mills and a member of the boards of both CRA and the GMMHC, asked the GMMHC to invest $3 million to $5 million to take over CRA and prevent its bankruptcy. The GMMHC board rejected this request, saying there was not enough capital available for it.

The federal government also withdrew its support from the New Town growth coalition. In December 1974 HUD began having second thoughts about the New Town in Town project. The front-page headline above the fold in the December 16 *Minneapolis Tribune* indicated both a change in media perceptions and a real threat to CRA: "HUD REPORT INDICATES THAT CEDAR-RIVERSIDE PROJECT 'NOT VIABLE.'" HUD had been running computer simulations to test the financial viability of all its New Towns, and the Cedar-Riverside plan had come out as the only one that was "clearly not viable." The paper also reported, however, that city officials, CRA officials, and HUD's New Communities head questioned the validity of the report, saying that the model was based on assumptions of rural new towns.

Finally, the local papers showed a switch in "frames" (Gitlin, 1980) in late 1974 from negative coverage of the protestors to negative coverage of Cedar-Riverside Associates and Cedar Square West. News of the GMMHC rejection of CRA's bail-out plea received front-page coverage in the November 1 *Minneapolis Tribune*. An October 19 *Tribune* article recognized that the movement participants were not just protesting the New Town in Town but also had positive alternatives (p. B4). The June 29, 1975, *Tribune* even allowed residents space on the editorial page to present their alternatives (p. A13).

What vulnerabilities in the growth coalition allowed the movement to open such devastating fractures among the coalition partners? The main issue, identified by Stone (1989:227), is that capitalism divides rather than unifies authority in cities. Consequently, development projects must be undertaken "in the absence of an overarching command structure or a unifying system of thought." Recall that Feagin and Parker (1990) identified five categories of decision makers in this division of authority: corporate-location, development, financial, construction, and support decision makers. Because these categories of decision makers, to the extent that they are located in separate capital actors, can have different self-interests, conflict can develop. The most important of these conflicts are centered in the actions of the "rentier" (Logan and Molotch, 1987), or property-owning, class—the development decision makers in Feagin and Parker's analysis.

Harvey Molotch (1979) argued that the local rentier class is primarily responsible for the creation of the urban infrastructure. It is the rentier class that transforms urban space from a use value to an exchange value. The rentier class is not strictly a capitalist class in Molotch's analysis, since it controls not the "means of production"— the capital involved in making things—but only the "sites of production." Because their wealth is achieved through the sale or rent of space *both* to productive capital seeking sites of production and to workers seeking sites of reproduction, rentiers stand in a potentially antagonistic relationship to both. Rentiers are also, overall, much more dependent on other fractions of capital than those fractions are on rentiers. Rentiers often operate with little real capital, depending on the financial or corporate fractions to take the risk of a speculative venture (Feagin and Parker, 1990). Conversely, other fractions of capital can circumvent rentiers by going into the land and property business themselves or can influence the government to acquire and prepare property usable for production (Molotch, 1979). Large corporations, with vastly greater resources, are additionally less likely to be focused on short-term projects and less interested in short-term profits (Neubeck and Ratcliff, 1988). Rentiers are even often in structural competition with one another, since development of one part of town often jeopardizes development in other parts. The death of downtowns, blamed on the development of suburban retail malls (Sternlieb and Hughes, 1981), is a case in point.

Because rentiers are so vulnerable and capital-dependent, and because many potential conflicts exist among fractions of urban capital, the only way for them to succeed with any development project is to organize a growth coalition. The growth coalition attempts to make capitalism a plus-sum game, in which an advantage for one is an advantage for all, rather than a zero-sum game, in which any advantage for one must come from a loss for others. Those project proposals that cannot convince various fractions of capital of their mutual benefits are difficult to implement. Two examples in Chicago (Bennett et al., 1988) show the obstacles to getting other fractions of capital to sign on. The Fort Dearborn project, which proposed demolishing and replacing a large section of downtown Chicago, ground to a halt when major property holders thought their investments would be threatened by the plan. Another downtown Chicago development plan ran into opposition from businesses that believed that too many resources were being channeled to one developer. In both these cases antagonistic fractions of capital either did not see the project generating growth or did not see the growth benefiting them.

These fractional conflicts and vulnerabilities of the rentier class make any urban development risky. Cedar-Riverside Associates was probably more vulnerable than most. With virtually no capital, CRA was hoping to build enough high-rise housing for thirty thousand people, relying solely on investors. And because the project was to be built in ten stages, CRA had to organize those investors for ten consecutive projects. Problems that developed at any point jeopardized the entire remainder of the projects.

In the 1970s Cedar-Riverside neighborhood activists were able to attack the growth coalition at exactly its most vulnerable points. As the CREDF lawsuit brought further development to a halt, growth-coalition investors became skeptical that they would gain from their investment. And the Tenants Union actions, along with CRA's reactions, politicized the New Town project. Capitalists do not like operating in the public eye, especially when the exposure is over a controversial project, and they are likely to withdraw from growth coalitions whose activities they fear are or will be politicized (Mollenkopf, 1978). The PAC helped to fragment political leadership at City Hall, depriving CRA of talented political entrepreneurs and creating leadership fragmentation—two of the most important constraints on healthy growth-coalition functioning (Molotch, 1988). As the movement isolated CRA from other fractions of capital and from political leadership, the political-economic foundation of the New Town grew shakier.

Shifting the MHRA

By early 1975 the growth coalition was in accelerated disintegration. CRA, unable to fend off the CREDF suit even after rewriting the environmental impact statement, was in dire straits and turned to the MHRA for help. One of CRA's creditors had threatened to pull his money out, jeopardizing the subsidized housing in Cedar Square West, unless he received a lien on a piece of property that did not already have a lien on it. As a result, the MHRA paid CRA $200,000 for the "air rights" above the Cedar Square West parking lot, allowing CRA to pay off enough debt to provide the reluctant creditor with a clean lien. Interestingly, the PAC supported the MHRA and HUD to "protect the people in that housing any way they could," not knowing about the money the MHRA was going to contribute (Snoose News, March 1975:2).[2]

Two other, more expensive bail-out plans were proposed in 1975. In the first the city would create a nonprofit organization to invest $100 million of public money in the project over two years to preserve the tax shelters of investors. This scheme was soon replaced by a plan to cut the city's cost to $48.5 million and have the MHRA buy the Stage II land for $5 million and lease it back to CRA. The City Council voted down this proposal but, by July, approved a plan committing the city to $21 million (with HUD matching funds) to purchase CRA land in the old neighborhood with no necessary commitment to developing it according to CRA's plans. Community activists, outraged that this plan "was, once again, formulated and drawn up in the back rooms of HUD and the city coordinator," called meetings and then met with council members and the mayor's office. The mayor was able to include a stipulation that the entire plan was subject to the outcome of the newly agreed-on review of the 1968 Urban Renewal Plan (Snoose News, July 1975:1).

The MHRA position began to shift in April 1975 when the neighborhood movement persuaded the MHRA to conduct a reevaluation of the 1968 Urban Renewal Plan. This reevaluation would be organized "to give residents and area business people a clear voice in the re-viewal process" (*Snoose News*, July 1975:1). The PAC and the MHRA hired architects to assist in this joint review and cosponsored a series of all-day Saturday workshops for resident review of the 1968 plan.

The first workshop was held in July with more than one hundred neighborhood, government, and institution people in attendance. The neighborhood institutions pushed for increased parking space and higher housing densities, and neighborhood residents and businesses pushed for increased parks and preservation of the existing com-mercial strip and housing. The second workshop of about eighty-five people attempted to work out some agreement between the neighbor-hood and the institutions. The third workshop resulted in new Urban Renewal Plan "objectives" that emphasized involving neighborhood residents and businesses in proposal initiation and review, using rehabilitation of housing when possible, encouraging community-based development, meeting the consumer needs of the neighborhood people before meeting institutional needs, protecting the Mississippi River gorge, deemphasizing automobiles in planning, and encourag-ing development that controls crime. These objectives were an im-portant shift from the 1968 plan, but it was some time before they became policy.

On its face the MHRA shift seems dramatic and surprising, espe-cially in an organization that was created specifically to limit ac-cess to urban planning. But it must be remembered that, since the historic role of urban renewal agencies has been to channel federal funds to private redevelopment projects (Levine, 1989), those agencies are most likely to support projects that will clearly produce growth. Projects that cannot promise growth will not receive the strong politi-cal support needed to take them from the drawing board to reality. Increasingly, it became clear that the New Town plan could not deliver that growth. Even Cedar Square West was not renting at expectations, and the legal and financial difficulties of CRA created skepticism that further development could be completed.

It is also true that, although redevelopment authorities are only "quasi-public" agencies and relatively insulated from citizen pres-sures (Squires, 1989a; Levine, 1989; N. Fainstein and S. Fainstein, 1986b), they are not completely protected from the political vulnera-bilities of the local state that appoints their boards and determines their budgets. Renewal agency support for projects that fail to deliver on promises to enhance either the tax base or the job base brings the entire agency into question. The New Town was clearly failing to deliver, and the project was being publicly politicized through the local press, creating a hot potato for City Hall and the MHRA. Since activists can target accountable public officials, both on the MHRA board and in the city government that appoints them, especially in more accessible, unreformed local states such as Minneapolis, project politicization is very undesirable from the renewal agency's perspective.

The MHRA perspective was also being pushed by a shift in the overall attitude toward neighborhood-based development throughout the Twin Cities, and it was reverberating downtown.

> There were some forces in the city at the time, in the inner-city neighborhoods, that were promoting the idea of grass-roots, non-profit corporations having the capacity. . . . And at the same time there was the Greater Minneapolis Housing Corporation, this big nonprofit in town, who was actively assisting and encouraging, financially and every other way, in making that happen. (Dick Brustad interview, 1991)

The citywide movement advocating democratic, community-based urban planning was probably one of the strongest forces changing the MHRA. Ross's (1976) study of advocacy as a specialty within urban planning, based on self-assessments of its adherents, found that social movement organizations were highly influential in getting people involved in the approach. Advocates were making inroads through the outspokenness of Tony Scallon, a member of the MHRA board and later in the decade one of Cedar-Riverside's City Council members, and Dick Brustad, who was to become the executive director of the MHRA and then of Brighton Development Corporation, which provided the capital for democratic, community-based development through the CDC in the 1980s.

None of these things, by itself, seems great. But Cedar-Riverside activists, along with those of other neighborhoods, were able to make an impact on the MHRA through each of these routes. With the loss of the previously unswerving MHRA support, and already at odds with HUD and other capital actors in the city, Cedar-Riverside Associates was sinking deeper and deeper into disrepute.

The Beginning of the End

In September 1975 the *Snoose News* front-page headlines said it all: "CREDF WINS LAWSUIT" Federal District Court Special Master Edward Parker, to whom Judge Miles Lord had referred the case, recommended to Lord that "HUD, MHRA, and Cedar Riverside Associates be 'permanently enjoined from taking any action in furtherance of the Cedar Riverside project as proposed both Stage II and any other part of the project' until an adequate environmental impact statement is completed and the court is satisfied that the decision to proceed with the project 'is not arbitrary and capricious.'" Parker found, consistent with CREDF, that the revised environmental impact statement did not adequately address environmental impacts, present alternatives, discuss economic impacts, or provide fair evidence.

Much to activists' initial surprise, Judge Lord gave in to Mayor Hofstede's request to wait ninety days before signing the order in hopes that a new Urban Renewal Plan could be passed. At the end of 1975, however, the ninety-day hold on signing the order for a new environmental impact statement expired and there was no new Urban Renewal Plan. The MHRA had strayed from the new urban renewal objectives, specifying more high- and medium-density housing, retaining the possibility of a "mini-centrum" mall, and weakening community participation requirements. The MHRA later shifted back to the original agreement, but outgoing mayor Hofstede rejected the plan as financially unfeasible, and the MHRA voted to send the whole thing back to committee. CRA, the MHRA, HUD, City Council members, Mayor Hofstede, Mayor-elect Charles Stenvig, and the PAC and CREDF met in hopes of reaching agreement before Lord signed the order.

CREDF and PAC did not immediately press for Lord's signature, since the MHRA was agreeing to democratic community-based redevelopment if the city could avoid lengthy appeals on the environmental impact suit, which Judge Lord's signature would bring into motion. But HUD insisted that new construction in the neighborhood continue to be at high-density levels, and the MHRA valued CRA's land at a "fair market value" of $20 million, while CRA and HUD valued it at twice that much—conspicuously equal to CRA's debts (*Snoose News*, January 1976:3). With no agreement on the horizon, on March 9, 1976, the PAC voted unanimously to request Judge Lord to sign the finding.

In April, Judge Lord signed the environmental impact statement suit. The signing set precedents of national importance. First, "failure of a project to meet pressing housing needs is a negative environmental effect," and in the case of Minneapolis that meant failing to create housing for large, poor families. Second, "absentee ownership results in negative environmental effects." Other findings included problems of pollution, congestion, inefficient energy use, and too little open space—all the result of high-density development (*Snoose News*, April 1976:1). On May 14, 1976, Judge Lord signed an amended order that allowed "noncontroversial" projects to go ahead, such as neighborhood park expansion, rehabilitation of the West Bank Co-op grocery space, repairs to historic Dania Hall, and continuing CDC planning.

Then the New Town plan unraveled. Green Tree Corporation foreclosed on a $1 million loan to CRA. HUD decided to foreclose on all of CRA's property except for Cedar Square West. Because of HUD's foreclosure decision, the PAC voted to ask the Eighth Circuit Court of Appeals, to which HUD had appealed the environmental impact statement decision, to declare the case moot, which would dismiss the appeal and remove the injunction against further development. Since HUD was foreclosing on CRA's land in the old neighborhood, the CRA threat was removed and declaring the case moot would allow redevelopment to proceed. After lengthy negotiations in late 1977 Judge Lord declared the case moot and sent his decision back to the appeals court for its final ruling. The appeals court agreed with Judge Lord, though allowed refiling of the suit if HUD revived the New Town scheme. HUD finally began foreclosing on CRA properties in the old neighborhood in late 1977, nearly a year after it had first decided to do so.

To celebrate, the Tenants Union sponsored a demonstration in front of CRA headquarters, where Father Bill Teska gave a eulogy to CRA, beginning with the biblical reading of the story of David and Goliath and foreshadowing what lay ahead: "David's victory over Goliath was really the beginning of his public life. And likewise, for us this victory over the philistine forces which threatened us is only the beginning of our work. Now the more subtle task of building and creating something entirely new is before us" (*Snoose News*, November 1977:2). Little did neighborhood residents know that the threats would expand along with the opportunities through the end of the decade.

The Political Opportunity Structure in Chaos

The political opportunity structure remained volatile through the remainder of the 1970s. The destruction of the New Town growth coalition left a power vacuum in Cedar-Riverside, and a collage of power brokers, including the University of Minnesota, Augsburg College, private developers, and CRA, tried to salvage what they could from the neighborhood before the dust settled. The local state, attempting to weather the fiscal crisis imposed by the 1970s international economic collapse, found itself coming to blows with the neighborhoods of Minneapolis.

Multiple Fronts

Beginning in late 1976 neighborhood residents constantly had to shift their attention to ward off dangers on multiple fronts, the neighborhood institutions saw the opportunity to expand, and the University of Minnesota announced its intentions to use the People's Center building for office space and demolish three adjacent houses for a parking lot. It began moving the Studio Arts Department into the building, but as Tim Ogren explains, "as the profs moved their stuff in, we moved their stuff back out." After pressure from council people and state legislators, an agreement was reached: the university was allowed to tear down the houses, but it had to provide the displaced residents with relocation funds, give the People's Center building to the community for one dollar, and offer a long-term lease on its land. This compromise was the beginning of a new realism among activists: "We were idealistic about fixing and saving everything. . . . It was a very painful decision to allow the university to knock down three houses in order to get the People's Center for one dollar" (Ogren interview, 1987).

The neighborhood's community-controlled social reproduction base was threatened by continual barriers to establishing, and then maintaining, the West Bank Co-op Grocery. In late 1976 HUD had tried up $70,000 in CDBG monies for the co-op, but it succeeded in opening in December of 1977. Six months later, however, the owners of the building, which had reverted from CRA's control, demanded a 300 percent increase in the co-op's rent. The PAC, the Tenants Union, and the co-op organized a petition drive. By October 1978 "hundreds" of petition signatures, postcards, and City Hall allies had helped the co-op negotiate a new lease.

Augsburg College was also attempting to expand across the neighborhood and began demolishing houses. This action provoked one of the conspicuous uses of the "uncontrollable elements" strategy that neighborhood activists had established during the Cedar Square West dedication ceremony uprising. Not being able to gain satisfactory negotiations by any other means, activists warned that there could very well be disruptive demonstrations during the college's spring commencement. The resulting negotiations were able to save two houses.

Meanwhile, Cedar-Riverside Associates had not given up on getting what it could out of its remaining neighborhood land. In mid-1976 CRA's property management arm, UCPI, was planning to renege on an agreement to preserve the historic firehouse building just north of Cedar Square West. The firehouse provided community space and housed Mixed Blood Theater, the Twin Cities' premiere progressive, multiracial theater company. UCPI planned to install a commercial restaurant. The PAC, CDC, Tenants' Union, Cedar Riverside Arts Council, Snoose Boulevard Festival, Mixed Blood Theater, and concerned residents met with CRA president Robert Jorvig and persuaded the prospective restaurant representatives to meet with community representatives before closing any deal with CRA. By October the neighborhood had obtained a six-month reprieve from CRA on the firehouse with pressure from ninth ward alderman Zollie Green and sixth ward alderman Earl Netwal. The save-the-firehouse movement eventually grew to a coalition of twenty organizations, which worked to get the building placed on the historical register to protect it. The coalition succeeded, and the firehouse and Mixed Blood Theater were saved.[3]

Also in 1976, in the Seven Corners section of the neighborhood, Inn Management, Inc., was proposing to tear down neighborhood housing and businesses to build a motel with a surface parking lot that "looked like a long freeway in Kansas somewhere" (Mungavan interview, 1991). Although some argued that allowing the motel could be used to wrest concessions from the city, the PAC voted not to approve the idea until there were detailed plans. The PAC sponsored workshops to address residents' and businesspeople's objections; by December it approved the motel but limited the land that the motel and its parking could occupy. This was one more concession made by the neighborhood, and though it would lead to future benefits, it exacted a cost in neighborhood unity. PAC architect and organizer Tim Mungavan, who worked the neighborhood workshops to review the plan, described the atmosphere of one meeting as "a riot" in which the residents who were threatened with displacement voiced their opposition loud and long.

The Struggle for the Local State

The end of 1976 also brought a new set of struggles with the City Council as city officials attempted to cut social service and housing programs, replace the community advocate on the MHRA board with an appointee the neighborhoods found unacceptable, and cut funding to the PACs in the city. When the city did cut funds for social service and housing, neighborhood activists across the city formed the Coalition for the Defense of Neighborhood Priorities. In February 1977 the coalition filed an administrative appeal with HUD in hopes of tying up the city's Community Development Block Grant (CDBG) funds. Also in February PAC delegate Jackie Slater ran for one of the three City Council seats representing areas of the neighborhood, and she went on to win that seat in November.

The political pressure, along with CRA's financial collapse, led to a city-created Cedar-Riverside Task Force in February 1977 in another attempt to develop a new Urban Renewal Plan for the neighborhood. The task force was composed of two PAC members, two MHRA members, two council members, a mayor's representative, and two Chamber of Commerce members. The April 1977 *Snoose News* estimated that 150 people turned out for hearings on development proposals by the PAC, the MHRA, and the city planning commission (p. 2). Once again, neighborhood institutions attempting to expand ran into resistance from neighborhood residents.

> The fights were between the institutions and the neighborhood people and downtown. One of the speakers I remember . . . said that land was worth 50 cents a square foot out in some suburb and the land we were living on was worth 20 or 25 dollars a square foot. So why didn't we move out to where land was only 50 cents a square foot, because we were such totally worthless people to be living on such valuable real estate. And everybody's there going, "Holy shit, is this guy as bad as he sounds?" (Dorothy Jacobs interview, 1991)

Residents, two of the three council members representing the neighborhood, and State Senator Allan Spear all supported a PAC-sponsored plan, which provided for the lowest densities, the most rehabilitation, and the most community participation. The task force was still tending toward higher densities and a public corporation not controlled by residents. By mid-1977, however, the task force report, with much lower densities and a greater emphasis on rehabilitation, was approved by the PAC and adopted by the City Council by an eight-to-five vote above the objections of CRA and its major creditor, First National Bank of St. Paul.

In the face of one victory, however, the City Council chopped CDBG funds to neighborhood and housing projects once again in December 1977. The approval of the Cedar-Riverside Task Force report and the cut in funding to neighborhoods opened up every vulnerability of the local state to citizen legitimation, capital pressure, and coercion from higher state tiers. HUD sent an "official letter of warning" threatening to withhold all of the $17.4 million in CDBG funds allotted to the city unless it reviewed its handling of those monies (Snoose News, December 1977:6). Also in December 1977 CRA entered the fray and filed suit against the City of Minneapolis, the MHRA, and HUD, asking for $105 million and attempting to stop foreclosure. CRA charged that HUD did not keep its promises and failed to revise the EIS adequately, and that the city and MHRA had interfered in negotiations by adopting the Cedar-Riverside Task Force report. In February HUD countersued for the more than $30 million CRA owed.

Citizen-legitimation interests triumphed. In December 1978 the City Council passed, by a vote of nine to four, the PAC tax-increment proposal, allowing the community to have access to the increase in taxes resulting from redevelopment in the neighborhood. This proposal included almost $1.6 million for city acquisition in the old neighborhood, another $100,000 for a "revolving fund" to purchase other properties that came on the market, $94,000 for the PAC budget, and some money for the purchase and rehab of buildings in the business district and improved parking.

This victory was not just the result of political pressure. Neighborhood activists had been shifting attention toward planning alternative redevelopment. The PAC and CDC organized neighborhood planning meetings in hopes of actually implementing democratic, community-based redevelopment. At planning meetings held in the Riverside Park section of the neighborhood, "PAC staff provided each participant with a large map of Riverside Park and scale drawings of housing types to 'cut and paste' on the map. . . . Imaginations ran wild and the results were interesting and exciting ways to increase the density and yet maintain the character of existing housing" (Snoose News, April 1978:8). The "over fifty residents and a few absentee landlords" participating attended eleven meetings. By October they had a plan to prevent displacement, create cooperatively owned housing, and protect the area against speculation. The Riverside Park Task Force plan was adopted by the PAC in November. With a detailed, developed, affordable alternative to the New Town, neighborhood residents provided the city with its only hope of getting out from under the New Town fiasco.

In mid-1979 the city also responded to the Neighborhood Priorities Coalition administrative appeal to HUD, which HUD had eventually upheld, and the two-year lawsuit charging that the city was misusing CDBG funds. The City Council adopted a resolution committing the city to providing substantial subsidized housing for families and implementing adequate relocation practices. The fall 1979 city elections brought further optimism. Tony Scallon, a neighborhood ally from the MHRA, was elected over Zollie Green in the ninth ward, adding to Jackie Slater's influence on the City Council. Don Fraser, former congressman and neighborhood supporter, had been elected mayor after a heated and volatile campaign, with help from the turnout for the ninth ward race.

The movement's most significant impact during this period was in pulling City Hall out of the growth machine. Some of the transition in City Hall's posture occurred through electoral victories, as across the city neighborhood activists elected officials who were at least more opposed to the influence of big capital, if not more sympathetic to neighborhood autonomy.

> There was clearly a change at the elected official level in city government toward being very comfortable with that whole approach, from the mayor on down—Hofstede. And he kinda viewed the whole thing—he didn't view it so much as a grass-roots, block-by-block democracy type of thing. . . . He viewed it sort of more in terms of, well, his background—kind of a northeast Minneapolis union kind of model. And he saw the whole thing in terms of being like a company town. The Keith Heller thing was a company-town model, and he knew that was very bad and believed that sort of the rank and file should determine their own destiny.   (Dick Brustad interview, 1991)

The movement made great strides in obtaining more solid allies at City Hall through the election of Jackie Slater, Tony Scallon, and Don Fraser. These individuals were not always well regarded by neighborhood activists, however. Jackie Slater was seen as a moderate on the PAC and was approved of less and less during her tenure on the council. Rosabeth Moss Kanter (1977) has suggested the vulnerability of tokens in maintaining commitment to their minority group peers when they are alone in a hierarchical organization. That may be what happened to Jackie Slater. As the number of allies in city government grew, the neighborhood movement seemed to have fewer disputes with its local state representatives.

Through the latter half of the 1970s, activists were able to bring to fruition the contradiction between "accumulation and legitimation" in the local state, a topic that has often been discussed. Some argue that the local state's primary role is to enhance social reproduction in order to maintain legitimation among the population, and it is the job of higher levels of the local state to respond to accumulation pressures from capital (Cockburn, 1977; Broadbent, 1977; Saunders, 1981; Boddy, 1983; Katz and Mayer, 1985). Though it is clear, as we have seen, that the local state does get involved in supporting accumulation through providing tax abatements and infrastructural improvements to attract and retain capital, it is also the case that citizen demands are most prominent at the local state level (Markusen, 1978; Dearlove, 1979; Schulz, 1979). Regardless of the local state's actual behavior in supporting accumulation versus reproduction, citizens seem to have greater expectations from the local state than from higher-level states. Thus, the local state is probably more vulnerable to citizen-legitimation pressures than are higher-level states, especially when barriers have not been erected through local state reforms that replace mayors with city managers and district council members with council members elected at large.

The contradiction between accumulation and social reproduction is also more intense when demands rise or the local state's ability to meet those demands falls—that is, when the local state can no longer afford to meet both demands (O'Connor, 1973). During good times the state can at least appear to be meeting citizen demands for social reproduction services. But as the economy founders, the local state is less able to keep up appearances. In the late 1970s, though the Minneapolis economy was still far from its lowest point, significant financial pressures were developing in the city which would collide with citizen interests. The pressures developed around the newly created Community Development Block Grant (CDBG) program.

After 1974 the increasingly conservative federal government shifted the fiscal burden, and the struggle, to the local level. The Housing and Community Development Act of 1974 established the Community Development Block Grant program and the smaller and more focused Urban Development Action Grant (UDAG) program. This program was targeted more specifically to benefit low- and moderate-income people. More important, however, money was not provided directly to development projects, as under the 1949 Housing Act. Instead, cities received funds based on their size and demographic characteristics (Feagin and Parker, 1990). Although the critics of the CDBG program have portrayed it as weakening the influence of neighborhoods by giving grants to cities rather than to projects and by not requiring funding for neighborhood-based organization staff (N. Fainstein and S. Fainstein, 1986a), it still contained leverage points, especially in Minneapolis. The most significant point of leverage was the shift of decision making from the national state to the local state, where neighborhoods could have more potential influence over the allocation process itself. In Minneapolis not only had the multineighborhood Coalition for the Defense of Neighborhood Priorities formed to politicize the CDBG allocation process, but the city had enhanced neighborhoods' abilities to push local state legitimacy buttons by responding to that politicization. The city established "City-wide Citizen Advisory Committees," one of whose duties was to make recommendations regarding how to allocate CDBG money. The mayor's and council's rewriting of nearly half the allocation recommendations of those committees brought the full weight of citizen-legitimacy pressures on the City Council. The same thing happened in the 1977 CDBG planning process, setting up the showdown for the 1979 council and mayoral elections.

As neighborhood activists turned to electoral strategies, with increasing success, they began gradually to reshape the political opportunity structure. Like electoral participation in cities such as San Francisco and Boston, where votes were able to influence political appointments or the creation of new citizen-oriented agencies (Mollenkopf, 1983), in Minneapolis voting was able to affect multiple levels of the state and increase the support for Cedar-Riverside activists' positions. The movement pursued electoral strategies in a successful attempt to oust the sixth ward's conservative council member and later elect Jackie Slater and Tony Scallon to the council. The movement also contributed to the elections of Mayor Don Fraser, State Senator Allan Spear, and State Representative Lee Greenfield. Robert Fisher (1984) describes the development of electoral strategies as part of the neo-Alinsky strategy of not just pressuring those in power but gaining direct access to power. These electoral victories helped to create the neighborhood–City Hall alliance that worked to regain control of Cedar-Riverside.

More than anything else, the destabilization of the political opportunity structure came as the unintended result of the local state's role in urban redevelopment. As John Mollenkopf (1978:122–23) notes generally, "local government's role in stimulating central-city development contradicted its role as the guarantor of social peace and political cohesion." Because top-down, capital-conscious urban redevelopment often threatens social reproduction directly by displacing residents, or indirectly by shifting resources from citizens to capital, it easily creates controversy. That was the case in 1977, when the city was seen as moving $2 million of its $17.4 million CDBG application away from neighborhoods to make up for the losses of previous top-down, capital-conscious redevelopment projects. The continuing conflict over the New Town destroyed what remaining stability existed in the political opportunity structure.

Without the destruction of the growth coalition, the tentative alliance with City Hall, and the chaos created in the political opportunity structure, the neighborhood would have been in dangerous waters. The two final battles of the 1970s almost wrecked the movement. But in the absence of a solid growth machine or a local state captured by capital, these two battles instead marked a transition.

The Final Battles

Wresting Control of the Old Neighborhood from CRA

The most intense struggle during this period involved the Tenants Union. On October 29, 1976, the Minnesota State Supreme Court ruled against the Union in the second rent strike. The court ruled that tenants could not withhold rent because a landlord had violated a collective bargaining agreement regarding rent raises, but could strike only to protest code violations.[4] Angered but undeterred, the Tenants Union continued organizing Cedar Square West residents and delivered five hundred petition signatures to the local HUD office protesting Cedar Square West maintenance and security. The Union won a meeting with Tom Feeney from the area office at Cedar Square West—"We put his chair next to a bucket collecting drips from a sewer pipe" (Ogren interview, 1987). Instead of better maintenance, however, Cedar Square West residents got a hefty rent hike approved by HUD over residents' objections.

Tensions grew. By March 1977 the Tenants Union was in its eighth month of negotiations with UCPI over a collective bargaining agreement without resolution. By August the interim agreement between the Union and UCPI had expired with no collective bargaining agreement.

On August 25 strike preparations began. Cedar Square West residents collected strike pledges from 220 people in 180 apartments by early September. Tenants of the old neighborhood were also preparing to strike. CRA had taken the opportunity of the expiration of the earlier agreement with the Tenants Union to raise rents across the old neighborhood and was allowing the homes there simply to deteriorate.

This was the fourth rent strike and the most dangerous. Tim Ogren, a Tenants Union organizer, describes it as "the longest year of my life." The strike started dirty and stayed that way. CRA charged, in a letter, that the Tenants Union was misleading tenants by telling them that CRA could not evict them. The October 1977 *Snoose News* countered by citing a memo from the Legal Aid Society and stated that "in an action similar to ours, no one has ever been evicted in Hennepin County when showing up in court with their rent money in their pocket" (p. 1). A rumor circulated that foreign students and residents who participated in the rent strike could lose their immigration status. *Snoose News* responded by citing the reassurance of "a law professor who specializes in immigration problems" and charged that the MHRA had "implied" that subsidized tenants could lose their rent subsidy if they were evicted. A subsequent letter from the MHRA, reprinted in the November *Snoose News*, supported the tenants' right to strike and clarified the confusion over rent subsidies (p. 2).

Through October 150 units struck, joined in November by an increasing number of strikers from Cedar Square West. Thirty-five to forty Tenants Union members picketed the home of new CRA head Robert Hoffman. CRA had already sent out eviction notices to Cedar Square West strikers and was now sending unlawful detainer eviction notices, or "U.D.'s," to residents in the old neighborhood, including the New Riverside Cafe: "And the sheriff came and served the U.D. Steve took a piece of bread and some sprouts and put it in and he ate it. And then that night we had a mass meeting . . . . We called it 'the war council.' And then we had court training that night for unlawful detainer individual actions the next morning" (Ogren interview, 1991). By December the number of striking units had grown to 160 and was still climbing, and three hundred people demonstrated in front of the Cedar Square West rental office. The December 1977 *Snoose News* reported that some strikers were considering going beyond "nonviolent resistance" (p. 1). Tenants of Cedar Square West filed a class action suit in federal court to attempt to prevent UCPI from collecting the HUD-approved rent increase. Across the neighborhood the signs went up: "WE STAY."

The strikers won their first victory in December when Judge Peter Albrecht[5] dismissed all the eviction cases in Cedar Square West, finding that two-week notices did not follow federal guidelines. State Representative Martin Sabo, State Senator Allan Spear, and council members Zollie Green and Tom Scott urged CRA to cease the eviction action and negotiate. Numerous Twin Cities organizations voiced their support of the strikers, including groups as diverse as the Minnesota Coalition for Welfare Reform, the Farmer Labor Association, and the Guild of Taxi Drivers.

In early 1978 the New Riverside Cafe wound up in court. In response, about one hundred residents and cafe supporters posted an "eviction notice" on CRA's door, to no avail, however. Judge Albrecht ruled that the cafe, as a commercial tenant, could not legally withhold rent based on maintenance complaints and code violations. The cafe considered appealing but instead asked the court to allow it to pay its rent due and stay, and the court agreed. CRA appealed that decision, apparently hoping to remove the cafe altogether. Judge Donald Alsop also ruled against Cedar Square West residents who were attempting to rescind the October 1977 rent increases.

In March 1978 the mayor's office finally brought CRA to the negotiating table with the mayor and two aides, two representatives from HUD, the executive director of the MHRA, and council member Jackie Slater—one of the rent strikers. CRA and the Tenants Union were finally talking, though CRA's neglect of the houses in the old neighborhood meant that two houses were facing condemnation. The April 1978 *Snoose News* strongly warned tenants not to call the inspections department without first contacting the Tenants Union to avoid condemnation of the entire old neighborhood (p. 1).

The rent strike went into its eleventh month in mid-1978. Although Cedar Square West tenants had lost their lawsuit to stop rent increases, in the first of the eviction trials of the fifty Cedar Square West strikers the jury awarded a 17 percent rebate of rent to the tenants, far beyond denying an increase. But eventually, two tenants lost their cases. When CRA announced its intent to evict one of those tenants, the community exploded. "We had a meeting at the New Riverside Cafe and were wondering if we should camp out in front of Pam's door to stop the sheriff from coming in. Elaine . . . said, "Why should we wait for the sheriff to come in? Why don't we go occupy their offices now?' " (Ogren interview, 1987).

The next morning 125 Tenants Union members marched down and occupied the Cedar Square West rental office. By moving in the morning, they had the element of surprise on their side. "The standard joke was if Heller bulldozed the neighborhood before nine o'clock, he could have pulled it off. No one believed we got up before ten" (Ogren interview, 1987). They left without arrest when the mayor's office agreed to a meeting. Eventually, the evictions were dropped and the Cedar Square West rent strike stopped.

The Cafe also escaped eviction, but only by the luck of timing. After numerous delays HUD had finally taken action on its decision to place the old neighborhood into receivership, but HUD and the PAC fought over whether the MHRA or a private company would take over management of the old neighborhood. The PAC was hoping for a quick resolution, since the First National Bank of St. Paul had begun foreclosing on CRA properties in the Riverbluff and Seven Corners sections of the neighborhood and was considering auctioning them off to the highest bidder. Another CRA building had reverted to its original owner when CRA refused to continue payments and HUD declined to pick them up. The possibility existed that thirty-five other properties in the neighborhood could also revert.

Judge Alsop eventually appointed Thorpe Brothers receiver for the old neighborhood, gave them the right to back rent (thus depriving CRA of any rent-strike money), and ordered the receiver to pay operating expenses and repairs before insurance, taxes, and contract payments. But the Minnesota Supreme Court gave CRA the right to evict the Cafe even if it did pay back rent. "CRA could have then attempted to evict the Cafe, but the next day, CRA itself was evicted when the new receiver took control of the older properties" (*Snoose News*, July/August 1978:7). On July 1st, 1978, Thorpe Brothers took over the old neighborhood, just in time to save the New Riverside Cafe. But relations with Thorpe Brothers got off to a rocky start over recognition of the Tenants Union, maintenance, and the continuing rent strike. In October 1978 an agreement was finally signed, which including a 20 percent rebate on rents withheld during the CRA portion of the strike and a commitment by Thorpe to use half the rent money for major maintenance.

The strike had left the Tenants Union in disarray and had burned out its organizers. The other organizations had done their part, eliminating the threat before the Tenants Union could succumb. But there was still one more battle left to finish off the New Town.

The New Town's Last Gasp

In March 1980 HUD revived the New Town in Town.

We thought that things were turning around in our favor. We had stopped them. And all of a sudden—I think it came as kind of a shock to people—we got word that HUD was essentially giving CRA a second chance. They had already squandered uncounted millions of dollars and hadn't successfully done anything. We thought that we had stopped it . . . but then all of a sudden HUD's going to give CRA a second chance. (Ogren interview, 1991)

HUD proposed a settlement of both its foreclosure suit against CRA and CRA's countersuit, which involved selling the $35 million CRA owed it to First National Bank of St. Paul for about $2.7 million. The bank, in turn, had an agreement with CRA which could continue the original project. The city's initial response was to counteroffer that the MHRA acquire, at low cost, all but the Stage II land and the land bordering Cedar Square West, on which CRA could continue to build high-rises.

The community's reaction was swift and militant. Less than twenty-four hours after residents heard of this plan through the city grapevine, the Community Union called a meeting attended by more than one hundred people. Residents threatened to picket, glue locks, and call in the television news show "60 Minutes." Two hundred demonstrators leafletted citizens on April 15, tax-deadline day, protesting plans to bail out CRA using tax dollars. Activists picketed the First National Bank of St. Paul. The New Riverside Cafe handed out pre-printed postcards, five hundred of which ended up at HUD. And activists descended on City Hall.

And we had a meeting at City Council chambers with representatives from HUD. I remember Jack getting real mad and storming out. I remember I took one of those big heavy chairs and threw it over and stamped out. . . . City Hall believed we still could turn out people, and the mythology of the reckless crazies, and who knows what they could do, affected city hall. Plus, Cedar-Riverside was very active politically. And of everything we did, that was the most important thing. (Ogren interview, 1991)

Aware that there were both voters and crazies in Cedar-Riverside, the city made a counterproposal to get HUD to sell its liens on the old neighborhood to the city, instead of to the bank, for $3.5 million and CRA to sell its land to the city on request. The city obtained the right of first refusal to acquire all residential land at 20 percent of market value, provided that a development proposal and the money to finance it was already in place, and the commercial property would be sold at market rates to anyone. It was a compromise engineered by practical politicians who realized that they had to reckon with the neighborhood.

By the mid-70s, the council under the leadership of Lou DeMars, I
think, recognized that . . . the city's backing of the Cedar-Riverside
project as it had been originally constructed was no longer viable—
because of the rent strikes and the environmental defense attack
and litigation, etc. And so DeMars, being a smart politician but certainly not anyone who would characterize himself then or today as
being in favor of community-based development . . . but being in
favor of the best political solution that serves the most people, negotiated . . . a compromise. And the compromise was the settlement
agreement.   (O'Brien interview, 1991)

The switch in city sympathies against CRA but not necessarily in
favor of the neighborhood may also have had its benefits. Because of
the state's dependence on funding from capital, it rarely acts against
the interests of powerful capitalists. The ability of officials at the city
level to avoid a lengthy lawsuit by negotiating a settlement among the
federal government, powerful bankers, and CRA required moderation
and apparent neutrality on the part of city officials. Kathy O'Brien,
another neighborhood activist who was elected to the City Council
after the settlement decision, argues:

In a sense, I sort of think of it as Richard Nixon going to China.
Probably if I, as former West Bank Tenants Union newsletter editor,
had been the council member for the area, I might not have been
able to affect the settlement or to bring that about. But the sort of
traditional . . . centrist Democrat council president not from the area
was able to bring about a settlement that sort of everybody could
live with.

The New Town in Town was finally, irrevocably stopped. The extent of the victory was not yet apparent, since the new Urban Renewal
Plan had not been approved at the time and the Cedar-Riverside residents had not begun to take control of the neighborhood housing.
But the primary threat had been removed, and residents had gained
a reputation, and a legitimacy, that would provide the foundation
for rebuilding the old neighborhood. In the 1980s the struggle would
drastically change character. Having successfully defended the neighborhood, the movement was now faced with the task of rebuilding it.
Much of the groundwork was already in place. Neighborhood workshops had instituted the planning. Funding strategies, and some of
the funding, were in place. The settlement agreement of 1980 signaled

the presence of a powerful neighborhood movement. It was clear that the neighborhood residents could not be ignored.

> We didn't, at that point, have the power to do anything, but we could stop anything. And I think that was literally true at that time, though the financial structure [of the New Town] was always the trump card. We could have moved to the desert and it still wouldn't have worked. That was slowly coming out. But I think there was a very broad perception on both sides that we could stop any project that they attempted.   (Ogren interview, 1991)

Actually accomplishing redevelopment was to bring a whole new set of problems for the neighborhood movement, however. It was in this third period of the neighborhood movement that Father Teska's warning—that the hardest part was yet to come—was realized. How do communities move on to conduct democratic, community-based urban redevelopment that serves community needs, preserves democracy, and reflects the diversity of interests in the community? That is far more difficult than stopping urban redevelopment, since communities are relatively weak by virtue of their lack of control of capital and their lack of access to the local state. Can communities create their own coalitions? The answer is yes, but not unproblematically. Cedar-Riverside provides a textbook example of how to stop urban redevelopment—amazing enough by itself. The real lesson, however, is still to come and provides a whole new perspective on the contradictions between capital and community.

The counterculture community. At the rear are homes later demolished to build Cedar Square West. *Photo by Ralph Wittcoff.*

An early Community Union press conference to oppose CRA's attempt to evict The Whale leather-goods shop. Seated from left to right are the Reverend William Teska; Ralph Wittcoff; "Jonah" (Robert Friedman), the shop's proprietor; and Jonah's assistant. *Photographer unknown.*

The New Riverside Cafe Collective, 1971. Photo by Eve MacLeish.

333-9924   IN MEMRY

22nd wed. mpls. hindustani
23rd thu. c. jirousek, b. bergland 12 string nite!
mike cass
24th fri. middlespunk creek boys
25th sat. midwest hayride shitkicker #3 folks!
26th sun. baroque ensemble

NEW RIVERSIDE CAFÉ

Beauregard, a member of the New Riverside Cafe collective in the early 1970s who was struck and killed by an automobile, is memorialized in a New Riverside Cafe poster. *Poster by Eve MacLeish.*

NEW RIVERSIDE CAFE

in ⊙ DIRE WOLF ♍ est. 1970

ANARCHISM NOW

2nd ANNIVERSARY!

Tuesday, August 22nd — Open Stage — sign up at 7:00 pm

Wednesday, August 23rd — A Rainbridge

remember we still got anarchist prices!

Thursday, August 24th — Becky Riemer

Friday, August 25th — Roy Alstad's Mill City Blues Band

Saturday, August 26th — Ed Beatty & Ted Unseth

Sunday, August 27th — Betty Boop & trackin' friends

open from noon, music at 9:00 p.m., 329 Cedar   333-9924

An early New Riverside Cafe poster. Anarchism was the guiding philosophy, marijuana (symbolized by the cannabis plants at the top) was the drug of choice, and the Grateful Dead (symbolized by the roses) was the defining music of the time. *Poster by Michael McKenzie and Zack Zniewski.*

A People's Pantry poster, before the organization grew into North Country Co-op. Poster by Zack Zniewski.

Another early New Riverside Cafe poster. Note the caption at the bottom: "There's No Gov't. Like No Gov't." Poster by Eric Monrad.

BEWARE

SABOTAGE

The original watchcat. Poster by Zack Zniewski, who states, "I am proud to have carried forward an image traditional to American anarchism by reintroducing the old IWW 'sabcat.'"

Left: A poster commemorating the Cedar Square West dedication ceremony uprising. *Photo by Debbie Wolking.*

Below: Riverside Plaza, previously named Cedar Square West, the first and only stage of the New Town in Town, at dusk. This view shows only five buildings of the eleven-building complex. *Photo by Debbie Wolking.*

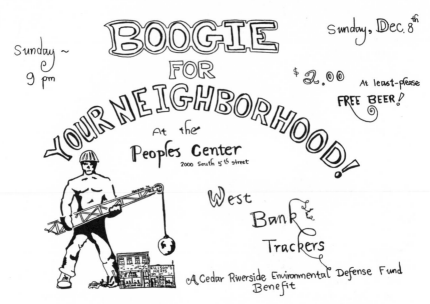

A fundraising poster for CREDF, advertising one of the neighborhood's infamous "boogies." *Poster by Norman Peterson.*

A Tenants Union sign that hung in rent strikers' windows. *Poster attributed to Richard Hofacre.*

A Tenants Union strike poster. Note the watchcat. *Poster by Eric Monrad.*

A publicity poster for the CDC. *The Towering Inferno* was a disaster film about a high-rise fire. The name ultimately chosen was "West Bank Community Development Corporation." *Artist unknown.*

The community's response to the MHRA purchase of "air rights" above Cedar Square West in order to channel funds to CRA. The drawing appeared in the Winter–Spring issue of *Common Ground*, an alternative publication on work and community issues in the Twin Cities. *Drawing by Chuck Logan.*

Deteriorated housing in the Cedar East section of the neighborhood. *Photo by Debbie Wolking.*

The tools of community-based planning. Residents would move, remove, and add these wooden houses on block diagrams to see what different redevelopment plans would look like. *Photo by Tim Mungavan.*

The first neighborhood groundbreaking celebration, October 17, 1982. *Photo by James Lotzer.*

The same house before and after rehabilitation. In addition to improvements in the exterior, extensive renovation was often done to roofs, insulation, windows, foundations, and interiors. *Photos by Tim Mungavan.*

Tim Zniewski and Ralph Wittcoff of the Durable Goods store collective. Durable Goods was one of the businesses displaced by business-strip redevelopment. *Photo by Debbie Wolking.*

Entertainment at Cedarfest, the annual neighborhood festival. *Photo by Debbie Wolking.*

The watchcat preserved in concrete. *Photo by Debbie Wolking.*

CHAPTER

6

Building the Foundation for
Community-based Development

I think . . . they were very aware at that point in time where sort
of the opposition battle was won, and they were now being told by
everybody that "you guys are so goddamn smart, you do it"—that
sort of thing. And, I think, by and large they were very much
aware they had to change everything. They had to go from an
exciting intellectual exercise of being in opposition and finding
good reasons why the project shouldn't go ahead and all that
analysis and grass-roots politics; to not only having a dream about
how the neighborhood should function but then learning how to be
a production force, to literally go out and do it—be the producer of
the housing.
                                        —*Dick Brustad interview, 1991*

One of the problems with success is it's always a lot of work.
                          —*Tim Mungavan at September 1989 PAC meeting*

T HE STRUGGLE against the New Town in Town was over. A disorganized group of hippies believing everything was lost had
become an organized group of activists believing anything was possible. The seemingly impenetrable growth coalition that was to level
their neighborhood had been shattered, creating an urban redevelopment policy vacuum in the local political opportunity structure.
Suddenly, how to plan urban redevelopment, what kind of urban redevelopment to plan, and where to plan it were open to question
throughout perhaps all levels of the city bureaucracy, except for the
Planning Department, which stuck tenaciously to top-down, capital-
conscious planning models.

In 1980 the neighborhood movement began to move toward democratic, community-based redevelopment. And residents were in an enviable position to begin that redevelopment. The 1980 settlement agreement provided enormous resources. Not only would the city be able to purchase the land for 20 percent of its cost, but the development that had been completed would create an increase in tax payments—a "tax increment"—that would be channeled back into the neighborhood. In return, the residents agreed to give up the Seven Corners section of the neighborhood for a hotel, parking ramp, and high-density housing.

Before the neighborhood activists could make full use of those resources, however, they would have to do battle with opponents inside and outside the neighborhood. They had to transform their community movement from one whose solidarity was based on opposition and confrontation to one that had to build solidarity out of suddenly diverse interests and enlist the cooperation and support of former targets. Organizing against a mutual threat is easier than organizing a diversity of interests that may have contradictory self-interests (N. Fainstein and S. Fainstein, 1974; Saltman, 1990). This transition from neighborhood defense goals to neighborhood development goals made even the relatively minor differences among activists on the West Bank seem, at times, impossibly incompatible. And the need for resources to accomplish democratic, community-based development necessitated alliances with capital and the local state which were seen as at best distasteful and at worst corrupt.

Thus, the twin problems associated with moving from neighborhood defense to neighborhood development were new internal dissension and altered external relations. Internal dissension can tear a movement apart and is especially dangerous when there is no longer a clear common threat. Although all residents agreed on the undesirability of Cedar-Riverside Associates and its New Town in Town plan, they could not easily agree on the direction redevelopment should take. Much of the effort in the early 1980s was devoted to resolving difficult conflicts in the neighborhood over both the process and the product of neighborhood redevelopment. And while residents were working toward a fragile consensus within the neighborhood, they were painfully aware of the need for establishing a strong political foothold at City Hall. Activists struggled over how to maintain that foothold and still preserve community autonomy.

During these early years of neighborhood-based development, residents succeeded in isolating their antagonists within the neighborhood and gained far more than a foothold downtown, helping to establish a new neighborhood-focused governing regime at City Hall that would channel enviable resources to the neighborhood throughout the 1980s. In this chapter I describe the struggle to build a neighborhood consensus around development planning and establish a supportive governing regime downtown.

Prelude to Community-based Development

As usual in Cedar-Riverside, nothing came easy. Beginning redevelopment was not as simple as creating a neighborhood consensus and gaining local state support to implement it. The disrupted political opportunity structure had not yet settled down in the early 1980s, and the instability confused relations and allowed continual threats to the neighborhood to surface. Cedar-Riverside activists could never focus all their energies on positive action, as they needed to guard against both nuisance hassles and dangerous threats from within and without.

Confronting Outside Threats

Although the main threat, the New Town in Town, had been laid to rest, its creator continued to haunt the neighborhood. In 1979 Keith Heller attempted to sell off the homes he owned in the Riverside Park section of the neighborhood—at speculative prices, activists charged. When two other homes went up for sale in the neighborhood, activist residents organized the Anti-Displacement Housing Organizing Committee (ADHOC), put up fake "for sale" signs in Riverside Park to protest speculative selling, and were able to get one house taken off the market. Cedar Riverside Associates attempted to evict the Free Store, a stable neighborhood institution providing free consumer goods, apparently with some pressure from the neighborhood businesses, to "improve" the area's image. CRA had also lost some neighborhood properties to Northwest National Life, which activists were struggling to reclaim. And one of Heller's employees had become manager of the properties in the old neighborhood, through Thorpe Brothers, although the settlement agreement had specified that a separate manager be appointed. The final straw came when, activists charged, CRA's maintenance crews moved into several boarded-up homes in the neighborhood and smashed plumbing fixtures, cemented drains, and otherwise made the houses uninhabitable.

In April 1981, about one hundred people gathered at the New Riverside Cafe for a meeting of the Community Union, which had reorganized to replace the defunct Tenants Union, and voted to begin another rent strike to protest CRA's actions. By May CRA had filed unlawful detainers against ninety strikers, but all were thrown out of court because there was no clear manager consistent with the settlement decision. By September 1981 the amount of rent being held in escrow had climbed to nearly $100,000. In October CRA appointed Realty Management Services as independent manager and agreed to pay $670 in legal costs. Satisfied with this response, the Community Union voted to end the rent strike.

The perceived nastiness of neighborhood activists was having an influence on urban capital. The investors who were reclaiming commercial property from CRA hung onto it, likely worried that the movement would go on the attack if they sold it to speculators, and attempted to negotiate with the CDC about selling it to the local business tenants of those buildings. But the banks would not risk much to help those local businesspeople purchase their buildings, especially since neighborhood businesses, less ideologically militant than the residents, had only ambivalent support from the PAC.

Relations with City Hall also became strained as the neighborhood movement struggled with the transition from neighborhood defense to neighborhood development. Council member Jackie Slater, who had always been seen by militant activists as a political moderate, came to be regarded as an adversary. Her disputes with militant Tenants Union activists over Union strategy had won her few friends in the neighborhood. Tempers flared further when PAC member Bruce Rubenstein wrote a letter of protest to the Minneapolis headquarters of Honeywell Corporation, known among antiwar activists for its role in the manufacture of cluster bombs and nuclear weapons technology. Honeywell was considering becoming the new management entity in the neighborhood. Rubenstein's letter, written as a PAC staffperson and on PAC stationery, suggested that Honeywell send its top executives to Vietnam to "crawl over minefields on their hands and knees, exploding these grisly weapons." Other suggestions were equally colorful. City Council people were appalled. The PAC executive council voted that Rubenstein write a letter of apology, though "the neighborhood was very happy—the slap on the wrist was only a show for City Hall." Rubenstein apologized only for implying that the letter came from the PAC, and Honeywell backed away from its interest in managing property in the neighborhood.

Additionally, activists feared changes in the MHRA. There had been rumors in the mayor's office since the beginning of the year that the old MHRA was going to be combined with the Minne-apolis Industrial Development Commission (MIDC) to save money. Neighborhood activists were trying to assess the impact of this development. Minneapolis had been considered a "strong council, weak mayor" city government by activists, even with some increase of the mayor's budgetary powers in 1977. Some saw this plan as exacerbating mayor-council tensions, others saw it as streamlining the development process, and some feared it would dilute citizen participation. Regardless of people's fears and objections, however, the MHRA and MIDC were combined as the Minneapolis Community Development Association (MCDA), under joint mayor-council control. On June 1, 1981, the MCDA was created with a board of six—three from each organization—and the staffs of both retained. Although community-based development in Cedar-Riverside was not appreciably disrupted by the restructuring, it provided an added grievance around which Twin Cities neighborhoods were to mobilize two years down the road to build a new governing regime.

Defusing Internal Threats

While the outside antagonisms were, for the most part, nuisances that had to be contended with before they flared into bigger problems, the internal threats were potentially more damaging. Ideological disputes had always existed in the neighborhood, particularly between socialists and anarchists, but there was more agreement than disagreement, and differences were set aside for the greater consensus on the need to defend the neighborhood against the New Town. With the demise of the New Town plan, however, disputes between diverse leftist ideological adherents made for long and tense discussions over the coming course of community-based development. Nevertheless, the initial internal threats did not arise from leftist factioning. Rather, the threats came from structurally based factions in the neighborhood—namely, property owners.

John Davis (1991), drawing from Peter Saunders's (1978) discussion of "domestic property classes," argues that differential access to property creates different objective interests. Ultimately, as Logan and Molotch (1987) and Feagin and Parker (1990) maintain, rentiers occupy a much different property class than renters: the first makes income from property; the second pays income for the right to occupy, but not *control*, property. Most interesting in Davis's (1991) use of the property-class notion, however, is his discussion of homeowners. Homeowners, according to Davis, occupy a middle position between renters and rentiers. Though homeowners own their property, they derive no income from it. Homeowners thus occupy a "contradictory class location" that makes them politically unpredictable (Wright, 1985). Homeowners vehemently fight threats to the community that may reduce their property values, but they are unwilling to take political risks because of the social-control functions of the mortgage, which places effective control of their property in the hands of the lender. Davis argues, consequently, that we have to look beyond the cultural homogeneity that lies on the surface of neighborhood relations to explore the diversity and potential internal conflict rooted in structurally differentiated property classes.

In Cedar-Riverside three different property classes took shape. First were the remaining homeowners, who had gradually come to oppose the New Town on the side of the radical neighborhood residents. Second were the radical residents, who were not planning for individual homeownership, but were developing a model of collective control of the neighborhood housing through co-op ownership and control strategies. And third were the renters in Cedar Square West, who had no hope for either ownership or control of their units. The neighborhood was also structurally divided by more traditional class boundaries based on the control of productive capital. On the one hand most residents by this time had come to occupy more traditional employment patterns as wage workers. But some residents and nonresidents, members of the worker-controlled co-op businesses such as the New Riverside Cafe, Freewheel Bike Co-op, Durable Goods hardware store, and North Country Co-op, remained committed to neighborhood control of the neighborhood. Finally, there were the traditional small businesses in the neighborhood. While retailing exotic fashion, books, cutting-edge outdoor gear, or creative dining, and adopting liberal notions opposed to big capitalism, these businesses nonetheless had to attend to their bottom lines and were as resistant to neighborhood control of their activities as they were to outside control. Like homeowners, these businesspeople occupied a contradictory class location. Although they owned their businesses, they did not employ a large work force and so their profits did not come primarily from the exploitation of a wage labor force. Thus, also like homeowners, small business owners were fickle allies in the neighborhood.

Within Cedar-Riverside in the early 1980s the exchange-value pressures of homeowners and small businesses were pitted against the use-value pressures of activist residents. Conflicts came as residents attempted to limit the impact of exchange-value pressures on community-based development. Hostility escalated when activists charged that one neighborhood businessman, believed to be allied with Keith Heller, controlled four PAC seats because his friends and relatives were strategically placed in combined Cedar Square West–business strip districts. Neighborhood activists on the PAC led a move to redraw the boundaries to reduce his influence and increase the representation of Cedar Square West residents, a measure that passed the PAC by only one vote and set homeowners and businesspeople against the activist residents. The West Bank Business Association (WBBA), representing about a third of the neighborhood's businesses, was also pushing for a parking ramp in the neighborhood which would displace at least four units of housing.[1] Radical businesses in the neighborhood, such as the New Riverside Cafe, became involved on the residents' side, leading to a bitter stalemate.

Businesses, homeowners, and institutions, having been dealt two setbacks over the parking ramp and the PAC redistricting, organized a "Reform Caucus" party slate for the 1980 PAC elections. Activists had more support, however, bringing 650 residents to the polls—a turnout of about 10 percent, high for neighborhood elections by any standard. All but one of the candidates on the activist-sponsored "Community Union" slate were elected to the PAC. Activists recall, only partly joking, that "this produced the last of the great West Bank parties. We spent the night getting bombed in celebration and then began attending AA the next day."

Undeterred by the activists' electoral successes, homeowners, with business support, submitted a proposal to the MCDA in early 1982 which would have given the existing PAC only one vote on a new PAC dominated by businesses, property owners, and institutions. In response, the MCDA initiated a review of the PAC process through a series of meetings involving the PAC, the CDC, institutions, businesses, and property owners. The businesses pressed for further power by collecting businessperson signatures on a petition calling for a separate PAC for businesses, even though the PAC had agreed to add four business seats, one homeowner's seat, and one property owner's seat. By April 1982 the PAC proposal was accepted and a Business PAC (B-PAC) was created. It was represented by four seats on the regular PAC, making it, as Ralph Wittcoff noted, "the only business organization in the city with citizen participation funding."

Other difficulties, not structurally based, also developed within the community. Though these conflicts were more easily resolvable, agreements remained shaky and provided the fuel for greater struggles later in the decade. The main quarrel at this point developed between residents who advocated low-density renewal and those who advocated letting things be. The older hippie anarchist residents were content once their houses were saved. More central activists, however, argued that they needed to proceed with democratic, community-based redevelopment in order to meet promises they had made to the city in the negotiations that led to the 1980 settlement decision. These residents also feared that if the community did not conduct its own redevelopment, much of the neighborhood housing could be condemned before long or another speculator could step in and the neighborhood would again face the danger it had just escaped. The redevelopment advocates prevailed, but they found it difficult to gain the full support of those who had little or no interest in rehabbing their housing.

> There was a strong anarchist feeling that land belongs to all of the people, and it should be turned over in total to the neighborhood and everyone should be free to develop as they please to provide their own housing. . . . And when we started talking about boxes and arrows and legal structures—we had this book from the Housing Law Project at Berkeley, it was like three hundred pages long on how to organize a CDC. That didn't stir anybody's imagination. (Steve Parliament interview, 1991)

Unless the residents took charge of redevelopment the neighborhood would likely be dismantled piecemeal by others. Augsburg College had purchased other houses in the neighborhood and hoped to demolish as many as forty buildings. Northwestern National Life Insurance Company reclaimed property from CRA when Thorpe Brothers refused to pay the money due to keep the land in receivership, allowing even more parcels to slip away. St. Mary's Hospital was making plans to tear down two houses for a parking ramp.

Shifts in the Political Opportunity Structure

Counterbalancing the threats in the neighborhood and underlying the conflicts and instability in the political opportunity structure were subtle changes that would shift the balance toward democratic, community-based development in the 1980s. At the federal level the shift from program to block-grant funding formulas moved the political burden to the local level. Although the CDBG program has neither benefited poor people as much as was promised (Levine, 1989) nor provided the same federal-level participation in decision making (N. Fainstein and S. Fainstein, 1986a), it has not been a complete loss. For the first time, organized neighborhoods had access to a program at the local level to conduct community-based development. Communities Organized for Public Service, or COPS, in San Antonio, Texas, pressured the city enough to direct more than half of San Antonio's CDBG allocation between 1974 and 1981 to COPS development programs (Reitzes and Reitzes, 1987). Cleveland City Hall maintained CDBG funding of neighborhood-based organizations even in the face of massive federal cuts (Keating, Krumholz, and Metzger, 1989). Under Mayor Harold Washington, Chicago City Hall doubled the number of community-based organizations that received CDBG support (Bennett, 1989). Into the 1980s, community-based development organizations increased their success in obtaining their share of CDBG, Urban Development Action Grant (UDAG), and Housing Development Action Grant (HoDAG) money, obtaining funding that sometimes reached more than $1 million per project (Center for Community Change, 1988). Cedar-Riverside benefited both directly and indirectly from this change in federal funding, because the neighborhood was able to mobilize the talent and expertise to make the most of this shift. Cedar-Riverside had achieved a credibility rarely attributed to community-based mobilizations. And the city was stuck with a land assemblage that would have to be dealt with. The New Town

> was such an obvious exercise in colossal stupidity that its utter, total, and complete collapse in a way gave the opposition a sort of mantle of credibility that it managed to carry for quite a while. It's not at all the same as if the Heller-Segal New Town in Town plan had never happened and instead the residents of that neighborhood had said, "Listen, this place is falling apart. We gotta fix it up and here's how we gotta do it." It simply isn't the same situation at all, because in the second situation you're sort of starting from ground zero and you're scrambling, and there's nothing that sets you apart from anybody else that's got a similar problem. (Jack Cann interview, 1991)

At the city level the backing of the local state for democratic, community-based redevelopment was set up through the 1980 settlement agreement and the new Urban Renewal Plan that followed. And with the 1980 ward reapportionment, four of the thirteen council members became responsible for areas of the neighborhood. The influence of council member Tony Scallon and Brighton Development executive director Dick Brustad had helped transform the MCDA's predecessor, the MHRA, into supporting neighborhood-based redevelopment. Consequently, the city government was more available than it ever had been, as the PAC staff and leaders were provided official access to negotiate development plans and funding through the city bureaucracy and political system. Not all city departments automatically fell into step with the new focus on community-based redevelopment, however. Dick Brustad argues that

> from about . . . 1978 on, the staff and the board of MHRA and then the MCDA were pretty much totally committed to the new approach—not only because that's the direction most of the elected officials wanted to go, but because they truly believed in it. . . . The problem was bigger in other city departments, actually, like the Planning Department, who had not bought into the new approach. They still liked the massive, large-scale project.

The more supportive city government created through the 1979 elections was also important in the final passage of a new Urban Renewal Plan for the neighborhood. The plan contained concessions to CRA and homeowners to exclude some CRA properties and all owner-occupied buildings from acquisition and to eliminate a "land trust" program that would have ensured that certain properties would remain available for low-income residents. But it also provided crucial concessions to the neighborhood. A "no-displacement" policy prevented current residents from having to move out of the neighborhood because their homes were being torn down or because of housing cost increases. It also drastically limited density levels to eliminate the possibility of high-rises and even walk-up apartments in all but the Seven Corners section of the neighborhood. With support from Mayor Fraser, the City Council finally passed the new Urban Renewal Plan on August 8, 1981.

Finally, West Bankers were fortunate that they were living in one of the Midwest's healthiest urban economies and expanding metropolitan areas. The city government was both willing and able to channel enormous resources into urban redevelopment in Cedar-Riverside. The Twin Cities were also in the process of developing a strong service sector. And it was economic gains in this sector that cities such as San Francisco and Boston used to direct funds into neighborhoods to stave off criticism of growth-coalition projects (Clavel and Kleniewski, 1990). Minneapolis did not adopt a "linkage" policy whereby downtown rents were increased modestly to fund neighborhood development, thus linking downtown development to neighborhood development, but it did adopt a tax-increment funding strategy. Tax-increment financing channeled the increased property tax intake created by development projects back into the neighborhoods where the development occurred. Thus, in Cedar-Riverside, Cedar Square West and the Seven Corners developments provided property tax increases that could be used for future development. City government was also willing to pass millions of dollars in bond issues for neighborhood development. And at least one council official argued that he supported downtown office-tower construction so that property taxes in the neighborhood could be maintained at lower rates, offset by increased property taxes paid by "those shiny new office towers."

The Beginnings of Democratic, Community-based Redevelopment

By the time the new urban renewal plan was passed, the neighborhood was poised for redevelopment. The CDC had already gotten its feet wet in the West Bank Co-op Grocery deal. It was growing both financially and organizationally, having loaned $25,000 to the West Bank Co-op Pharmacy to expand the collectively controlled social reproduction base, and $50,000 to other neighborhood businesses. The CDC had also joined a consortium of nonprofit, community-based developers to press the City Council for more low-income housing. The PAC was securely in the hands of neighborhood activists, and with the employment of a radically trained architect who was committed to maximizing resident involvement in planning, redevelopment would include some unique features—not the least of which was its participatory democratic character.

Participatory Democracy in Neighborhood Planning

When the citizens of Cedar-Riverside confronted the need to shift from neighborhood defense to neighborhood development, they once again faced the dilemma of finding a way to organize their movement. In this case the dilemma was focused on how to remain true to the democratic, community-based decision-making model while maintaining an efficient planning and implementation process that could encompass the complexity of the project, meet funding and planning deadlines, and make the most of the available redevelopment resources. Managing both those goals—the first of which the community insisted on and the second of which was imposed by the outside world—was an enormous challenge.

Much has been written about the counterculture's emphasis on participatory democracy—democracy that emphasizes the direct involvement of, and control by, individual citizens in shaping the policies that affect them. These participatory democratic practices were organized so that all authority resided in the group, rules were kept to a minimum, social control was maintained through personalistic and moralistic means, friendship and values were the basis for recruitment, incentives were symbolic, decision making was egalitarian, and there was minimal differentiation between members (Rothschild-Whitt, 1979). Participatory democracy in the counterculture, then, was not highly structured, but rested on informal agreement and a community of common interest and agreement. At the root of New Left participatory democracy was the ideology of participatory democracy, rather than any specific organizational structure.

This lack of formality and resistance to structuring was risky. Some argue that the stress on the process of decision making, as opposed to instrumental strategies and tactics, undermined the New Left (Breines, 1980). And indeed, it does seem that decentralization and "structurelessness," while supporting participation, undermine an organization's ability to act efficiently (Mansbridge, 1984; Freeman, 1972–73). A clear chain of command, stable structure, division of labor, and specific goals are widely agreed to be essential ingredients for social movement success (Useem, 1975). Overall, countercultural organizations seem to be limited to tasks that do not require high efficiency, memberships that are not diverse, and contexts that do not demand rapid responses (Rothschild-Whitt, 1979). Such organizations, if they are to remain countercultural, must also resist the pressures to conform created by funding needs (Davidson, 1983) and must be forever vigilant against the "tyranny of structurelessness," which allows hierarchies to develop in the absence of a specific structure to prevent them (Freeman, 1972–73).

The alternative to this informal participatory democracy is a more structured approach. Jo Freeman (1972–73) advocates a structure that distributes tasks, authority, and information widely and democratically using rational rather than personal criteria; rotates responsibilities; creates accountability mechanisms; and maintains equal access to resources. Some feminist organizations practice strict participation rules, including using chips that members "use up" as they speak, not letting anyone speak twice until everyone has a chance to speak once, and using a "rotating chair" so that leadership of the discussion is controlled by each speaker in turn (Mansbridge, 1984; Wheeler and

Chinn, 1984). The antinuclear movement divided its members into small groups, adopted rules preventing members from dominating discussion, and used consensus decision making (Barkan, 1979).

The neighborhood was in an interesting position in relation to this dilemma in the early 1980s. A community that had cherished its informality now confronted the reality that the two organizations best suited to planning, implementing, and overseeing democratic, community-based urban renewal were not structured to be participatory. The Project Area Committee was a representative democratic body, with members elected from neighborhood districts or special interest groups such as homeowners or newly forming co-ops. The CDC was organized to be even less participatory, with board members elected at large at annual neighborhood meetings. This form of "unitary democracy," in which all members are treated as having the same interests (Mansbridge, 1980), is appropriate only when all interested members do indeed have common interests. During this period of the CDC, board members could either live or work in the neighborhood, thus bringing the conflicting interests of businesses and residents into the CDC itself. The unitary democratic structure of the CDC could allow either group to organize a controlling interest. The economic forces impinging on the neighborhood were most dangerous for the CDC. As a redevelopment corporation, the CDC controlled significant resources—both knowledge and money—and was responsible for the financial viability of large investments. Consequently, the CDC's attention had to be directed toward its bottom line.

The concentration of the highly complex information required for conducting neighborhood redevelopment in the hands of the CDC staff, the centralized structure of the PAC and CDC and their accompanying economic and political pressures, and the decreasing rotation of leadership—the PAC chair, for example, occupied that seat for a decade—created the potential for one of the most tragic problems confronting social movements. That problem, as Roberto Michels (1962 [1915]) first recognized, is the "iron law of oligarchy." Michels argued that all social movement organizations were inevitably subject to the increasing centralization of power, which would eventually undermine the goals of the organization. Thus, the rise of an oligarchy of a few leaders would lead to goal displacement. Ever since then, centralized leadership has been feared. Since leaders are usually best acquainted with the operational details on which the organization is maintained, power naturally accrues to them (Kutner, 1950). In movements that become institutionalized, as occurred in Cedar-Riverside once the New Town was stopped, leadership is less likely to risk the costs of radical goals and strategies (Zald and Ash, 1966). It is partly the lack of leadership turnover in an institutionalized movement which signals the problem of oligarchy (Edelstein and Warner, 1976). As information centralizes in the hands of those leaders, the community is deprived of the knowledge necessary to make informed decisions (Katovich, Weiland, and Couch, 1981).

The problem is not quite as simple as Michels and others have framed it, however. Some research suggests that leaders can actually prevent the goal transformation assumed to follow from oligarchy. Leaders in the environmental movement, for example, were ideologically more radical and strategically more militant than less central members (Stallings, 1973). In research on neighborhood movements, Pamela Oliver (1983) found that full-time activists were motivated more by ideologic incentives, while part-time transitory members were motivated more by individual incentives. Leadership may also make a shift in radical directions if radical subgroups in the organization control needed resources (Barnes, 1987). This is particularly true of staff in organizations with volunteer boards, who can also shift an organization in radical directions if the staff itself is radicalized (Jenkins, 1977). And research on the largest United States women's movement organization, the National Organization for Women (NOW), found that although authority was centralized, goal transformation had not occurred. Both Kristin Jonasdóttir (1988) and Jo Freeman (1975) point to a strong ideology of democratic participation as one of the most important influences preventing goal transformation in NOW.

In Cedar-Riverside the strength of the community based on a radical ideology of participation permeated the structure and practices of even the PAC and CDC. The struggle to limit business representation and Cedar Square West representation was based on the belief that those who were most affected by neighborhood redevelopment should have the strongest voice in determining the course of that redevelopment. And the radical ideology of participation was maintained most strongly by leaders. The ability of leaders to organize the neighborhood vote and persuade City Hall to abide by drastically reduced representation of Cedar Square West residents illustrates the strength of the commitment to participatory democracy even in a representative democratic structure. These leaders played the role of "organic intellectuals." Drawing on the work of the Italian Marxist Antonio Gramsci, Allan David Heskin (1991:13) describes the organic intellectual as "a philosopher who both learns from and forms the bases of the philosophy of the people." As the outside world threatened to undermine participatory democracy in the neighborhood, these organic intellectuals preserved the memory and ideology of community control on which this new community was founded.

Leaders engaged in various strategies to promote and enforce participatory democracy (see also Stoecker, 1990). Activist leaders used pressure ranging from private confrontation to public discussion to enforce an ethic of citizen participation among both CDC and PAC staff. For example, a CDC staffperson who made design changes for new housing without consulting residents was taken aside by a PAC staffperson, who explained and emphasized the need to consult with residents. CDC board members were extensively trained in the history and practice of citizen participation. The training itself was participatory. At one training meeting, staff organized board members into small groups and asked them to sort through a collection of documents and their own memories to compile a list of important events in the neighborhood's history. Representatives from each group presented their lists of events and then created a collective list. A similar strategy was followed in training board members in the goals of the CDC and the overarching ideology of democratic, community-based redevelopment. This process continued through the entire training program. The CDC also funded numerous neighborhood activities, including an oral history of Cedar-Riverside, an annual community celebration, community-based recycling, and other community education activities at the Cedar-Riverside People's Center.

Leaders actively involved residents in the decisions that concerned them. *Snoose News*, published from early 1975 until early 1983, and again from 1988 to 1992, carried monthly minutes of neighborhood meetings, extensive discussions of neighborhood issues, and announcements of all neighborhood and city meetings. I would find two or three flyers stuck in my screen door every month requesting attendance at various PAC meetings to discuss such issues as liquor licenses, redevelopment planning, and City Hall politics. For important issues, such as when our block went through the planning process to close our street to prevent late-night bar traffic and create off-street parking, I would get a knock on my door from an organizer. And residents who were concerned with current issues did attend PAC and CDC meetings to help make policy. Although only board members could vote, concerned residents often dominated the floor for discussions of a half hour to two hours, and I cannot remember a PAC vote that did not reflect in a substantial way the desires of the residents who spoke. When a rail line was to be reopened near the Seven Corners area to carry trains hauling toxic waste, residents living next to the rail line were informed and invited to a PAC meeting. Based on their presence and their statements at the meeting, the PAC voted to oppose the rail line. In another case residents living in apartments above a business building were threatened with the loss of parking spaces to an absentee landlord. Those residents voiced their opposition at a PAC meeting, leading to negotiations with the landlord that succeeded in preserving the parking spaces. In yet another case PAC staff helped organize residents who opposed bar expansion to attend a PAC meeting and voice their opposition.

Participatory democracy was most evident in neighborhood planning for community-based development. The very earliest meetings to develop objectives for alternative redevelopment were created literally from the ground up. Late in 1978 residents in the Riverside Park section of the neighborhood were invited to neighborhood planning meetings. Over eleven Sunday nights some fifty-plus residents and a few absentee landlords participated in developing goals for redevelopment in that section of the neighborhood. Over the objections of property owners and a few renters, the group arrived at goals of one hundred rehabbed units and one hundred new units in Riverside Park, with an emphasis on co-op ownership structures and measures designed to maintain affordability, retain existing subsidies, and prevent speculation that would drive up land or housing costs. These goals were given extensive coverage in Snoose News and were treated as an ironclad policy by the PAC in evaluating any development proposals for the neighborhood. The emphasis on housing as a community use value pervaded the policy. Any property owners would, under the policy, be able to recover only their costs, and no profit. Developers as well would "be limited to recapturing only the amount invested" (Snoose News, December 1978:1).

Planning in the Cedar East section of the neighborhood in 1981 followed a similar participatory process. Here redevelopment was much closer to a reality, and the planning process was much more detailed and more emotionally intense:

> In the first round of block meetings, PAC staff provided a scale model of each block which allowed residents to consider demolishing each other's houses. First aid was provided and no serious injuries were reported. The ideas that rose out of these meetings

were evaluated for their planning and design merits and architecturally refined before being presented in a second round of block meetings. . . . After this second session with block residents, the resulting plans were given to the West Bank Community Development Corporation (CDC) to be used as a basis for future development proposals. . . . Most residents found this to be a painful process. (*Snoose News*, August 1981:1)

Then came the crucial step of actually organizing the co-ops. The residents who would be affected by the creation of the co-op, either because their homes were too far gone to save and would have to be replaced or because they would have to move out temporarily for the rehab to occur, were brought together to discuss how to redevelop their homes. Those who chose to leave the neighborhood were provided with relocation money. But all who chose to stay were guaranteed a new unit. Within economic and engineering limits they determined the design of their rehabilitated unit, advised by PAC and CDC staff. Residents were informed of the struggle that led to this process and were trained to establish their own cooperative housing organization for their new housing. The process involved night after night of meetings to present all the complex legal and financial information and actually to organize the co-op. The complexity of this process and its importance to a successful co-op means that a great deal of staff time and money must be devoted to it.

These procedures were as directly democratic as urban redevelopment could be. Encumbered only by zoning regulations, engineering principles, and financial constraints, residents collectively redesigned the neighborhood street by street, house by house. In addition to involving residents, the process led to innovation after innovation, as the neighborhood tapped into the diversity of creativity held by its citizens. Being involved in a truly democratic process not only increases democratic attitudes (Pateman, 1970) but has spin-off effects leading to progressive change generally (Mansbridge, 1984). And in Cedar-Riverside those spin-off effects led to progressive, environmentally oriented change and land-use principles.

West Bankers pioneered energy efficiency into their redevelopment, including using retrofit superinsulation (doubling the wall thickness for added insulation), sealing the building in plastic, redesigning houses to make the most of passive solar heating, and installing high-efficiency furnaces. The planning for this redevelopment was conducted through numerous workshops and over six months of serious work by the PAC Energy Task Force, which brought in consultants, studied other projects, and finally came up with recommendations for cost-effective, energy-efficient options that could be designed into the redevelopment.[2]

The neighborhood also pioneered the use of "infill housing," with some units built in the interior of blocks. Cedar-Riverside was organized with wide blocks. In some of them, in order to lower costs and boost densities just enough to increase political support at City Hall, residents designed three- or four-unit townhome buildings in the interiors of the blocks. So innovative was the concept that the fire department balked at the idea initially and remained so resistant that, in one case, the neighborhood actually lost five units of housing that were designed as infill.

The greatest test of neighborhood democracy came, however, when it was time to begin planning specific development projects. In March 1982 the City Council approved the PAC's Section 8 proposal with an $8.5 million bond sale. The proposal consisted of the thirty River-bluff units, seventy Section 8 units spread through the old neighborhood, and fifty-five units subsidized through tax-increment financing. The approval also authorized the MCDA to purchase the two blocks of neighborhood lost to Northwestern National Life by CRA. The housing was designed with passive solar and superinsulation principles to bring heating costs down to about $130 annually, with a projected increase in construction costs of only 1 to 5 percent for new construction units and about 10 percent for the rehabbed units. The project's promotional material billed it, apparently accurately, as "the largest rehabilitation-retrofit project incorporating superinsulation technology in the world."

No longer were the plans preparation for the future. Now it was time actually to build and tear down houses, move people around, and create at least some instability in the community. The Riverbluff site, whose planning had been in process since the late 1970s, was halfway down the bluff on the Mississippi River bank and cut off from the rest of the neighborhood by the university. Residents struggled over whether the site was safe for women and children because of its isolation and the danger of the river, and became unified only when the city Planning Department opposed the project.[3] Some residents

> said women with children shouldn't live in such an isolated spot. It's going to be dangerous for them. And then neighborhood people stood up and . . . accused us of not wanting poor people to live

on the river. . . . And we'd shut up and it was really pretty intimi-
dating. But then there was a lot of opposition from downtown to
letting poor people live on the river. The Planning Department
went berserk when that prime piece of real estate was going to be
used for housing poor people. So that activated the neighborhood.
(Dorothy Jacobs interview, 1991)

Other disputes surfaced as the PAC organized block meetings in
Cedar East to plan the rest of the Section 8 housing. That created a
new set of struggles, since these Section 8 units would be scattered
among the existing housing. Some residents feared that the neighborhood might "change" with a proliferation of Section 8 housing.
Others resisted agreeing to their houses being demolished after fighting so hard to save them from the high-rises, and there were fears that
the neighborhood culture would be lost.

There was a house on 19th they called "the sign house." There was
a guy in there who, you know, collected signs . . . and he always
had the signs all over the house. As we tried to decide what to do
with each house, we had to evaluate the condition of the building, not the signs. There were definitely houses that couldn't be
rehabbed . . . and that was sort of a realization and everybody said,
"Well, shit, now we gotta decide if we're gonna lose some of this
character that we're so fond of."   (Tim Mungavan interview, 1991)

The process began on the block level, as residents looked at the structural evaluations of their houses and the costs to rehab or replace
them and made collective decisions on what to do with each house.
The next step was to take the proposals, with any remaining disputes,
to the PAC. All the residents whose houses would be demolished
could choose to relocate within the neighborhood or receive funds
to relocate out of the neighborhood. The democratic process was not
without pain, however, as Tim Mungavan, Dorothy Jacobs, and Ralph
Wittcoff note.

Nobody wanted to move out of their houses. These people would
live in dumps, you know, and would not want to leave. Everybody was very determined to save their house.   (Mungavan interview, 1991)

My neighbor across the street, he wanted to stay in his house. His
place was literally leaning—it was in terrible condition. But people
were so nice to John. And I remember the night the decision was

made that his house had to come down. And people went to the bar with him—really took care of him. But they also told him the truth: "Your house is a piece of shit, John." (Jacobs interview, 1991)

I cried a tear when Freddy Case's house, known as "the sign house," came down. But I was willing to say at that point that it has to be done for the greater good—it was part of what has to be done. (Ralph Wittcoff interview, 1991)

Throughout this process there was no shortage of objections, conflicts, and tensions. But the procedures that were created to conduct the planning made certain that the objections were given voice, the conflicts were allowed to erupt, and the tensions were acknowledged. In the early going the neighborhood probably had the best combination of elements: a strong ideology insisting on democratic participation maintained by community leaders, and formally structured organizations that could act more efficiently than mass participation organizations. The formalized structure of the PAC and CDC created a clear chain of command visible to City Hall and identified responsible parties in the neighborhood who could be held accountable. At the same time, organization leadership could override the limited participation of the PAC and CDC structures to create more involvement.

The PAC really did things right. This series of planning workshops really worked. And it really did generate something close to a consensus amongst all of the participants. And because it was the right way to do it, all of those problems that became the focus of infighting and tension and so on were relatively minor problems. If the planning had been done less carefully and with less effort to build consensus, those problems would have been much more severe and it may well have resulted in the whole thing collapsing. (Cann interview, 1991)

Redevelopment Begins

It was never easy. Residents had to persevere once more against outside threats before they could begin construction. Keith Heller filed a lawsuit against the Section 8 project, arguing that the City Council approval was illegal, and refused to turn over CRA-owned land for the project. Both strategies were short-lived, however, and by the end of July 1982 the project was on the move again. Residents of Riverview Towers, a high-rise at the extreme northern corner of the neighborhood bordering Riverbluff, then objected to the Section 8 Project, but negotiations overcame their objections as well.

Groundbreaking was held on October 17, 1982, with a large community celebration in front of one of the houses to be rehabbed, with the watchcat banner draped across it. Council members, activists, and other supporters showed up for the day-long celebration. But the construction process was frustrated by complications, as activists had to oversee the contractor vigilantly as a constant reminder to live up to affirmative action hiring requirements, including neighborhood-based hiring, and to follow the rehab plans:

> I first realized we had a problem when I got a call from the architect, who said . . . "We wanna tear the back porch off—it's not in good enough condition to save." I said, "Tear the back porch off? We went through all of this design stuff, and you're telling me now you wanna tear the porch off?" We had a big confrontation with the construction people in a meeting where the residents of the building in question were able to talk over the problem in detail. This format later evolved into a regularly scheduled "watchcat committee" meeting where neighborhood residents reviewed all change order requests. As it turned out, the contractor was, when pushed, able to find a way to save the porch.   (Mungavan interview, 1991)

Nearly a year later, in September 1983, the buildings were occupied and the co-ops held their first election of officers. The Riverbluff project ultimately became the thirty-unit Riverbluff Co-op, financed through a partnership of the CDC and Canadian Financial Corporation. The development in the old neighborhood became the sixty-five-unit West Bank Homes Co-op, financed through a partnership of the CDC and Brighton Development Corporation. Both were to be lease-hold co-ops, meaning that the housing is actually owned by the partnership, which includes limited-partner investors who buy tax-sheltered shares in the co-op but have no voting rights. The partnership then leases the housing to the co-op, which controls the housing within the bounds of the lease. The actual degree of control allowed the co-ops varied: Riverbluff functioned much more like a traditional tenant–absentee landlord project, and the West Bank Homes functioned much more like a typical co-op. The dissatisfaction with Canadian Financial Corporation and the growing respect between ex-MHRA director Dick Brustad at Brighton Development and the neighborhood led to a continuing relationship between the CDC and Brighton in financing the subsequent co-ops.

With this project, activists had shown that they could produce affordable, superinsulated housing. They had pioneered infill housing, over the objections of the fire department and the planning department. The PAC and CDC also attempted to enforce, with mixed success, a strong affirmative action policy with the contractors for hiring women, minorities, and neighborhood residents for the projects. As residents developed experience, they also practiced a ninety-day notice policy so residents would have three months to find new permanent or temporary housing, subsidized moving expenses up to five hundred dollars for residents temporarily displaced, and provided payments of up to four thousand dollars for residents choosing to leave permanently.

The lease-hold co-op structure, with the city retaining title to the land, also eliminated the danger that speculators would buy up land and inflate neighborhood housing prices. This co-op structure and the creative planning supporting it held down monthly rents to typically one hundred dollars below market rate, a savings of as much as 25 percent in the Twin Cities. The Section 8 units received an additional subsidy so that occupants paid no more than 30 percent of their income on housing.[4] And the unique geographic arrangement of the co-ops, with their members scattered among units across the neighborhood, also served a purpose.

> When we developed the urban renewal plan and the settlement
> agreement, we were all afraid that if we had done it block by block
> it might allow Heller-Segal to come back and do somethin' sneaky.
> So what we did was we developed a couple houses in this block, a
> couple houses in that block, so as to prevent anything from happen-
> ing. . . . And we made West Bank Homes here, down Riverside, in
> these two blocks here—this block and the other block. . . . So it had
> all been done, and Heller couldn't take over a whole block and put
> a high-rise in it.   (Hal Barron interview, 1991)

Four other development projects took shape in the neighborhood in the early 1980s. The New Riverside Cafe began a fund drive to buy its building. It took a long time, but by August 1984 the cafe had organized the funding, through the CDC, to purchase its building and rehab it. The People's Center building, long in need of repair, was given a new lease on life in 1981 when it was rehabbed. The third development resulted from the compromise to allow a hotel and high-density housing in Seven Corners. In 1982 the city received a large Urban Development Action Grant (UDAG) to fund the creation of 250 units of apartment housing in Seven Corners in return for allowing a parking ramp and a 248-room hotel. The Seven Corners development was not a popular project, even though it would bring substantial resources into the neighborhood through the tax-increment increase created by the development. The catch was that three blocks of the area would have to be leveled for the development.

> It was somethin' the city was absolutely insistent on—"We gotta have some of that high-density housing there"—and that seemed the best place for it. But once it got time for the compromise to be carried out, the people who were specifically effected said, "Fuck the compromise. This particular three blocks is our neighborhood and fuck you, you aren't gonna do it."   (Cann interview, 1991)

But without organized resistance in the area, and with the realization among activists that the compromise had been necessary to get the Section 8 housing and the People's Center rehab project, the development went ahead. By the end of 1983 the 240-unit Seven Corners lease-hold co-op apartments were ready for occupancy. This project was organized as a management cooperative rather than an ownership-based cooperative, providing a resident board to review rents, policies, and personnel.

On September 24, 1983, the neighborhood held the groundbreaking for the next phase of redevelopment in the old neighborhood. This eighteen-unit project was constructed on land acquired with the Section 8 developments and was financed through the CDC-Brighton partnership. Its residents named it the "Union Homes" co-op, some recalling the legacy of the Tenants Union, whose members put signs in their windows with the Tenants Union logo and bold letters stating "UNION HOME." For others, the name celebrated the labor-union affiliations of some residents in the co-op along with the Tenants Union and the Community Union.

The neighborhood had turned the tide. From the almost certain destruction of their neighborhood a decade ago, residents now controlled their own destiny. It seemed, at the time, that there was no stopping them. Before redevelopment could remake the entire neighborhood, however, the remaining instability in the political opportunity structure had to be settled. Democracy within the neighborhood was not enough—it had to be expanded to the city itself.

Solidifying a New Regime at City Hall

While redevelopment was proceeding in the neighborhood, Reaganomics was taking its toll on the City of Minneapolis, and the impact was trickling down to the neighborhoods as the city budget became increasingly strained. Then the trickle became a torrent. The Reagan administration cut the city's Community Development Block Grants from $19 million to $15.4 million and eliminated any requirements that the money be tied to neighborhood groups. The city slashed neighborhood groups' budgets from $350,000 to $62,000 for 1982 in response to the federal budget cuts and loosened restrictions. Neighborhood housing office staffs were reduced from fifty to nineteen people from 1980 to 1981, and then to four in 1982.

The Cedar-Riverside budget was temporarily spared, since it came from tax-increment financing rather than from federal funds, but the reprieve did not last. At the end of 1982 the City Council cut the PAC budget by two-thirds, down to $34,000 with an extra $10,000 for the B-PAC. Jackie Slater, who voted for the cuts, was seen as betraying the neighborhood movement, especially when the other three council members representing the neighborhood, including Kathy O'Brien, a Tenants Union activist who had been elected to the council in 1981, voted to maintain PAC funding.

Thus, the new year arrived with sad news. The first issue of Snoose News in 1983 was also the last, and the issue itself was devoted to an obituary of the newspaper. The Elliot Park Surveyor agreed to take over neighborhood coverage and neighborhood distribution, but it did not provide the extensive coverage that Snoose News had. The CDC began publishing a newsletter, but it was much less politicizing than Snoose News had been. The PAC lost two staff members, leaving the organization with only one and a half positions.

From the outrage among the city's neighborhoods again sprang the city-wide Neighborhood Priorities Coalition, renamed from its earlier, clumsier moniker, with West Bank PAC chair Tim Ogren as chair. The coalition first enlisted the aid of State Senator Linda Berglin and State Representative Todd Otis, who threatened to sponsor state legislation to give neighborhoods more control over the MCDA or perhaps hold up the city's budget. The coalition also organized a neighborhood convention at which one hundred people representing neighborhood organizations in Minneapolis were expected, but two hundred showed up. The coalition platform demanded recognition of neighborhood and community organizations, more low-income housing money, 20 percent of development-generated jobs reserved for neighborhood residents, and more neighborhood representation on the MCDA board.

The Neighborhood Priorities Coalition was challenging the governing regime of the City of Minneapolis. The neighborhoods faced a City Council that wanted to balance the city budget on their backs, and the neighborhoods were not going to stand for it. It would not be enough simply to protest, however. As Stone (1989) notes, challenging a regime necessitates that the challengers organize enough opposition to undermine the foundation of the current regime. That requires, at least, voting the old regime out of office. But it also means electing new officials who have a working relationship with the challenging group. A regime is not simply a government, but also all the informal relationships between that government and other actors in the city (Stone, 1989). For the neighborhoods of Minneapolis, it meant electing neighborhood activists to the City Council. Some progress had already been made, with the election of Kathy O'Brien and Tony Scallon to the City Council and Don Fraser as mayor. But Cedar-Riverside had lost the allegiance of Jackie Slater, and there was a lack of firm council allies representing other neighborhoods.

In the neighborhoods' favor was the reality that had made the challenge necessary in the first place: urban fiscal crisis. It is under periods of fiscal crisis that existing regimes are most vulnerable (Pecorella, 1987; Castells, 1981). With the advantage of instability in the political opportunity structure, urban fiscal crisis, and effective organizing, the Neighborhood Priorities Coalition targeted the City Council in the November 1983 elections and won in a big way. The DFL party tallied up ten of the thirteen council seats, an increase of two. The "liberal south-side camp" dominated the council with seven seats. Brian Coyle, another West Bank activist, took the sixth ward to become the city's first openly gay council member.[5] Since Cedar-Riverside then was divided mainly between three council districts (with a sliver of the neighborhood in a fourth), the neighborhood movement had two council advocates who were trained in the neighborhood movement, a third who had supported the neighborhood movement since his MHRA days, and a fourth who also supported the neighborhood. In 1984 the council increased neighborhood funding 400 percent to 1980 levels, allowing two staff members to return to the PAC.

The transition in city government did not happen all at once. As in Santa Monica, California, where environmental and neighborhood activists gradually came to dominate the City Council from 1973 to 1981 (Clavel, 1986), the shift in Minneapolis had begun in 1977 with the election of Jackie Slater and continued with the election of council member Tony Scallon, Mayor Don Fraser, and council member Kathy O'Brien. With the 1983 election the neighborhood forces in the city achieved a majority on the City Council, with seven allied or sympathetic council representatives. And council members representing portions of Cedar-Riverside comprised four members of that majority.

In the second half of the 1980s, then, Minneapolis approached the definition of a "progressive" regime. As Clavel (1986) explains, progressive urban political coalitions grew from the deindustrialization, white flight, federal provision of poverty services, urban fiscal crisis, speculative redevelopment, and neighborhood organizing of the 1970s. In cities as diverse as Boston, San Francisco, Chicago, and Santa Monica, new urban regimes arose with characteristics and priorities much different from those of their predecessors. These new regimes were much more willing to take on direct or shared control of local enterprises, advocated collective control of housing and business, developed policies supporting progressive redistribution of wealth, managed budget cuts by restructuring rather than cutting services, supported regulation of capital in the form of rent control and affirmative action legislation, took an advocacy stance supporting city residents against suburbs and capital, and encouraged and even organized citizen participation in urban policy making (Clavel, 1986:10–12). Minneapolis city government took on ownership of neighborhood property to prevent speculation, channeled tax-increment funds to neighborhoods, supported co-op housing, maintained neighborhood organization funding, and eventually developed an expanded citizen participation planning process across city neighborhoods. Though not as progressive as San Francisco, Boston, or Santa Monica, since it continued to promote downtown development and growth generally, Minneapolis city government took a decidedly progressive turn toward neighborhoods in the 1980s which lasted into the 1990s.

Cedar-Riverside activists, through the PAC and CDC, became thoroughly involved as one of the informal partners in this new progressive regime, as the neighborhood movement entered an "institutional stage" (Turner and Killian, 1972) in its history. Allies in the 1980s were no longer protest organizations. Brighton Development Corporation has been the CDC's main for-profit partner. Parliament Management Company and other management companies provide housing co-op management services. The relationship with Brighton is particularly intriguing. A radical neighborhood movement, guided by socialist and anarchist principles that are antagonistic both to capitalism on the macro level and to profit-seeking on the micro level, found a positive working relationship with a for-profit developer. As Dick Brustad, Brighton's executive director, explains:

I think I started out, personally, with some residual goodwill because I had been part of leading the charge when the city officially flip-flopped from the Heller-Segal mode to the neighborhood plan mode. And I think [the CDC staff] were very committed to the idea of joint ventures with profit-motivated corporations, and that it was sort of a necessary evil that was well worth it, and that we were probably less evil than most of the others. . . . And then I think . . . they're all very sharp people, the neighborhood leaders. The thing we had going for us is we truly believed in this process.

Politicians also became strong allies, from state senators and representatives to the mayor and at least four City Council members. The neighborhood was seldom without the votes it needed downtown to get additional millions of dollars to continue democratic, community-based redevelopment. Rarely is a neighborhood movement able to participate so directly in city politics. The cost for these alliances, however, was a decreasing isolation of the movement and a consequent expansion of the diversity of interests within the neighborhood. The strained loyalties that are predicted to result from such outside attachments (Crenson, 1974) developed in Cedar-Riverside in both the PAC and the CDC. When three angry residents attacked council member Scallon at a PAC meeting for his lack of support for subsidized singles housing, neighborhood leaders seemed almost to come to Scallon's aid, explaining that the PAC meeting was not the place to attack council members.

The question must be asked whether Cedar-Riverside activists sold out for this participation in the new governing regime. John Mollenkopf's (1983) analysis of neighborhood movements in Boston and San Francisco found that neighborhood organizations were indeed co-opted. They gave up their militancy and confrontation for cooperative relations with city officials when the city government began to respond to their policy demands and funneled money their way. In the end, however, the neighborhoods were bought off and were not able to control the trajectory of development in their communities. William Goldsmith and Edward Blakely (1992), however, believe that it is possible for neighborhood-based political movements to gain official influence at City Hall which allows them to affect the policy agenda, provide support for neighborhood groups, bring other supporters into the governing coalition, and build a core of experts to push urban reform further.

West Bankers did give up their militancy for support from City

Hall, which would cost them later in the 1980s. But it is also true that they did not lose control of redevelopment in the neighborhood. To the extent that Cedar-Riverside activists became part of the system, they resisted compromising on the redevelopment plans that had taken so much energy, and so many Sunday nights, to achieve. For a time it appeared that the governing regime was actually institutionalizing support for the neighborhood's redevelopment process—providing political legitimation for democratic, community-based redevelopment and enormous resources for its implementation. That is especially astounding given the pressures that threaten the longevity of progressive impulses from urban regimes. Any regime "represents an accommodation between the potentially conflicting principles of the popular control of government and the private ownership of business enterprises" (Stone, 1987:269). Thus, as use values and exchange values clash, conflict is inevitable. Progressive regimes are also "activist" regimes, struggling to accomplish *new* policy, making their task much more difficult than that of "caretaker" regimes, whose primary and much simpler activity is maintenance of the status quo (Stone, 1989). Their more risky goals make progressive regimes unstable and lead them to face opposition in implementing policies, especially since their policies often run counter to the interests of capital (Stone, 1987). Under any conditions, capital exerts as much, if not more, influence from the shadows, as I have discussed. One of the ways that capital can stymie progressive regimes is by withholding the cooperation necessary to implement policy (Stone, 1989). Whether refusing to roll over short-term notes, which destroyed the progressive regime of Mayor Dennis Kucinich in Cleveland (Swanstrom, 1985), or threatening to disinvest from cities that refuse to bow to its demands, as occurred when the City of Detroit agreed to level Poletown for a Cadillac plant (Wylie, 1989), capital makes its influence felt not so much at the input end as at the output end.

It is the distinction between policy creation and policy implementation which makes the creation of a strong governing regime so important and Cedar-Riverside's achievements so amazing. Herbert Kitschelt's (1986) elaboration of the concept of the political opportunity structure makes the distinction central. All kinds of progressive policies can be created, but if there is not strength to implement those policies, they are doomed. It is because of these two facets of the policy-making process that it is so much easier to stop a policy than to make one. Policy making must succeed at both the creation and implementation stages, but it can be stopped at either stage. The Cedar-

Riverside community was able to implement urban redeve
that emphasized use values and to create policy that prevente
borhood land from being transformed into exchange values,
a grass-roots process that was coded into policy in the loca
Its success is partly attributable to the relative economic he
the Twin Cities, which allowed the city to spend money in Cedar-
Riverside without seeming to undercut downtown interests. One of
the determinants that allowed Boston's mayor Raymond Flynn much
greater success than Cleveland's Dennis Kucinich at implementing
progressive urban policy was Boston's far healthier economy. Kucinich was working with a city tottering on the brink of default, providing much greater leverage for the foes of the progressive regime. While
each was successful in creating progressive urban policy, Flynn was
far more successful in actually implementing that policy (Swanstrom,
1985). There was money in Minneapolis, and capital was at least
grudgingly accepting of democratic, community-based redevelopment. Some factions of capital were even supportive of the neighborhood movement, providing grants to the CDC for neighborhood
development work.[6]

Nevertheless, Cedar-Riverside activists did not control the local
governing regime in Minneapolis any more than they controlled the
federal policy they also used so much to their advantage. Their lack of
control would become more evident as the 1980s wore on. The influence of capital lurked in the shadows, gradually creating a contradiction within the redevelopment being conducted in the neighborhood
which would nearly tear the Cedar-Riverside community apart.

7

The Struggle Within

I think the biggest failure, and a very big one, was that we ended up with a neighborhood that was less of a community than when we started. We didn't sustain a political movement, and the sense of community has been fragmented. I can live with the mistakes in the financing and construction. But we ended up dissipating the political energy.

—*Tim Mungavan interview, 1991*

T HE NEIGHBORHOOD surged into redevelopment into the mid-1980s. Its membership in the governing regime intensified beyond connections to council members to include neighborhood activists hired to work with the MCDA. By December 1983, even under the burden of PAC funding cuts, plans had crystallized for other parcels acquired with the Section 8 project. The initial plans called for seven two-bedroom units, thirteen one-bedroom units, and two three-bedroom units, again designed by the residents. The project was another product of the CDC–Brighton Development Corporation partnership, with an estimated cost of $790,000. Financing for this stage was to come from limited-partner, or "syndication," funding and from roll-over from the Seven Corners apartments and Union Homes. It eventually became the Watchcat co-op, the most focused of all the co-ops, with nineteen units of housing, including eight Section 8 units, on a single block.

Neighborhood activists also succeeded in getting the city to approve a plan to rehabilitate a commercial building in Seven Corners for much needed "single-room occupancy" housing for low-income individuals in mid-1984. Cedar-Riverside had historically housed some very low-income individuals who were perpetually vulnerable to homelessness. Combined with rehabilitation of the Dudley Riggs comedy nightclub on the first floor, the second-floor space would be rehabilitated to preserve eight low-rent rooming units. Even this project involved more than providing low-rent housing. The impetus for the development came from the character of the residents of the building, who had lived there between five and twenty-five years and developed a community of mutual support that would be destroyed if they were forced to relocate.

While the neighborhood housing was being rehabilitated, however, the social fabric began to unravel. The businesses became financially independent from neighborhood residents. And the separate tasks of the PAC and CDC brought these two organizations into conflict. The CDC developed one focus to attract funding sources to maintain affordability. The PAC developed a different, and somewhat antagonistic, focus to maintain community control of the development process. Struggles between residents and businesses, between separate resident groups, and between the PAC and the CDC broke into the open. At issue was the direction neighborhood redevelopment should take and what direction it had already taken. The capital-community contradiction tore into the community with a vengeance in this period, disrupting the housing co-ops, threatening the neighborhood institutions, and expanding the disastrous impact of Cedar Square West.

Sources of Internal Conflict

The conflict that erupted in the late 1980s derived from pressures imposed on the neighborhood from without and from changes in the community itself. Kenneth Benson (1977, 1983) has developed an approach called "dialectical methodology" to study organizational change. Dialectical methodology is based on Marx's theory of social change, in which particular forms of social organization set into motion processes that result in contradictory outcomes, forcing new social forms to arise to solve those contradictions. Benson adapts this approach to study organizations, attempting to locate the source of contradictions between the goals of the organization and their implementation. In the case of Cedar-Riverside the contradictions between capital and community in the political opportunity structure created contradictions between the community-control goal and the housing-affordability goal of the neighborhood movement.

The pressures from without came from changes in the funding opportunities for urban redevelopment in general and for community-based development in Cedar-Riverside in particular. The power of capital to disrupt all the hard work of community building made itself felt through the economic constraints imposed on community-based development. After the planning of Watchcat co-op, funds in the city began to dry up. Urban fiscal strain had settled into the Twin Cities, producing not an acute crisis but a chronic condition. In one response the city centralized the tax-increment financing and redistributed it across the city, including to downtown. The neighborhood could no longer be assured of strong city funding and was forced to turn to more risky funding for redevelopment, funding that began to involve compromises. While the community defined the neighborhood from a use-value orientation, redevelopment required them increasingly to present their plans in an exchange-value framework.

Elaborating on the exchange value–use value contradiction, Kevin Cox (1981:438) distinguishes between communal space organized for the community and communal space organized as a commodity. The threat of commodification of communal space is omnipresent and overriding, since "the community can only be saved by treating the communal living space as a commodity. Banks redlining the area, for example, have to be convinced that the neighborhood is a good investment." As the CDC searched for new funding, it was drawn into presenting the neighborhood space as a commodity and accepting financing packages based on exchange principles that undermined community control. Increasingly, the community was forced to choose between community control and affordability.

Economic Contradictions and Community-based Development

One solution to the problem of decreased government funds for redevelopment was to build housing that required less subsidy. Consequently, the CDC pursued the strategy of building and rehabilitating owner-occupied housing. The CDC developed creative financing for eleven ownership townhomes and two single-family houses that were promoted as affordable to households with as little as $19,000 annual income. It was a popular strategy, and all but two of the townhomes were sold before they were even built, and with minimal marketing. Though they were by far the most affordable owner-occupied housing in the Twin Cities, only two of the homes were purchased by neighborhood residents. The prices ranged from $70,000 to $75,000—out of the reach of many West Bank residents—and available subsidies were limited to families with children.

In their search for new sources of funding, the CDC staff discovered the new federal Housing Development Action Grants (HoDAG), and the PAC passed a motion to set the CDC to work on obtaining a HoDAG for 260 units in the neighborhood. Many of these federal funds, especially through the UDAG and HoDAG programs, required cities to leverage private money before the funds would be committed. This policy ushered in the era of the "public-private partnership," allowing capitalists to all but dominate urban redevelopment, taking over planning and implementation. Government's role became subsidizing developers through tax abatements, utility deals, site preparation, and sometimes direct financial support (Feagin and Parker, 1990). The HoDAG thus superficially allowed the community to control the shape of the project but also required the CDC to sell the project to "limited-partner" investors who bought shares in the projects as tax-sheltered investments. Although these partners were "limited" in the sense that they had no voting power in the co-op decision-making process, their power exerted itself much like that of other investment capital—in their ability to withhold their investment until they were offered something they wanted to invest in. Since the project had to be attractive, its function as an alternative was constrained. With the HoDAG the community was no longer able to place the local state between itself and capital. Instead, the CDC-Brighton partnership had to appeal directly to outside capital and take its chances with shifting market forces.

In October 1984 the neighborhood was awarded a $1.2 million HoDAG to help redevelop 116 units. This project was to house many of the neighborhood activist leaders who had continued living in houses where the frost collected on the inside walls in the winter while the movement worked on housing for poor families. The City Council had taken seriously the neighborhood's early critique of Cedar Square West as not suitable for poor families with children, and it limited its support early on for those poor families with children. Thus, many of the activists who had opposed the New Town project by advocating for families with children found themselves shut out of the initial Section 8 housing. But the HoDAG funding, clearly oriented toward poor families with children, was equally unsuited for single adults whose wages were increasing or couples whose children had grown up.

This project, which we all celebrated on that warm summer day in 1986, was enormously complex and became a magnet for all the grievances that had built up in the neighborhood since redevelopment began. Selling limited partnership bonds as tax shelters to fund the project, at a time when the Reagan administration was attempting to eliminate those shelters, created delay on delay as investors waited to see whether the shelters would be preserved before they invested. Though all the bonds were eventually sold, the delays created disruptions that rippled through the project. Some residents resisted moving out to prepare for rehab. They had seen construction start dates pushed back too often and now were going to stay until they had to move out, especially after an MCDA foul-up gave residents new leases. As a result, the construction schedule was threatened, potentially increasing the costs of the project. Not wanting a few uncooperative residents to threaten the entire project, the Sherlock Homes co-op (the title of the HoDAG co-op) members instituted a policy preventing those who did not leave their units on time from being guaranteed a unit in the project. But they eventually rescinded the policy as the "revised" closing date of December 1985 was not realized until the middle of 1986.

Another problem was that organizing a ninety-two-member co-op had never been done in the neighborhood before. The co-op organizers, who were hired by the CDC, were relatively new to organizing, and many of the residents were experienced activists, creating clashes of style and disputes over process. The Sherlock Homes co-op membership became increasingly disorganized and disenchanted as delay piled on delay, and there was a continuing disagreement between PAC and CDC staff over who should take responsibility for organizing the co-op. Coming from a radical perspective that acknowledged and distrusted the influence of capital, even in the hands of the benevolent CDC, the PAC leadership was concerned that the CDC could not effectively organize the co-op because the CDC also had a financial interest in the project. The more organized the residents were, the less fiscal control the CDC would be able to exert over those residents. The CDC, however, had the funds for organizing and the staff availability.

The unsuitability of the HoDAG to the neighborhood's needs created the deepest problems. The HoDAG discriminated against the many single adults and couples without dependent children in the neighborhood, since the subsidy contained a clause that required twenty-six units to be occupied by families whose incomes were at or below 50 percent of the area median income. This policy could force residents to move out of the co-op if their incomes increased (or their family size decreased) past a certain limit and directly contradicted the neighborhood's no-displacement policy. "And at some point, somebody said, 'Well look, what if some of the people that are currently below the income limit go above the income limit?'

'Well, that means that somebody's gonna have to be kicked out.' 'That means that you've adopted a subsidy program here that could result in me being displaced from my home'" (Jack Cann interview, 1991). The CDC considered using internal subsidies on this project—some units would rent at the market rate to subsidize other units—to reduce the impact of the restrictive funding regulations. There were fears, however, that these units would be too expensive for residents. The economy of the 1980s was much different from the economy of the 1960s, and the residents were different as well. Their living expenses had increased, many were tired of living in poverty, and they were working more than they ever had before. They had become, said one neighborhood activist who was so embarrassed that he made me turn off my tape recorder, "middle class." With increased economic needs and desires, and with a lack of well-paying work in the neighborhood, activists were more and more earning their livings outside the neighborhood. The CDC argued that displacement would be unlikely to occur and that, if it did, the affected residents would be able to find another unit in the neighborhood. But PAC leaders and Sherlock Homes members saw the problem as a direct threat to the goal of community control.

In this final period of democratic, community-based redevelopment the CDC became more dependent on capital and less dependent on the community. The HoDAG funding required the CDC to sell the neighborhood to investors from the outside. Economic development interests among the CDC staff also created strong alliances with neighborhood businesses. In addition, the CDC needed to attract long-term loans, insurance, and support for its $300,000 annual operating budget. Thus, the CDC had to establish cooperative and supportive relationships with the financial community, philanthropic foundations, and other funders. This economic reality pulled the CDC away from the community. For one thing, the organization was increasingly dependent on funds and expertise from outside the neighborhood. For another, its own interests as an organization to produce financially practical redevelopment became separated from the neighborhood's interests to maintain community control. This was a problem across the country as CDCs were being transformed from advocates for the poor to development agencies with profit-based partners (Weaver, 1990).

As development proceeded in the neighborhood, community organizing was neglected. The shift from community organizing to community development, or neighborhood defense to neighborhood development, and the internal movement problems that accompany that shift, are not unique to Cedar-Riverside. Saul Alinsky (1971:130) argued that "the price of a successful attack is a constructive alternative." But "constructive," in the case of community development, must be defined within a political opportunity structure that allows only bricks and mortar to be considered "development." Community, for all the rhetoric of the Reagan administration, was at best ignored and at worst feared. The federal government in the 1980s shifted virtually all resources away from community organizing programs such as VISTA and the Community Action Programs and focused resources into Community Development Block Grants. Philanthropic foundations also increasingly emphasized physical development. Both the federal government, thoroughly under the control of conservative capitalists, and foundation officials guarding capitalist-generated treasures eventually decided that the funding of community organizing would jeopardize their ability to centralize power further and contain democracy (N. Fainstein and S. Fainstein, 1986a; S. Fainstein and N. Fainstein, 1986; Jenkins, 1985; Roelofs, 1987).

At the same time that communities were winning battles against displacement, discrimination, and domination, powerful actors within the political opportunity structure were withdrawing the resources those successes had been built on and shifting the burden for community maintenance and development to the communities themselves. In many cases communities were ill-equipped to take on the extraordinarily complex tasks of housing and commercial redevelopment. But even the communities that were prepared for the challenge were unable to prevent a wholesale shift of movement resources away from community organizing to community development within their movements (Giloth, 1985; Lenz, 1988).

The shift in resources generally took three paths. The first path is the most advantageous to community organizing, since it does not always necessitate a shift of internal movement resources. Here the community organizing group creates a set of development demands, presses for those demands, and then presses for power holders to implement those demands, rather than attempting itself to implement development. That keeps the community organizing group free to continue to devote its internal resources to organizing, holding others accountable for the implementation of the group's program. San Antonio's Communities Organized for Public Service, or COPS, is the most famous example of such a strategy. Between 1974 and 1981 COPS successfully pushed the City of San Antonio to spend over half its CDBG budget to implement COPS development programs, as noted earlier (Reitzes and Reitzes, 1987).

COPS is known not only for its success, but also for its uniqueness. Few community organizing groups have been able to avoid becoming swept up in the politically tricky currents of community development. A far more common path, then, is for the community organizing group itself to become transformed into a community development organization (Fisher, 1981). Both of Saul Alinsky's famous Chicago community organizing groups—the Back of the Yards Neighborhood Council and The Woodlawn Organization—were transformed into community development organizations focusing on housing rehabilitation. The shift never really succeeded in Woodlawn, as arson and gentrification increasingly threatened the neighborhood (Reitzes and Reitzes, 1987). The Mission Coalition Organization, in San Francisco, California, also saw its community organizing emphasis diminish as it took on an employment service and a language center that sucked up organizational resources and staff time (Weissman, 1981).

Finally, the community organizing group can spin off a community development corporation, or CDC, that is bureaucratically separate but often politically connected to the original community organizing group. That is what happened in Cedar-Riverside when activists got together to form the West Bank CDC. Distrusted from their earliest moments as offshoots of the 1960s Community Action Programs (Berndt, 1977), CDCs have not been held in very high esteem among community activists. Although they were designed around the principle of grass-roots control, in practice CDCs have a weak track record in maintaining grass-roots involvement and remaining responsive to grass-roots needs (Berndt, 1977; Kelly, 1977; Blakely and Aparicio, 1990).

In especially this third case the shift of resources results in a greater formalization and centralization of the movement, ultimately undermining community organizing itself. CDCs have to make decisions within strictly bounded financial circumstances within equally strict timelines. This circumstance leaves little time for the inefficiency of full democratic participation, which is the lifeblood of effective community organizing. The highly technical nature of the information that development decisions must take into account also does not allow for very effective participation by nonexperts (Fisher, 1984). And development does not hold the same excitement of organizing against a common enemy, making participation yet more difficult to maintain (Fish, 1973) while attracting supporters who are less disposed to militant action (Weissman, 1981).

> When you do community-based development, you have to have community organizers and you gotta have bankers. Opposite ends of the spectrum must be related to one another. People who were into community activism don't wanna spend the time and the energy on the financing stuff. It's just too boring, it's complicated, and it takes a lot of time. So you either have somebody who's a banker tryin' to work in a neighborhood or somebody who's a community organizer tryin' to get a handle on the financing. (Tim Mungavan interview, 1991)

Ultimately, CDCs are always in danger of becoming another source of outside control of communities (Berndt, 1977; Fish, 1973). This dilemma presented itself to the Cedar-Riverside community as problems developed with the co-ops and local businesses, and conflict broke out into the open.

The conflict within the CDC had been brewing since the advent of the problems with the Sherlock Homes co-op. As Sherlock Homes was first organizing, the other co-ops also began experiencing problems maintaining an organized resident base and good working relationships with their management companies, which handled the ongoing financial management of the co-ops: paying the bills, providing maintenance, and keeping the books. Riverbluff Housing co-op replaced Realty Management Services, charging that the latter neglected to inform new residents of co-op plans and treated residents in a "high-handed" manner. The co-ops' problems ultimately led to a critique of the entire lease-hold co-op funding strategy, seen as "identical to the one used by Heller which the neighborhood had opposed only a few years before," and a concern that the strategy left residents with little more power than renters but a lot more responsibility (Snoose News, November 1987:8). Strains developed between old and new residents, especially with the completion of Union Homes co-op, and the PAC staff began planning neighborhood mediation boards to attempt to settle neighborhood disputes and reestablish community ties.

Business Backlash

External pressures also played a role in expanded business organizing in the 1980s. Unable to survive on income generated by consumers in the neighborhood, local businesses increasingly looked to the rest of the metropolitan area for consumers for the growing number of entertainment-oriented businesses along Cedar Avenue. Although the residents no longer had to worry about a growth coalition outside the neighborhood, they had to worry about a growth coalition developing inside the neighborhood. This coalition attempted to expand its political and economic power by appealing to interests inside and outside the neighborhood. In early 1984 the B-PAC tried to increase its half-time staff position to a full-time position. The residents reacted angrily, and the PAC approved only a half-time position. Then one businessperson, whose influence had been reduced in the earlier PAC reorganization, led a lawsuit against the 1984 PAC plan to increase the PAC representation of those residents in the old neighborhood directly affected by redevelopment. The Minnesota Civil Liberties Union (MCLU) threatened to join the suit, motivating the PAC to pass a compromise restructuring to shift the Seven Corners and two of the five business seats to resident control. This move satisfied the MCLU but angered the B-PAC, especially when the lawsuit failed.

In mid-1984 the city provided $42,000 to help the B-PAC organize a "theater district" in the neighborhood to promote the local theater companies, after the B-PAC failed to land a $38,000 grant. Substantial advertising and promotion of the neighborhood businesses became directed, for the first time, outside the neighborhood, allowing them to be less dependent on neighborhood dollars. A smaller proportion of the businesses catered to the material needs of low-income neighborhood residents, and neighborhood employment consisted almost entirely of low-wage, part-time service work. As a result, local businesses received less structural pressure to adapt to residents' needs. And as the theater district idea took root, neighborhood bar owners began pushing for license upgrades to allow them to offer live entertainment. The bar issue became heated in the neighborhood as the developing family atmosphere came into conflict with the late-night noise and vandalism associated with the bars, and the PAC continually resisted increasing or upgrading liquor licenses in the neighborhood.[1]

While the businesses were stymied in the PAC, they were gaining influence in the CDC. The CDC was exploring "economic development" and was taking advantage of new funding opportunities for businesses.[2] Staff time, board time, and CDC newsletter space were increasingly devoted to neighborhood businesses. In July the CDC hired a staffperson specifically to promote commercial development in hopes of preventing the First National Bank of St. Paul from repossessing commercial buildings owned by what was left of Cedar-Riverside Associates and selling them to another speculator.

In spite of this effort, new business developers did begin buying up the business strip in 1986. Mark and Don Smith bought the commercial buildings along Cedar Avenue that the bank was unloading: three major commercial buildings and one walk-up apartment building. They narrowly missed acquiring the Durable Goods hardware store building only because of the resistance of the Durable Goods collective, which put out a flyer that read, "If the CDC succeeds in giving this building to the Smiths, it will mean the loss of thirty jobs." The Smiths increasingly evoked the rage of the PAC by neglecting neighborhood historic preservation criteria in remodeling the commercial buildings and by their resistance to signing a tenants' agreement to protect the residents of the walk-up apartment building unless it included a no-strike pledge. Neighborhood activists attempted to resurrect the Community Union, again, but the call for a meeting drew only about thirty people.

By this time the neighborhood had lost the ability to turn out en masse or to threaten targets with "uncontrollable elements." The cooperative relations that had developed with local government and local capital had taken their toll on the neighborhood's militancy. As in Hartford, Connecticut, where neighborhood militancy died as activists were drawn into meetings with city power brokers over establishing a development linkage program (Neubeck and Ratcliff, 1988), Cedar-Riverside activists had not organized a militant action since 1980, when the movement shifted to community-based development. The old Tenants Union would have gone out on strike. This time the residents discussed a rent strike, but the fear of eviction prevented it. Even Keith Heller returned to purchase some commercial property in the Seven Corners area. The neighborhood movement was not the dreaded monster it had been during its second period. Consequently, much of the task of attempting to negotiate with the Smiths fell on the leadership of the PAC, especially the B-PAC.

The turmoil in the neighborhood business strip broke in numerous directions by the late 1980s. Savran's Bookstore, a West Bank institution, closed its doors. Savran's financial troubles were exacerbated when the Smiths' purchase of his building drove his rents up. The Coffeehouse Extempore, which had become a valued West Bank folk music outlet after it was wrested from CRA's control, also shut its doors. The West Bank Co-op Pharmacy, funded by the CDC as an extension of the West Bank Co-op Grocery, was sold to a private businessperson after serious financial losses that were beginning to threaten the grocery store. In August 1992 the members of the West Bank Co-op Grocery, unable to recover from their financial problems, voted to sell out to a private grocer. And At the Foot of the Mountain Theater, a twenty-year-old feminist theater company in Minneapolis, whose productions were given at the People's Center, also closed down because of financial difficulties.

The Changing Community

Adding to the difficulties within the neighborhood was the rapidly changing face of the community. In the midst of the established counterculture residents, whose voluntary poverty was understood in a context of in-depth, radical theoretical knowledge, entered residents who shared the poverty but not the theoretical perspective, or who shared neither. New residents moving into the ownership townhomes from outside the neighborhood were attracted by the funky culture of the neighborhood but had neither the financial need for nor the ideological interest in participating in the often tedious internal negotiations about further redevelopment in the neighborhood. Other residents moving in from the outside had not had the counterculture lifestyle experience and did not have the depth of alternative vision. Pejoratively referred to as "liberals" by neighborhood activists, these new residents did not see necessary contradictions between businesses and residents, did not share the perspective of Cedar-Riverside as an island against the world, and did not support the preservation of militancy in the neighborhood to scare off outside threats.

Residents moving into the co-ops from outside the neighborhood also brought diversity. Many of these residents were members of the truly oppressed, particularly in the Section 8 housing. Their poverty was not voluntary, and many had been denied access to education in general, let alone education in radical perspectives. Building Section 8 housing for poor people was a conscious goal of redevelopment, as was increasing the racial diversity in the neighborhood.[3] But the two goals combined to create awkward results, bringing into the neighborhood impoverished and oppressed single Anglo and African-American women with children. They lacked the life experience that would encourage their involvement in neighborhood decision making, and the time, energy, and childcare resources that would support such involvement. As they spent more time in the neighborhood, these women did become involved, particularly as CDC board members and co-op leaders. But this participation also created difficult dynamics, since both their material interests and their organizational involvements pulled them increasingly in the direction of supporting the goals of affordable housing more than the goals of community control in the neighborhood.

What was occurring in Cedar-Riverside during this period was a breakdown in community. If we return to Logan and Molotch's (1987) measures of community, we can see the problem. To begin with, the neighborhood had become less of a focal point for residents. New residents did much of their shopping outside the neighborhood at discount grocery stores rather than at the neighborhood food co-ops. And old residents increasingly left the neighborhood for consumer goods, especially as outsiders began frequenting neighborhood businesses. Cedar-Riverside, long feared by the outside world, had been transformed into a fad neighborhood. And with the influx of new residents and the reduction of exclusive neighborhood "free spaces" protected from the outside world (Evans and Boyte, 1986), informal support networks were either weakened (for old residents) or prevented from developing (for new residents). There were growing perceptions, partly founded, that crime had increased in the neighborhood, especially around Cedar Avenue. This lack of a sense of security was heightened by the number of new faces in the neighborhood. When I first moved into the neighborhood in 1983, the streets were full of characters whose clothing, jewelry, and hair made them immediately recognizable. As time passed and some of those characters moved out of the neighborhood and were replaced by anonymous and unremarkable residents, the sense of predictability diminished. The neighborhood's identity shifted also, from a strong sense of countercultural values to an emphasis on diversity. As the neighborhood's 1987 annual celebration was organized, "diversity" became its dominating theme— certainly a more inclusive identity than before, but without as much depth and elaboration. This new identity, of course, also signaled a reduction in the shared ethnicity within the neighborhood, as white liberals, counterculture radicals, and African Americans struggled to forge an identity of diversity from the new neighborhood population. Finally, the changing population led to a reduction in the agglomeration benefits as community-based services closed or were sold.

Social reproduction activities that brought the neighborhood together could have reversed this process. But a subtle transition had occurred in how the neighborhood organized these activities. Social reproduction became increasingly individualized through the 1970s, and the trend accelerated in the 1980s. Communal living had all but disappeared, the New Riverside Cafe was no longer as likely to cater neighborhood events, and the explosion in the number of children in the neighborhood made meetings difficult to organize. At one neighborhood meeting a resident expressed the sentiments of the group by speaking against a motion that would have required a long discussion: "Some of us have children to get home to—and leaving your children with a babysitter past ten o'clock is borderline child abuse." Each of these characteristics of community breakdown intensified the others and aggravated the tensions generated by pressures imposed on the community from the outside.

Conflict in the CDC

The CDC was seen as the source of many of the problems developing in the neighborhood with the Smiths and local business closings, and the hostility escalated in the fall 1986 CDC board elections, for which the PAC leadership organized "the largest turnout for a CDC election in many years," according to one CDC staff member. The PAC-nominated slate swept the open CDC seats, and the new board members were determined to reemphasize community-control issues and direct the CDC less toward economic redevelopment. The tension within the CDC grew to the point where CDC staff offered to participate in dispute mediation, but splits within the board and between the board and the staff prevented any agreement on even the form of mediation.

With the CDC in turmoil and morale in the co-ops at a dangerous low, the final phase of redevelopment of the 1980 settlement properties was put on hold while the PAC undertook a lengthy review of the earlier redevelopment. The evaluation showed that current co-op members were burned out by the number of meetings required by the co-ops, were angry at the lack of general participation, and were skeptical that their co-ops would ever generate enough money to buy their buildings from the CDC-Brighton development partnership. Tensions also built as redevelopment brought more low-income children to the neighborhood, and vandalism and juvenile misbehavior in the streets increased.

On the heels of this dispute, divisions between the PAC and the CDC, and then within each organization, grew very deep. At the root of these conflicts was a structural contradiction between the movement's two goals of community control and affordable housing. Community control means control over design, maintenance, and tenancy. It means, ultimately, economic control so that residents cannot be displaced by foreclosure, condemnation, speculative selling, or other practices. But the subsidies that make the housing affordable and the highly specialized knowledge required to finance an affordable project—especially a problem in the HoDAG and Section 8 development, which had strict family-size and/or income requirements—undermine community control. The local state, federal government, and local capital all became involved in creating that contradiction.

Cedar Square West and PAC Conflict

Cedar Square West increasingly took center stage in the second half of the 1980s and shifted the ongoing tensions into the PAC. Serious problems developed there as early as 1984. Keith Heller, $165,000 behind on city water bills on Cedar Square West, bounced a $50,000 check, and the city turned the water off to fifteen hundred residents of the complex for five hours before negotiations restored service. The problems with utility payments and lack of maintenance led the PAC to pressure HUD to begin foreclosure proceedings. In November Heller was ousted as manager of Cedar Square West. By May 1985 the entire project was in the hands of a receiver, and financial disclosures showed that Keith Heller was not even paying the rent on his own units in the complex.

HUD foreclosed on Cedar Square West in 1986. Fears were mounting in the neighborhood that HUD would sell the complex to the highest bidder, again leaving the tenants with an absentee landlord, no maintenance, no rent control, and no recourse. In the worst case, Keith Heller himself could buy the complex back. Cedar Square West was the neighborhood's own Pruitt-Igoe,[4] beset by the alienation bred by superdensities and probably without salvation. But as bad as the project was, the neighborhood was stuck with it, and activists wanted to keep it from becoming a worse problem and improve it if possible.[5] Without local control, activists believed "it would be much more destabilized and you get somebody from Dallas to come in here and own this thing, and we could have, you know, no handle whatsoever on the kind of social problems that would develop there. And then you probably would lose all the people there who do have some potential for leadership" (Mungavan interview, 1991). The PAC leadership, Cedar Square West tenants, and council member Brian Coyle began the fight to secure local ownership and resident management participation. But HUD resisted selling the project to the city, and activists were horrified to learn that HUD wanted to recoup its losses by increasing the number of Section 8 subsidized units in the complex. The neighborhood leadership had stopped the New Town by citing the lack of facilities for families with children in high-density housing, and now HUD was attempting to create more such units for low-income families. The city and the PAC filed suit to stop HUD from increasing the number of Section 8 units and unloading Cedar Square West to the highest bidder. But in June attorneys from Legal Aid filed a class action lawsuit to increase the number of Section 8 units in Cedar Square West from 667 to 1,079 of the 1,299 units, allowing people on Section 8 waiting lists to move into vacant units in the complex. This move put both the city and the PAC in the uncomfortable position of appearing to oppose low-income housing, as the July 1987 *Surveyor*, which had taken over neighborhood news coverage from the defunct *Snoose News*, made a point of emphasizing (pp. 1, 3).

Finally, in August 1987 HUD agreed, under pressure from the city, Minnesota Republican senator Dave Durenberger, and the neighborhood, to sell the complex to the city, which would in turn sell it to a developer partnership the PAC had organized. On December 26, 1988, for $15 million for the purchase and another $7.5 estimated for necessary repairs, Cedar Square West was renamed Riverside Plaza and became the neighborhood's problem. The new owner partnership included Sherman-Boosalis Corporation (a private developer), Brighton Development, Parliament Management, the Twin Cities Housing Development Corporation (a citywide nonprofit developer), and the PAC, which was standing in for the Riverside Plaza Tenants Association (RPTA, pronounced "ripta") until the group was organized to take over. The deal ended all the lawsuits and held the line on the number of Section 8 units, with HUD agreeing to provide other Section 8 units elsewhere in the city.

The PAC's role in the purchase of Riverside Plaza raised tensions higher. Cedar Square West had always been the Achilles' heel of political organizing in the neighborhood, and a name change to Riverside Plaza would not eliminate the anomic qualities of the project. No matter how hard neighborhood activists tried or how many resources they poured into the project, RPTA would not become a stable, effective organization. As time dragged on and the PAC still had not turned over its interest in Riverside Plaza to RPTA, critics of the PAC became increasingly skeptical of PAC activists' motives. One member of the business opposition on the PAC charged that the PAC had a conflict of interest because it was both part owner and the neighborhood review organization. The December 1987 *Surveyor* accused the PAC of not allowing RPTA to take its rightful role as a management partner in the project (p. 2). PAC activists' motives were also severely challenged, with some portraying the situation as a power grab and others portraying it as a money grab. The PAC was blamed for, on the one hand, not turning over control to RPTA and, on the other hand, not successfully organizing RPTA to be able to take over.

The role of the PAC in the purchase of Cedar Square West was unusual, since one would have expected the CDC, as the neighborhood-based developer, to assume that role. But by the time it became clear that someone would have to take responsibility for the concrete towers, the CDC was paralyzed by internal and external conflict, and the PAC tried to play the CDC's role. "I think if it would have happened nine months earlier or nine months later, the CDC probably would have been the partner. It would have made sense for that to be. I think the way the PAC tried to handle that issue was by saying, 'We're involved through the planning stage and then our seat is taken by the residents' group'" (Dick Brustad interview, 1991).

The conflict, once it moved into the PAC, created further tears in the community fabric. A long-time staff member of the CDC and promoter of the economic development emphasis left the CDC to work with the City of St. Paul. Tim Mungavan, for many years a neighborhood housing activist and PAC staff member, left his formal position with the PAC to become a less-central PAC consultant. One other PAC staff member and two CDC staff members resigned suddenly. Tim Ogren, long-time PAC chair, received a Bush Grant to study union organizing and resigned from the PAC.

A Shift in Neighborhood Organizing

The movement's organizational structure changed greatly in this third period and undermined the neighborhood's ability to manage the organizing, recruitment, and tactics dilemmas. The more militant protest organizations withered away. With their target removed and therefore their specialized functions gone, the Tenants Union and CREDF disbanded. The Community Union remained available for neighborhood crises but never again succeeded in organizing large numbers. The Riverside Plaza Tenants Association never really got off the ground. On the other hand, the development-focused organizations expanded their power and scope. As we saw, the CDC grew to employ a thirteen-member staff with a $300,000 annual budget, while the PAC, after fighting for its life in the early 1980s, achieved a $100,000 annual budget and complete power for making development decisions at the neighborhood level. As the housing co-ops were completed, residents' attention was also drawn to their own co-op organizations.

The organizational structure that developed in this late period of the movement resembled the Gerlach and Hine (1970) decentralized-segmented-reticulate, or DSR, structure. Increasingly, the movement became composed of separated constituencies divided into separate organizations, as opposed to the unified movement of the second period. Community-control advocates were attracted to the PAC, while affordable-housing advocates were drawn to the CDC. Community-control advocates did create a strong presence on the CDC board after the fall 1986 elections, but the staff, increasingly recruited from outside the neighborhood, remained focused on the issue of affordability.

The unity of the earlier federated frontstage structure became entangled with the contradictory goals of the CDC and the PAC in this period. Community development corporations have always been viewed with suspicion by neighborhood activists as being too tied to bottom-line economic interests, requiring too much specialized knowledge, and not organizing residents effectively enough (Stever, 1978; Lauria, 1980; Berndt, 1977; Kelly, 1977; Blakely and Aparicio, 1990; Twelvetrees, 1989). These fears existed from the beginning of the CDC in Cedar-Riverside but were held in abeyance. Before the 1980 settlement decision the CDC had little to do and was primarily involved in assisting the PAC and the Tenants Union, creating a high degree of task overlap between the CDC and the PAC in the planning workshops. Before 1980, moreover, the CDC staff was recruited from highly regarded neighborhood activists who were among the most militant members of the movement. The initial trust of the CDC staff was combined with a disinterest on the part of many activists in the complex financial machinations required to fund development:

> The people who ran for the CDC board were different than the people who ran for the PAC. They were the straighter people in the neighborhood. . . . It was seen to be kind of boring by the activists. . . . You know, your control is there, but you usually kind of end up making the hard decisions between two bad things and a lot of details that you don't wanna get involved with. . . . Nobody wanted to learn it; it's awful, you know.   (Dorothy Jacobs and Tim Mungavan interviews, 1991)

As the 1980s progressed, the lack of task clarity between the PAC and the CDC, the hiring of staff from outside the neighborhood, and the separation of the affordability and community-control goals led to conflict. The initial disputes came as the CDC began hiring and supervising organizers and was seen as taking independent policy positions. From the perspective of Dick Brustad: "The CDC—and I think it has been more so in the recent years, say the last five years—has from time to time clearly crossed over into wanting to be involved in the policy neighborhood decisions. And so then it's the PAC and the CDC stepping on one another's toes—never in their own minds having what I thought was a clear distinction." The conflict moved into the PAC with its involvement in the purchase of Cedar Square West. The PAC was then blamed for a lack of maintenance, unfinished repairs, and other development problems in Riverside Plaza. And it was the PAC that was charged with having a financial interest in the complex which contradicted its citizen-participation role—the same criticism that was leveled against the CDC in funding co-op organizers. The lack of strict differentiation between the two organizations allowed each to cross into the other's territory, exacerbating internal conflict.

The overlap of duties in the PAC and CDC carried over from the oppositional stage of the movement, but their goals became increasingly distinct. The goal specialization of the PAC and the CDC put the contradiction between affordability and control into two separate organizations. Thus, a structural economic contradiction became an interorganizational conflict. Rather than attempting to manage this contradiction, PAC members and other community-control advocates targeted the CDC as the culprit, and the CDC returned complaints about the PAC. A single neighborhood organization would have had to deal with this contradiction directly, since the competing interests would have clashed *within* the organization.[6] That would have made the economic contradiction more clear. Even with the PAC and CDC separate, a stricter separation of roles requiring the CDC to relinquish control over community organizing funds and to better inform the PAC of its proposed funding mechanisms for the co-ops, and restricting the PAC from becoming a development partner, would have controlled the resultant conflict.

The incentives motivating leaders and members split with the factioning of the movement during this period. Leadership was inspired by strong ideological incentives. But the ideological goals were divided between the affordability proponents in the CDC and the community-control advocates in the PAC, and the two factions competed for the allegiance of residents. The greater relevance of ideological incentives for movement leaders as opposed to the movement constituency is not problematic in itself, but in the case of Cedar-Riverside there were competing ideological incentives even among the movement leaders. Consequently, internal disputes came to be more ideological and polarized than had been the case earlier.

For the mass of residents in the neighborhood—new and old—the important issues became controlling the children, maintaining the affordability of the housing, reducing crime, and obtaining basic services. Countering capitalism, creating a sustainable community based on anarchist self-determination principles, resisting the encroachment of the state—all the values that had guided the opposition movement and the planning that went into democratic community-based redevelopment—were lost in this period. New residents, in particular the large number of undereducated single women with children housed in the Section 8 housing co-ops, did not read Marx, or Mao, or Bakhunin, or Kropotkin and were not motivated by the ideological incentives that inspired those who did study alternative and radical philosophies.

Increasingly, then, residents were recruited to movement activities only on the basis of material incentives, rather than by a guiding ideology. Thus, they were unlikely to vote in PAC elections as long as they believed their interests were being cared for. As soon as they perceived their material interests at stake, residents turned out en masse. But there was no organization, such as the Tenants Union in the second period, that could help residents translate their material interests into ideological commitment to the alternative vision of the movement leaders. Even the New Riverside Cafe, once it purchased its building and became involved in the theater district promotion, attracted an increasing number of people from outside the neighborhood and lost its "living room" quality. The movement lacked a means by which to recruit members to the community. "Organizing used to be easy. People would respond, come to meetings. Now you have to work on self-esteem issues. You have to work with single mothers who don't have enough money. They have time, but no self-esteem. Political organizing won't work right now. You need to work on building community—provide food, music, and socializing" (Jacobs interview, 1988).

Tactical flexibility also was lost as a consequence of maintaining membership in the governing regime in Minneapolis. As in Hartford, where militant neighborhood organizing forced city officials and capitalists to the table to discuss a development "linkage" program, both militancy and mass organizing gave way to meeting after meeting of tedious negotiation requiring expert knowledge (Neubeck and Ratcliff, 1988). The new relationship of the neighborhood movement to the political opportunity structure required new tactics and inhibited the use of a diversity of tactics. Without a mass participation organization that could engage large numbers in militant tactics and could do so without threatening the legitimacy of the PAC and the CDC, the neighborhood was not in a good position to push the political opportunity structure. Although the neighborhood movement had four allies on the City Council, other council members were becoming irritated that so much money was being spent on Cedar-Riverside. Militant tactics had alienated even Jackie Slater during her time on the council, so it was clear that anything more militant than negotiation could turn the council against the neighborhood, especially without a mass neighborhood organization to back up demands for plan approval and resources. With each compromise, the next one was easier. The movement, especially the CDC, had returned to viewing the political opportunity structure as immutable: "The law comes down and HUD says, 'This is the law,' and the staff says, 'OK, do it.' But, of course, that's not ever true. I mean this is the law, but there's no such thing as *the law*. You can always compromise. You can always make different kinds of agreements" (Hal Barron interview, 1991).

The internal conflict generated by the contradiction between affordability and community control could have been headed off more effectively had activists framed the conflict as generated by the political opportunity structure rather than within the movement. The movement was characterized by strong and passionate personalities, a quality that served them well in escalating the conflict against the New Town. But when the focus shifted to community development, those same personalities clashed with one another. The goal contradiction created by the outside became enmeshed with quarrels between exlovers, jealousies, and personal animosities. Increasingly, other activists were seen as the problem, rather than the political opportunity structure. Once again, if there had been a more strictly defined relationship between the PAC and the CDC, or if the organizations had been combined, the restrictions imposed by the available funding would have been seen more clearly earlier, directing the movement's anger outward rather than inward. But that did not happen, and by the end of the 1980s the community was dangerously close to civil war.

Conflict Breaks Out

In late 1987 *Snoose News* returned to the neighborhood—this time funded by the CDC, the co-ops, and the MCDA—and fanned the flames of conflict. An article in the December 1987 issue, lamenting the loss of numerous neighborhood-based businesses, charged the CDC with serious misdirection.

> It is the role of community development corporations, in this case, the West Bank Community Development Corporation, to provide community-based and resident-owned businesses with working capital. . . . This has not happened on the West Bank. The West Bank Community Development Corporation has created a situation where speculation is rampant and community-based businesses of long standing are closing down.   (pp. 1, 3)

This accusation evoked a storm of protest from neighborhood businesses, even from a New Riverside Cafe member, and from some residents, who responded in the February 1988 *Snoose News* (pp. 4, 6, 7).

Conflict grew between the management companies and the housing co-ops as well. Though the co-ops needed to work with the management companies, the self-interests of the two parties contradicted each other. Conflicts erupted even with Parliament Management, led by one of the early organizers in Cedar-Riverside:

> We have to be the bad guy. We got in the position of having to enforce these regulations that say if you're using HoDAG money, for instance, in Sherlock Homes, you've gotta keep a certain number of the units occupied by very low-income people. If . . . the family's income goes up, they're in a big house, and all their kids move out, we've gotta move that family out and move somebody else in who meets the requirements. Well, if the person you move out happens to be an old neighborhood organizer who feels like they're getting evicted after they did all this work to get all this stuff in place, then you're a really bad guy.   (Steve Parliament interview, 1991)

That scenario has not taken place in Sherlock Homes yet, though some activists have moved out, fearing they would face displacement, and blame the CDC and the management companies for not protecting their rights.

In January 1988 it all broke loose. The CDC board voted seven to four to dissolve the corporation.[7] Radical board members, frustrated at their inability to change the direction of the CDC, made the move to dissolve. Their motives after the fact are unclear: some say they really wanted to dissolve the CDC, others say they wanted to restructure the corporation, and still others say they wanted to do something extreme that would activate the community.

Regardless of their intentions, their action did activate the neighborhood. Dissolution action could not be taken by the board alone but had to be voted on by the community. The CDC staff distributed a flyer throughout the neighborhood, warning that all community control of past and future redevelopment could be lost and inviting people to a general meeting. Bold letters on the bright yellow, two-page flyer announced: "SPECIAL MEMBERSHIP MEETING OF THE WEST BANK COMMUNITY DEVELOPMENT CORPORATION TO CONSIDER WHETHER TO DISSOLVE THE CDC." The February 1988 *Snoose News* carried a two-page pro-con debate on dissolution (pp. 6, 7). The Union Homes co-op drafted a compromise resolution that involved large-scale restructuring of the CDC toward issues of community control and away from economic issues. The neighborhood prepared for the meeting.

Two hundred fifty people came out for the meeting—73 percent residents and 27 percent businesses. It was the largest group attending a neighborhood meeting since before Keith Heller was ousted from the neighborhood. Bill Teska, the neighborhood's Episcopal minister and perhaps the only person left who was trusted throughout the neighborhood, chaired the meeting. A dispute broke out at the very beginning over whether those who did not live in the neighborhood would be allowed to vote, since the CDC had recently learned that community development corporations receiving state grant money were required to limit voting to residents only. The practice in the CDC up to that time, however, was that anyone who worked or lived in the neighborhood could vote. The businesses scored their first victory when, by a vote of seventy-four to sixty-seven, they were allowed to vote. After that the neighborhood activists continued to lose ground. The Union Homes co-op attempted to introduce its compromise resolution, but it was tabled. By a unanimous voice vote, the membership voted to retain the CDC in its present form. Even those who had originally voted to dissolve voted in favor of the CDC.

Nevertheless, the meeting did not result in a clear defeat for the neighborhood activists. After the members voted to continue the CDC, board members were elected. Those who spoke out against the CDC most strongly were voted in as board members. One of them was Scott Vreeland, whose nomination speech emphasized the need to preserve the CDC for neighborhood residents, focused on the conflict between businesses and residents, and hinted at the "growth" pressures impinging on the CDC: "Businesses want more cars, more bars, and more people. Residents want less bars, less cars, and less density." The Union Homes CDC restructuring proposal obtained a serious hearing in the following months. One of its recommendations, that the CDC hire an executive director, was carried out in late 1988.

The cost of the turmoil was a great deal of bitterness and the loss of a development project. With all development at the CDC on hold, Brighton Development had gone on to plan redevelopment of the "Trinity block," the worst housing in the neighborhood, owned by Trinity Lutheran Church. After negotiations with the PAC to reduce the density, an agreement was finally reached to demolish the entire block except for two businesses and to build a thirty-seven-unit apartment building and seventeen ownership townhomes. The church would retain title to the land, making the entire project more affordable. Even though the Trinity block was redeveloped by Brighton Development (a private, for-profit developer) rather than the CDC, the PAC was involved directly in altering and approving the plans.

The PAC also moved on with planning the "Parcel B" development, the last remaining CRA land in the neighborhood. Along with thirty-four co-op units and two ownership units, the planning included block meetings to plan the closing of 19th Avenue to create off-street parking and a park for the residents of the development. There were still a few residents who resented any redevelopment in the neighborhood, however, preferring to live in houses literally falling down around them rather than give up their extraordinarily low rents, in some cases under one hundred dollars a month. The Parcel B and Trinity projects brought out that resentment and combined with the business opposition for one last stand.

As splits grew between those who advocated affordable housing and those who advocated community control, these dissenting voices amplified leadership divisions throughout the neighborhood. The movement's participation in the governing regime in Minneapolis provided ammunition for this increasingly vocal countermovement. Countermovements arise in opposition to change in an attempt to maintain the status quo or roll back change (Lo, 1982; Zald and Useem, 1987). In Cedar-Riverside the countermovement organized against collective decision making and citizen participation, trying to reassert the power of property rights. The offensive against the PAC began in response to the 1988 PAC elections, when only 87 residents voted— a not unusually low number but low enough to allow antagonists to question the democratic legitimacy of the PAC (*Star-Tribune*, April 8, 1988, pp. 1, 14A). A resident facing displacement from the Parcel B project, a businessperson who had struggled against the PAC's refusal to increase the number of liquor licenses in the neighborhood, and another resident filed a lawsuit charging that the elections were invalid. Though the suit was dismissed initially, and again on appeal, it signaled the beginning of war on the PAC.

Businesses and the residents allied with them were further angered when the PAC voted to disband the Business PAC and refused to request funding for a business staffperson on the PAC, leading to a dispute that brought the MCDA into the fray. In the spring 1989 elections the conflict fanned by the opposition, organized as the Committee for Open Government (COG), brought out 378 voters. COG-endorsed candidates did well in the Seven Corners and Riverside Plaza election districts. The dispute became both personal and ideological, with COG claiming a position "as the champion of free enterprise and the American way" (Platt, 1990:10).

Neighborhood activists' tenacious adherence to a vision of collective decision making and community control was increasingly challenged by those who argued that property, not citizenship, should vest people with power. Countermovement members argued that property owners and business owners, by virtue of their control of property, regardless of where they lived, should exert greater control over the PAC and the CDC. They also objected to the PAC's enormous power with the City Council, which allowed it to determine who would get a liquor license, be able to expand a business, or build a parking lot (and under what conditions). The movement's alliances with the city and Brighton Development were then used to portray the movement as an oligarchy in bed with powerful and unaccountable interests (Vogel, 1991).

With the rise of the COG countermovement, both the mainstream press and the two urban weeklies adopted the countermovement perspective (*Star-Tribune*, April 8, 1988, pp. 1, 14A; Platt, 1990; Vogel,

1991). No longer was the neighborhood movement seen as the little guy who defeated the big bad developer; it was the powerful beast that was oppressing the little people. Separated from its history, and without reference to the decade of collective planning, monthly proposal reviews, and interminable efforts to build consensus on development, the movement lost its legitimacy. The countermovement's success in achieving the support of the media came too late to do damage to the redevelopment in the neighborhood, but it contributed even further to the social breakdown in the community.

The countermovement leaders had opposed collective decision making from the beginning and were able to organize the resentment of Riverside Plaza residents over the PAC's inability to organize RPTA effectively. Riverside Plaza had become a quagmire. It had always been impossible for activists to organize, even in the days of Keith Heller, and the change in ownership did not help. The character of the complex changed, as increasing numbers of people with mental and physical challenges moved into the towers without adequate services or accommodations, increasing their frustration level. A shoot-out in the complex brought things to a head, and residents blamed the PAC for not providing services. "A flyer went out saying the PAC wouldn't set up community crime blocks in Cedar Square West. Well, we tried for years, but we can't set it up. The neighbor on the block has to set up the block" (Tim Ogren interview, 1991).

Even in the face of all this pressure, political heat, and eventually lawsuits, activists persevered. The community stayed organized just enough to finish off democratic, community-based redevelopment in style, with adherence to the alternative vision that had guided activists from the beginning.

Finishing Off the Neighborhood

The limitations imposed on the redevelopment by City Hall were a major source of the tensions that developed within the movement. But after the 1983 City Council elections, when the movement had four unwavering supporters on council, it was friends at City Hall that helped save the movement from being torn apart. First, City Hall increasingly approved plans to develop ownership units and subsidized housing for poor singles in the neighborhood. But more important, Cedar-Riverside's three main City Council members—Kathy O'Brien, Tony Scallon, and Brian Coyle—worked hard to prevent the movement's internal conflict from becoming an issue downtown.

There were people on the City Council and in the mayor's office who had no idea what the divisions were in the community. The fact that Tony, Brian, and I did shelter the community and the fact that we absorbed some tension and didn't let it become more publicly visible, we really sheltered the community. Tony and Brian and I would never make a decision on a Cedar-Riverside issue without talking to each other. And so we, by trying to remain allies on issues in that neighborhood . . . absorbed that shock a little   (Kathy O'Brien interview, 1991)

Ultimately, as the city political system became more stable and supportive of the neighborhood movement through the middle 1980s, it counteracted the movement's internal dissension, which had been catalyzed by capital and government-imposed funding and planning restrictions in the early 1980s.

Making the most of this political support, one movement strategy in the middle 1980s was to create a five-year plan that outlined the neighborhood's funding requests for the remaining redevelopment. Activists feared that the City Council's resistance to neighborhood planning and funding needs would only grow as time passed and that the tax-increment money (which was no longer reserved for the neighborhood but was put into a general fund) would be more difficult to get in the future. PAC representatives politely showed up at subcommittee meetings, committee meetings, and council meetings, waited to speak, and typically ended up with less time than they wanted to make their pitch.

Neighborhood activists persevered beyond the troubles with COG and Riverside Plaza to enact one last project from this five-year plan, over COG's objections. The Parcel B project was approved by the City Council on June 30, 1989. Again financed through the CDC–Brighton Development partnership, the project provided thirty-four lease-hold co-op units and twenty-five ownership units. The West Bank activists pioneered another alternative with this project. Four housing units were to be designed as children's daycare locations to care for up to ten children each, with the care providers receiving free rent in their unit. The approval of this project also included funds to close 19th Avenue, long a sore spot among residents because of the bar traffic that roared down the street at closing time. By the end of 1990 the "Blue Goose" co-op and the daycare homes were up and running.

The PAC also organized residents to come up with a plan for using the money the PAC had earned from its development work in Cedar Square West. A series of neighborhood forums held to decide how to prioritize community needs settled on building a sense of community, improving access to goods and services, and enhancing the quality of life in the neighborhood. The $200,000 fund was given to the Minneapolis Foundation to invest and disburse grants to the neighborhood, using an advisory committee of eleven appointed by the PAC to review proposals. Digging back into a more activist history, residents named the program the Unicorn Fund after a logo on an old Greater University Tenants Union meeting poster.

That was the last unity the neighborhood could muster. In the 1990 elections the COG-PAC dispute again brought 318 voters to the polls and another lawsuit. A long-time neighborhood activist lost his PAC seat in this election, signaling the beginning of the unraveling of activist control of the PAC. Two Trinity block residents, who were going to be temporarily displaced, charged that the PAC was not protecting their interests.

With the housing all but done, and infighting taking a continuing toll on the community's social fabric, it was time for a change.

> Now what we would call the *raison d'être*—the reason for existence—of the PAC disappeared because the housing was done. . . . But of course, it's hard to see that. You can see it now only in retrospect. Now, instead of fighting about means, they were fighting about who should have the power. And that came in as a result of all the controversy concerning the acquisition of the high-rises. (Barron interview, 1991)

Activists got together one evening and came to a decision, for all practical purposes, to disband the PAC. The neighborhood would be divided into four districts: Riverside Plaza, the seniors' high-rise, Seven Corners, and the old neighborhood. The PAC would meet only quarterly, and all business would essentially be conducted within each district. The hope among activists was that it would prevent the opposition from continuing to create problems for the old neighborhood residents. With support from the neighborhood's City Council members, on April 3, 1991, the restructuring proposal passed the PAC by the required two-thirds vote. It was over, without a celebration. "We went over to the bar by the railroad tracks and had a couple of drinks and then went home. It was real anticlimactic" (Ogren interview, 1991).

The Rise of Community-based Development: The Decline of Community

Understanding this period of the movement requires understanding activists' disappointment with what appears from the outside to be tremendous success. Few neighborhood movements can boast the liberation of a neighborhood and the transformation of its housing from rental tyranny to co-op control. The movement had accomplished what Castells (1983) sees as the greatest sign of success of an urban social movement: taking control of its locality through the creation and maintenance of cultural and political autonomy founded on new definitions of its local space. Virtually the only reason anyone would ever need to leave Cedar-Riverside was to buy underwear—a point of contention in business development planning. But many of the people who helped achieve the alternative vision left the neighborhood disillusioned and angry. Lovers separated, neighbors moved away, participation at collective activities declined. People sought their work, friends, and entertainment increasingly outside the neighborhood. Friendships were shattered, ideals were compromised, and the community identity was severely strained.

> We were able to save the tangibles—save the houses physically—and we managed to save and expand the institutions. And, amazingly, the reason it's a great success story is that everything we said we were gonna do happened. We got control of the land. We rehabbed all of the houses . . . affordably so the rents were low and people that lived there could afford to continue to live there, and many did. We are not abandoning the New Riverside Cafe or the Cedar-Riverside People's Center, and they're still there, and they're still doing in most ways what they're meant to do. But what we didn't succeed in maintaining, in saving if you will, is the intangibles—all those things we took for granted and never put down on paper ever—that dealt with relationships and interpersonal bonds, and ethics of how you relate to other people. . . . All of those things faded away. (Ralph Wittcoff interview, 1991)

A neighborhood had been rebuilt. The central community-based institutions—the People's Center, the New Riverside Cafe, and North Country Co-op—remained in place. New institutions were added. Parliament Management developed the Meridel Le Seuer Center for Peace and Justice to house Twin Cities peace and justice organizations, and the PAC helped develop four daycare homes and establish the Unicorn Fund. Space was rehabbed to house KFAI "fresh air" alternative radio, and Legal Advocacy for West Bank Women was founded. The movement had created 254 units of lease-hold, low-density co-op housing distributed among six co-op organizations; 248 units of management co-op apartments in Seven Corners; and 53 units of ownership townhomes. They helped Brighton Development construct 54 additional housing units. All the housing was financed to be affordable to low- and moderate-income families, with co-op rents ranging from $165 for single-room occupancy units to $319–$425 for one–two bedroom units; the highest rents were in resident-created housing in the Seven Corners apartments at $640. A "co-op summit" emerged in the late 1980s to coordinate street and sidewalk upkeep, and to maintain neighborhood security, saving the co-ops tens of thousands of dollars and enhancing neighborhood unity.

And there was change. According to estimates, at most half, and perhaps as little as 10 percent, of the original activists remained in the neighborhood.[8] Kathy O'Brien chose to not run for City Council again. The home I had left behind for an academic job in Toledo, Ohio, was demolished to make way for new townhomes, giving me a feeling, when I returned briefly in 1991, of what it is like to have a symbol of your life disappear.

Other changes occurred in 1991 while I was back on the West Bank. I watched the Trinity block be demolished. I watched as the site of the first protest in the neighborhood, the historic Dania Hall, burned from arson. I learned that, while I was on my way back to Toledo, Brian Coyle, the former PAC member and Tenants Union organizer who rose to become the vice-president of City Council, had died of complications from AIDS. And I received my last *Snoose News* at my new home in Toledo in October 1992, when publication ceased.

And life goes on. People immediately began discussing the restoration of Dania Hall, the building of the Coyle Community Center,[9] and the organizing of a party to celebrate the fiftieth birthdays of four neighborhood women activists. The community—the web of social relationships that held the movement together in the face of incredible odds—had suffered, but it had not died. And the struggle was not over. The co-ops still have to be managed, and the residents still have to learn how to buy out their units or buildings down the road. That process has already partly begun at Riverbluff, the least empowering project and the only one not developed with Brighton Development Corporation, where residents bought out Canadian-American Realty (formerly Canadian Financial Corporation) to form a lease-hold co-op. The community institutions still have to be maintained, especially as they attempt to weather the weak economy of the 1990s. That is especially true of the People's Center, which cut back on staff and programs and even resorted to pull-tab gambling at area bars for some funds. The exciting part is over, but now the next stage starts.

> There's the opposition, takeover, and control stage that we all went through. There's the development and ownership stage. But there's really a third, which is long-range management and operations to make this stuff livable. And it's clearly a third stage which has a whole 'nother set of requirements and obligations on it which has to do with meeting all the regulations of the financing and keeping the buildings preserved and doing the maintenance work and keeping the co-op organized and setting up processes for decisions. (Parliament interview, 1991)

In many ways the experiment is just beginning. Now that the neighborhood has rebuilt the housing, can it rebuild the community? And can it rebuild community in a way that returns the sense of power developed in the fight against the New Town? "I like the word 'experiment' because it implies that tinkering can still be done—that the things that didn't work aren't the end point, failure, and you turn out the lights and go home" (Ogren interview, 1991).

CHAPTER 8

The Role of Community in Urban Insurgency

The search for and/or struggle to defend community, both
the "sense" of community and actual community institutions,
becomes political in the context of the changes that capitalism has
brought in the everyday life of the individual—changes characterized by lack of control at work, school and play; impersonality
and competition in all areas of life. The desire for connectedness,
meaningful personal relationships and direct participation and
control over economic, political and social institutions on the basis
of the needs of the individual and community takes on radical
meaning in a period such as ours.
                    —*Wini Breines*, Community and Organization
                       in the New Left, 1962–1968

T HE PEOPLE of Cedar-Riverside discovered their power even as
they watched the housing west of Cedar Avenue bulldozed to
make way for the first stage of the New Town. For it was not just
the power of creating democratic, community-based redevelopment,
or even of stopping the remaining stages of the top-down, capital-
conscious New Town plan, that Cedar-Riverside exhibited. First and
foremost it was the power of creating a community on which a strong
defense could be built. And the movement that built and defended
that community produced both a culture and a social structure that
allowed Cedar-Riverside to expand its power beyond all predictions.
A megadevelopment of high-rise, high-density concrete ground to a
halt, and in its place grew more than five hundred units of human-
scale housing, the vast majority of it controlled by residents through
lease-hold or management co-op structures, all created by a commu-

nity. Not by a government bureaucracy or a capitalist corporation, but by a community.

In the earliest period of this neighborhood movement, up through the Cedar Square West dedication ceremony uprising, a well-organized growth coalition allowed the movement little agency. But in the second period the movement built on the community base created in the first period and was able to make the most of the financial vulnerabilities of Cedar-Riverside Associates and foiled the rest of the New Town plan. In the third period, after the 1980 settlement agreement, the neighborhood movement used the aura of power it had generated for itself in the second period to create democratic community-based urban redevelopment. But the movement also lost momentum through the 1980s as the political opportunity structure refused to support the goals of both affordable housing and community control, and the movement was unable to contain the conflict caused by the contradiction of those goals.

In this chapter I bring together the analyses of the three periods of the neighborhood movement to explore the underpinnings of community that channeled the neighborhood movement's power, or "agency."[1] The agency the movement was able to practice derived from two characteristics of community: community culture and social reproduction. Community culture is the initial source of all agency, since cultural beliefs and values define movement goals and strategies. Social reproduction, or the way in which people realize their biological and emotional needs, builds on cultural values and results in community practices that help reproduce individuals and the community collectively.

Community Culture and Urban Social Movement Action

The role of community culture in guiding social movements springing from communities has been long neglected. The early collective behavior theorists were willing to admit that social movements have cultural components but were less willing to see those social movement cultures as rational and viable (Jenkins, 1983). Resource mobilization theorists, attempting to counter the collective behavior theorists' view of social movements as irrational, portrayed social movements as almost heartless, rational, self-interested calculating machines (Klandermans, 1986; Hannigan, 1985; Evans and Boyte, 1986). Resource mobilization theorists are beginning to recognize the importance of culture, though they see it as a resource to be used the same way as money, such as providing for member satisfaction (Taylor, 1989).

It has been left to the new social movement theorists to discover the role social movement culture plays in the dynamics of social movements. New social movement theory developed with the perceived growth of movements focusing on cultural issues, such as protest against high-risk technologies and environmental destruction (Halfmann, 1988; Rucht, 1988), movements attempting to enact alternative modes of production and reproduction (Lipietz, 1988; Rucht, 1988), and especially urban social movements (Castells, 1983). As these movements became more prominent, it was apparent that culture was an issue. The civil rights movement, for example, while insisting that African Americans be given the same cultural opportunities that white Americans had, did not demand that the country change culturally as much as that it live up to its cultural rhetoric. The new social movements, however, began calling for a wholesale shift away from the values of patriarchy, capitalist exploitation and domination, consumerism, destruction of nature, and individuality. It is this demand for cultural change, rather than simply for political rights, along with a refusal to adopt the organizational and action forms of the dominant culture, that distinguishes new social movements and makes movement culture an important theoretical issue (Klandermans, 1986; Hannigan, 1985).[2]

How is culture used by social movements and how does it affect movement agency? First, culture has a profound effect on how the movement organizes itself: creating new organizational forms is part of the goal of new social movements. Movement organizations are exemplars of the society the movements want to create (Rucht, 1989). Culture also shapes the communities, individual identities, and tactics of new social movements in important ways because those communities, identities, and tactics are nontraditional and nonconventional (Szabó, 1988). The "prefigurative politics" of new social movements, which make the movement not just a means but an end in itself (Breines, 1989), guide the movement through the maze of contacts and negotiations and compromises with the outside world by providing a highly elaborated reference point against which the movement can judge its actions. Manuel Castells (1983) goes so far as to argue that the success or failure of urban community-based social movements is dependent in large part on the movement's ability to articulate its goals clearly and to act on them.

Urban social movements, especially those neighborhood-based

community movements organizing to preserve a culturally specific way of life, add even more importance to the concept of culture. These movements, in contrast to the portrayal of most new social movements as attempting to change a dominant culture, are attempting to *defend* their culture. Often that is an ethnic culture, but it can also be an alternative culture (Castells, 1983). In either case Castells identifies three cultural issues around which urban social movements develop: collective consumption, local cultural autonomy, and political self-management. Collective consumption refers to the collective goods necessary for community maintenance, a resource and service base available to the community as a whole. In bad times collective consumption is one of the first things to be cut by city governments. With an autonomous community culture, the community is able to resist the encroachment of capital and the state and their culturally antagonistic goods and services. Under political self-management, the community is able to resolve disputes among its members, maintain social control, and make community decisions, without interference from the outside and often with the provision of resources from outside sources such as the local state.

Overall, however, the role of culture in social movement dynamics is amorphous. Castells remains at an abstract level of analysis, but I believe his three cultural components can be developed more concretely. Collective consumption is expressed through those practices designed to reproduce the community itself on a daily basis, its "social reproduction" practices. Cultural autonomy is expressed through the ideology that guides community practice. And political self-management is expressed through the community's movement structure. The Cedar-Riverside neighborhood movement community, through much of its history, exhibited both an elaborated movement ideology and highly developed social reproduction strategies on which activists built an extremely sophisticated organizational structure. I consider each in turn.

Community Ideology: Anarchism, Socialism, and the Problem of Populism

Overcoming the problems inherent to neighborhood-based political organizing—limited issues, constrained leadership and financial resources, internal divisions, neighborhood population mobility—"requires an overarching ideology as potent as patriotism" (S. Fainstein, 1987:328). Building and maintaining a strong community that can withstand external assaults and overcome internal instability can only be accomplished by establishing bonds that go beyond basic neighboring. Those bonds are created through a community ideology. That ideology may be based in ethnicity or in a less traditional culture.

Ideology was an important motivating force in Cedar-Riverside and illustrates the "cultural autonomy" component in Castells's (1983) model of community movement culture. Many of the internal disputes during the early stage of the movement revolved around ideological issues. There were anarchists, Maoists, Castroists, socialists, and many other splinter ideologies operative in the neighborhood. In between mobilizations during the first two periods of the neighborhood movement, the tensions grew so strong that, as one resident said, "the anarchists would stay on one side of the bar and the socialists on the other." Even into the third period of the movement, ideological debates drove the discussions over whether to plan neighborhood development or to let residents develop or not develop their housing as they wished. A socialist influence was dominant in developing planning for neighborhood housing, while an anarchist influence maintained a strong foothold in the neighborhood through the New Riverside Cafe, North Country Co-op, and Durable Goods hardware store.

Overall there was more overlap than division. Even in Durable Goods, formed by a split from the New Riverside Cafe, one could find T-shirts ranging from a graphic of the Marx Brothers along with Karl Marx proclaiming, "Sure, I'm a Marxist!" to a graphic of the anarchist Emma Goldman asserting, "If I can't dance, I don't want to be part of your revolution." All residents considered themselves leftists, and even those who considered themselves socialists did not support centralized planning in the neighborhood but demanded that the planning process be as participatory as possible. And a socialist ideology decrying the accumulation of productive property in private hands effectively complemented an anarchist ideology of a community free of outside regulation.

> Back when Cedar-Riverside was a monolithic community, and it really was, we envisioned a different way of doing it . . . [that] it was possible to operate the neighborhood, the community, the city, the nation, and ultimately the world in a totally decentralized, self-sufficient fashion. And that people would, in fact, buy into the idea that their self-worth is not tied up with their possessions and property. "Property is theft," we used to say, "property is theft." (Ralph Wittcoff interview, 1991)

The community ideology elaborated quickly through the first period of the movement. Residents were opposed to both bureaucratic hierarchies and capitalist exploitation. Thus, from the beginning they sought to provide community services that could bypass both hierarchy and capitalism, leading to the New Riverside Cafe, the People's Center, and North Country Co-op. They also insisted on establishing relationships based on trust and self-regulation. Thus the New Riverside Cafe, for a time, practiced a policy of "eat what you need, pay what you can afford." Community sharing extended to all facets of life, from wage earnings to drugs to sex to childcare. Much of this ideology was developed by the hippies in the neighborhood. But antiwar activists were also settling in the neighborhood. The early ideological disputes between these factions involved issues more than broad-ranging political programs. The hippies mobilized to save their neighborhood, while the antiwar activists focused their energies on stopping the war in Vietnam. But as more and more study groups formed in the neighborhood, these ideologies began to overlap. And then HUD Secretary George Romney's plans to dedicate Cedar-Square West gave material presence to the developing community ideology beginning to understand the common role of the military-industrial complex in domination and exploitation both at home and abroad.

In the second period of the movement the cry for basic citizen control of the neighborhood became the most obvious outward expression of the community ideology. This ideology was clearly defined, as shown by the neighborhood's resistance to other movement organizations that attempted to infiltrate from the outside. In 1975 the infamous "co-op wars" hit the Twin Cities, which by that time had become a center for commercial co-ops. A Stalinist group calling itself the Co-op Organization, though referred to by Cedar-Riverside residents as "robot communists," attempted to infiltrate the co-ops throughout the metropolitan area. Since Cedar-Riverside was the political center of the co-op movement, the neighborhood became a target for the Co-op Organization's activity. Co-op activists in the neighborhood maintained an ideology clearly opposed to the dictatorial ideology and style of the Co-op Organization and succeeded in repelling the Stalinists (Wittcoff interview, 1988; Estep, 1979).

In other cases outside movement organizations attempted to enter the neighborhood and organize residents. Though these movement organizations also criticized the New Town, residents generally opposed these groups, seeing them as outsiders that would undermine neighborhood-based organizing power. Sometimes residents tore down flyers advertising such outsiders' meetings or sent organizers to oppose the group vocally at their meetings. The trust between residents in the early period developed into a greater distrust of the world around them. Cedar-Riverside defined itself as a unique community, opposed to capitalism but also opposed to Stalinism, emphasizing self-sufficiency and community-based control of the neighborhood.

Through the first two periods of the neighborhood movement, community ideology provided well-developed justification for opposition to the New Town. But in the third period, divisions between left-anarchist and left-socialist ideology, and the contradiction in the political opportunity structure between the twin goals of affordable housing and community control of neighborhood redevelopment, made implementation of democratic, community-based redevelopment problematic. Many anarchists did not support such a rigorous planning effort, especially one restricted by state-imposed funding requirements and family sizes. And there were also people in the neighborhood, not usually organized, who wanted only to be left alone. They opposed the New Town but also opposed any attempt to redevelop their building. These individuals made the most of the populist-sounding rhetoric of the movement to charge that the movement's "old guard" had become an invincible, power-hungry oligarchy bowling over the rights of individual citizens. But even here Cedar-Riverside activists developed a thoroughly elaborated ideology codified in the new Urban Renewal Plan: maximizing the participation of affected citizens in planning redevelopment, maintaining low density, preventing unwilling displacement, concentrating on energy-efficient rehabilitation and construction, and promoting racial integration.

The problems of ideological maintenance in the third period reinforce the need for a developed and elaborated ideology to support movement agency. This ideology maintained community support for the New Riverside Cafe, the People's Center, North Country Co-op, the West Bank Co-op Grocery, the Durable Goods collective, and a growing number of other co-ops. The sometimes tense combination of anarchist and socialist principles supported all these organizations in opposition to profit-based production and state-dominated services. But as increasing numbers of the ideologically committed activists moved out of the neighborhood, fewer residents were left who understood, cared about, and acted from those ideological commitments. What remained was more of a populist rhetoric opposing anyone who had power and supporting individual rights at any cost. The vision of community in populism was significantly different from the vision of community sought by the New Left which spearheaded the original opposition to the New Town.

Much has been written lately about populism and community-based movement mobilizations. Populism has been increasingly promoted, centered on the work of Harry Boyte and his collaborators (Boyte, 1980, 1984, 1989; Boyte et al., 1986; Boyte and Riessman, 1986). In its briefest form "populism calls for the return of power to ordinary people" (Boyte, 1986:3). But it is more complex than that. Populism is also based in a conception of community—usually a traditional community—that is threatened by an outside elite (Boyte, 1986). Populism is the belief in the justification of defending a way of life simply because it is a way of life. Beyond that, populism advocates no particular economic or political system except to oppose accumulation of economic or political power that might undermine established communities. Rooted in a defense of traditional values, populism thus acts as an ambiguous ideology that can be adopted by the political right or the left (Riessman, 1986). The right can use populist appeals to oppose housing or educational integration, sex/gender equality, and other progressive reforms. Although these applications undermine the broader intentions of populism for power to *all* the people (Boyte, 1984; Boyte et al., 1986), it is difficult for populism to reconcile the principle of power to all the people with the principle of defense of tradition—especially traditions steeped in racism, sexism, homophobia, and other oppressive and paranoid bigotries (West, 1986; Boggs, 1986). And since populism does not have a developed critique of capitalism as an economic system, and even supports small-scale capitalism, it does not deal effectively with how to prevent the accumulation and centralization of economic power (Boggs, 1986; West, 1986).

The localized movements rising from traditional communities based on populist appeals provide questionable outcomes. The anti-busing movement in Boston, with no conception of the class dynamics of forced busing, practiced a racist appeal (Novack, 1987). Alinsky's Back of the Yards neighborhood also turned to racist populism (Reitzes and Reitzes, 1987). There are numerous other examples of populism gone to the right (Boyte et al., 1986; Fisher, 1984). But even the cases of progressive populism show only small change or status quo maintenance that does not attack structures and cultures of exploitation and domination (Boggs, 1986). Those movements do not point to alternatives or better ways. Though Boyte and his colleagues (1986) believe that the practice of democracy in progressive populism will have progressive consequences that reach beyond the immediate issue to promote democracy generally, the critics remain unconvinced.

In contrast to populism, which resists ideological elaboration in order to integrate with community tradition, is the New Left. New Left activists attempted to create alternative communities consciously, based in alternative values, through their political organizing. This process of prefigurative politics gave life to countercultural ideals, even in such seemingly traditional community organizing projects as the Economic Research Action Project (ERAP). New Left politics was based in a positive utopian vision of what society should be, beyond sexist, racist, and class exploitative traditions. That meant creating new forms of community based on new values and new practices opposed to the accumulation of productive property in private hands, the control of individuals through an alienated bureaucracy, and the domination of some groups by others. It also meant opposing the traditions supporting capitalism, bureaucratic domination, and traditional authority (Breines, 1989). Opposing traditional community was consistent with left perspectives all the way back to Marx, which saw traditional institutions generally as providing a means for supporting capitalist ideological hegemony (Boyte, 1989).

As Wini Breines (1989) notes, many argue that the New Left's attempts to create a community liberated from oppressive traditions not only failed but never could have succeeded. Not least among the critics are the populists, who argue that the New Left's insistence on creating new countercultural institutional forms divorced community from roots and realities and thus could be nothing more than fantasy (Boyte, 1989). But although the New Left disintegrated as a *movement*, its prefigurative politics remained and developed through the women's movement, and sustainable counterculture communities liberated from oppressive traditions did prosper. People have lived the fantasies of progressive, countercultural communities that were anticapitalist, antipatriarchal, and antibureaucratic (Saint-Jean, 1986).

In Cedar-Riverside it was the elaboration of a countercultural leftist ideology that built a community where a less elaborated populist ideology would have at best only helped to stop the New Town. The vision that Cedar-Riverside activists had for their community was opposed to all mainstream American traditions. The American cultural cornerstones of private ownership and private control of housing and commerce were overturned on the West Bank, for both ideological and practical reasons. For example, Cedar-Riverside residents did not believe that traditional homeownership would counter the influences of capitalism in their neighborhood. Activists had watched as Seward, the neighborhood to their south, attempted to redevelop based on a homeownership model.

> As Cedar-Riverside redevelopment was just starting, the Seward neighborhood was just ending. And it provided a real useful example of what could happen if you're not careful. . . . It was done right at the time that middle-class flight from the city was a huge issue. So all the programs were designed to retain working-class and middle-class residents or to invite them back. . . . The problem was, as it got implemented it was right at the start of the back-to-the-city movement. And you had all kinds of people speculating on—pocketing large amounts of public subsidy.   (Jack Cann interview, 1991)

The declining ability of residents in Cedar-Riverside to elaborate this alternative community ideology liberated from tradition was what proved problematic in the third period of the movement. It was the resurgence of a populism promoting traditional conceptions of individual property rights and capitalist accumulation, building on the pressures created by a political opportunity structure that refused to allow residents both to retain community control and to maintain affordability of redevelopment, which disrupted democratic, community-based redevelopment in this period. Those who asserted that they had an inalienable right to stay in their housing, even if it meant that redevelopment in the neighborhood was stymied, saw the PAC as the epitome of accumulated power crushing the common citizen. These members of the Committee for Open Government, or COG, argued that the "socialists" who controlled the PAC were imposing redevelopment on hapless citizens who had no say in the process, and were taking personal gain in the process (Vogel, 1991). The dangers of populist ideology illustrate the importance of providing a more elaborated ideology that emphasizes alternatives to traditionalism.

The first source of agency in Cedar-Riverside, then, was the elaboration of a community ideology that provided a vision for an alternative community, a vision that emphasized mutual obligation and participation and the protection of community housing, commercial resources, and community services from capitalist exploitation. This ideology clearly defined what was wrong with the New Town plan and the process that created it, and what the alternative was. Developing alternatives to traditional models of urban redevelopment required a clear ideology that would serve as a guide to determine whether the community was still on course and to resist the impact of social forces that continued to threaten the neighborhood. Just how clearly alternative that ideology was can be seen in the community institutions that were built from that vision. Cedar-Riverside enacted an alternative vision not only of productive life, but of reproductive life. The New Riverside Cafe, the People's Center, North Country Co-op, the West Bank Co-op Grocery, and the daycare homes created in the last redevelopment phase signify a movement not just believing in an alternative culture, but successfully enacting that culture. The institutional bedrock that was created from the community's alternative culture constitutes the second important source of agency.

Social Reproduction

The way in which a movement community organizes "social reproduction"—how physical and mental health, cooked meals, personal services, education, living conditions, biological reproduction, and childcare are organized (Markusen, 1980)—constitutes the second component of Castell's model of community culture. And of all the facets of social movement culture that have been overlooked by analysts, none has been so thoroughly neglected as social reproduction. The relevance of social reproduction has only recently even become a topic of research in social movement theory. As is the case in much of social science research, "women's work"—all the tasks carried out behind the scenes to care for society's members, work that is unrecognized and unrewarded yet without which society would fall into chaos—has not received its share of attention in social movement research. Only recently have we noticed the crucial role that social reproduction activities play in social movement dynamics (Stoecker, 1992; Taylor and Rupp, 1991).

As analysts have thought about the role of social reproduction in political mobilization, they have begun with the household as the unit of analysis. Households are thought of as mediating "the links between individual behavior and collective action" (Smith and Tardanico, 1987:100). For impoverished African-American women, the establishment of a "homeplace" is the primary source of political resistance (hooks, 1990). But this idea of a domestic sphere as a source of political organizing and political power has been expanded to entire geographically located communities such as neighborhoods. Roberta M. Feldman and Susan Stall (1991) argue that the appropriation of the physical space of urban neighborhoods is in itself an empowering activity that leads to further action. Their research in Wentworth Gardens, a Chicago public housing community, shows how the creation of community-controlled services such as a community-run laundromat provided both resources and a sense of efficacy that led to effective resistance against displacement by the new Comiskey Park, home of the Chicago White Sox baseball team.

Social reproduction is important even beyond the community level. C. G. Pickvance (1977) expands a Marxist analysis of the "social base" of urban dynamics to go beyond the class locations of individuals. A crucial characteristic of the social base here is the social structure of the population itself: networks of kinship and friendship, and institutions not only of work but also of education and religion, among other things. Moving in an even more macro and theoretical direction, Barbara Laslett (1981) argues that society is shaped by both the production of goods and services and the reproduction of people on a daily and generational basis. Within capitalism these two systems are contradictory. Capitalists and workers strive to obtain a "surplus" of resources beyond what is needed to meet their individual daily needs. Capitalists take the surplus in the form of profits. Workers take the surplus in the form of wages to support nonwage-earning family members such as children, the unhealthy, or those who perform the family's social reproduction work. The competing demands for a surplus by workers and capitalists sets up a "struggle over the surplus."

How this struggle is worked out in community settings is where social movement power comes into play. Both capitalists and workers can secure some of their surplus, or reduce their need for a surplus, outside the direct worker-capitalist relationship. Capitalists have become increasingly adept at procuring their surplus through mergers and buyouts. Workers can secure some of their needed surplus through welfare payments or private donations. But perhaps most important, workers can reduce their need for an income surplus to support social reproduction work by reorganizing social reproduction work in the home and in the community. Within the home unpaid domestic labor normally provided by women, such as baking from scratch, sewing family clothes, and hanging the laundry out rather than using the dryer, can reduce the family's social reproduction costs (Hartmann, 1981; Luxton, 1980).

Of course, reducing the family's dependence on capitalists for a family surplus carries a cost in that it reduces the family's discretionary time. Social reproduction work, on average, eats up about fifty-five hours a week for women and eleven hours a week for men and children (Hartmann, 1981). The more time a family must spend on social reproduction labor, the less time it has available for social movement activities. That becomes more problematic as you move down the income ladder, where families are less and less able to purchase social reproduction services and appliances that reduce their time burden. Thus, those who have the most need to mobilize have the least time. When you add the gender imbalance in social reproduction labor, women have even less access to social movement involvement. This problem is often compounded in social movement organizations, where women perform the social reproduction labor for the movement (Sargent, 1981; Evans, 1979) and become stuck in the lowest organizing levels (Lawson and Barton, 1980).

Reorganizing social reproduction at the community level begins to overcome these problems. Within the community, collectivizing social reproduction can dramatically reduce the burdens otherwise placed on individuals and provide a source of community integration. It can also eliminate the isolation of those who would normally provide social reproduction services alone and reduce the total expenditure of resources on social reproduction activities. Such a reorganization, however, requires that communities carefully develop an alternative ideology to support the shift to collectivized social reproduction. As social movement activists recognize the role social reproduction plays in the lives of their constituents, they become aware of the need to incorporate social reproduction issues into movement mobilization. How social movements take on these issues affects four facets of movement activity: goal formation, structure, member recruitment, and tactical strategy.

Analysts studying the new social movements are increasingly pointing to crises in social reproduction as providing the justification for the goals of those movements (Touraine, 1988; Klandermans, 1986). Movements for environmental protection, health care, reduction of nuclear weapons and power generation, animal rights, and other issues arise directly from threats to people's ability to provide for their own social reproduction. Manuel Castells (1977, 1978, 1983) expanded this perspective to urban social movements, showing that a local community's ability to reproduce itself *culturally* involved its ability to provide for the social reproduction of its members, an ability that was increasingly threatened in the modern city. Counter-culture movements were explicitly concerned with developing new forms of social reproduction—alternative family structures, intimate relationships, sexualities, and provision of basic services such as food, housing, and health care—as central movement goals.

The Cedar-Riverside neighborhood movement clearly began as a new social movement, arising, like other such movements, from a base of the 1960s civil rights, antiwar, and student movements (Cohen, 1985). Its goals were directed not at the outside world, as in the more political movements of the 1960s, but at developing and defending an alternative community against the outside world. The community organizations that sprang up in the early 1970s, especially the People's Center and the New Riverside Cafe, reflected the movement's social reproduction goals. Organizations such as the Cafe, People's Pantry, the People's Center, and individual communes, however, were created not only to meet residents' social reproduction needs, but also to *collectivize* those reproductive needs. These activities brought residents together to build a strong community base out of which more outward-directed political activity could develop.

> And as an organizing strategy, we knew that we had to provide medical care and co-op food stores as a way of keeping the neighborhood together. . . . So in the context of opposition, or defensive adaptation, or however you want to characterize it, of hostile, aggressive, anti-developer, anti-governmental authority community organizing, there was a base of service and food underneath that it was building on.   (Steve Parliament interview, 1991)

Social reproduction goals also figured prominently in the outward-directed activities of the movement. CREDF's environmental impact statement lawsuit focused on the "unhealthy family environment" that would be created by high-density, high-rise housing. PAC formulation of a new urban renewal plan emphasized the importance of low-density housing and open space for child development and family living, and CDC plans that grew out of this process reflected that goal. Though this conventional-sounding position was partly pragmatic strategy on the movement's part, there was a strong belief among activists that low-density living was more healthy. The Tenants Union existed because of one of the most basic social reproduction goals: preserving low-cost housing.

Social reproduction goals clearly provided the impetus for the

Cedar-Riverside neighborhood movement. Intriguingly, however, those goals had to shift from proactive in the early period of the movement, when the People's Center and New Riverside Cafe formed, to reactive in the middle of the movement's history, as the neighborhood had actively to protect its very existence by creating defensive organizations, to proactive again, most recently as the housing co-ops formed. The solid community base that was established through those early alternative social reproduction activities was necessary for the ultimately successful mobilization against the New Town plan. The erosion of those social reproduction activities and of the community base was at least partly responsible for the conflict that erupted as the movement implemented democratic community-based redevelopment.

As social reproduction goals develop, they also inform the development of movement structure. Normally, we consider movements to be of the single-issue variety, such as the movement to stop the Vietnam war or women's rights movement. But as more movements organize around social reproduction goals, they find common ground that may otherwise be invisible. The Citizens' Clearinghouse for Hazardous Wastes, Inc. (1989), explicitly linked its issues with the 1989 HOUSING NOW! mobilization, asserting that "some people, especially those whose homes are contaminated by pesticides, *have* abandoned those homes and become homeless." Animal-rights activists and feminists are also beginning to link their movement goals, seeing the treatment of animals as objects as parallel to the treatment of women as objects and connected to a common patriarchal belief system (Sanbonmatsu, 1989). An isolated community movement, then, need not be so isolated if it joins other movement organizations with related social reproduction issues.

The Cedar-Riverside neighborhood movement produced its own movement structure based on related social reproduction goals: affordable housing (the CDC), community-controlled housing and commerce (the PAC), macrobiotics (the New Riverside Cafe), community-controlled medicine (the People's Center), and environmental protection (CREDF). With the elaboration of the federated front-stage structure, in which the multiple organizations were all backed by a single unified membership, the movement was provided with maximum flexibility to pursue each goal. The Cedar-Riverside movement is a localized example of what happens when movements link social reproduction goals. The movement was able to stop the New Town plan only because all the residents simultaneously supported all the social reproduction goals and backed all the neighborhood organizations. If only the environmentalists had backed CREDF, and health activists had backed the People's Center, and so on, there would have been desperate resource shortages, interorganizational conflict, and ultimately failure.

Perhaps the most important role played by social reproduction in affecting social movements is in the area of recruitment. Social movements have to compete with family obligations for members' involvement, and it is often family commitments that prevent people from being involved (Walsh and Warland, 1983). This competition is much less of a problem if the movement can attract members who have enough income that they can buy social reproduction services, have less need for social reproduction services, or have more time. Individuals with flexible work schedules and singles, for example, have greater "biographical availability" for movement activities (McAdam, 1986). But more often than not the social movement constituency lacks those advantages. In this situation people cannot become involved unless the movement can ease their social reproduction burden. Collectivizing childcare and other domestic labor through the social movement can attract recruits to the services at the same time that it allows them to participate in movement activities because those services are available (Markusen, 1980). Thus, providing social reproduction services through the movement both removes barriers to involvement and provides incentives to become involved.

The Cedar-Riverside neighborhood movement's highly developed social reproduction goals had a profound impact on movement recruitment. The collectivization of reproductive needs in the early phase of the neighborhood movement greatly eased the reproductive burdens of individuals, providing food, clothing, shelter, and time. Collectivizing social reproduction needs built on the new residents' ideology of voluntary poverty and the fat economy of the time. Cheap rents, cheap heat, cheap food, free health care, and free childcare were available. Between one-third and one-half of the residents were living communally by the early 1970s, allowing them to collectivize childcare, home maintenance, meal preparation, and bill paying to accumulate more readily the "family surplus" to which Laslett (1981) refers. The New Riverside Cafe also reduced residents' reproductive costs and provided a gathering spot as "the West Bank's living room." Most residents worked less than full time and many made what income they needed by playing music or selling arts, crafts, or drugs. Some single mothers in the neighborhood received AFDC payments. Other residents worked at the People's Center, the neighborhood's open school, neighborhood bars, or other small neighborhood businesses. The beer boogies, open school, commercial co-ops, and other neighborhood services continually brought residents together, reinforced alternative values and practices, and cemented the community networks and identity that enhance recruitment to social movements (Freeman, 1983a; Wandersman et al., 1987).

The importance of the social reproduction *organizations* such as the New Riverside Cafe, the People's Center, and the food co-ops became even more crucial for recruitment in the second phase. By the late 1970s the neighborhood movement's informal reproduction strategies of communes, taking in strangers, and sharing automobiles, kitchen utensils, and drugs had diminished greatly. Activists had for the most part finished college, their children were growing up, and their material demands were increasing at the same time as the economy made it more difficult to live off "the fat of the land." The 1975 co-op wars between the commercial co-ops and the Stalinist Co-op Organization also reduced the trust levels between political factions. And communal living produced its own tensions. One activist mentioned, "It was a relief to live by myself again. One of the things you give up [living communally] is privacy." Parents also wanted to develop a different relationship with their children: living communally "bothered me as a parent. My daughter didn't have a sense of being mine" (Dorothy Jacobs interview, 1988). Thus, recruitment networks were held together formally through gatherings at the People's Center, the New Riverside Cafe, and other neighborhood services rather than in homes, which increasingly housed more nuclear families than communal groups. But the movement still maintained its sense of community, especially in times of crisis. In the midst of the Tenants Union's last and most wearing rent strike, when all the organizers were preparing for demonstrations and court appearances, one of the organizers, Brian Coyle, was nowhere to be found.

And Brian wasn't around, and I said, "Son of a bitch. Where is he? He hasn't called in or anything yet." And I went out to dinner with my girlfriend at the time and got back for the mass meeting. Brian wasn't around, and where is he? We're partners in this! Right in the middle of the meeting he comes in with this great big cake with the Tenants Union symbol on it and "Happy Birthday Tim" and, of course, that's what he's been doing all day. (Tim Ogren interview, 1991)

Maintaining the community through the ties provided by social reproduction activities became even more difficult after the New Town was defeated. Fewer social reproduction organizations were reserved exclusively for the community, as businesses such as the New Riverside Cafe attracted more and more clientele from outside the neighborhood, at least half the old neighborhood population turned over, and the steadily increasing cost of living all affected recruitment. Residents were more often working full time outside the neighborhood. In contrast to the first and second periods, neighbors were less likely to meet each other through their work; through collective living, cooking, and childcare; through neighborhood meetings; and through time not spent in wage work. New residents were more isolated from old residents and from one another, and the New Riverside Cafe and food co-ops were less able to compete financially with discount chains that new residents did not find so politically distasteful. The People's Center continued to provide sliding-fee health care, and shared childcare remained available in some parts of the neighborhood, but funding for these activities became tenuous. Even old residents had problems making ends meet as they sent their children to college, paid more for their homes, bought their own cars to get to work, and desired greater economic security. As a result, people had less time for meetings and organizing.

Finally, social reproduction activities become part of a movement's tactical strategy. Organizing a movement to provide social reproduction sustains not only the movement but the community as well. Those social reproduction activities create a community culture that can be increasingly independent from outside influence, creating community "safe spaces" (Hartsock, 1979) or "free spaces" (Evans and Boyte, 1986). They also produce resources for the movement both in terms of membership and in terms of freeing up financial resources that would otherwise go to services provided outside the movement community. Social reproduction activities themselves can become political tactics. Women in the Chilean resistance movement constructed *arpilleras*, pieces of material sewn together to depict scenes of poverty, repression, and resistance. They exhibited and sold the *arpilleras* both to raise consciousness and to earn income (Moya-Raggio, 1984). Similarly, the Boise Peace Quilt Project (1987) has produced quilts depicting scenes of the costs of nuclear war and has displayed those quilts worldwide.

Social reproduction activities became central to the neighborhood movement's tactical strategy. In almost every case such activities were also political education, partly because the neighborhood had to fight to create many of its social reproduction services. The People's Center was established after a struggle with the University of Minnesota, which owned the building where the center was located. The New Riverside Cafe was moved down the street when the university leveled its first location for a parking lot, and the neighborhood's vocal protest forced the university to persuade CRA to rent the Cafe a new space—making the Cafe a CRA tenant just like the neighborhood residents. The commercial co-ops provided invaluable education in government regulations and economic self-management. The New Riverside Cafe, by serving as a gathering spot, used social reproduction as an organizing strategy. And all the residents were continually educated in the practices and values of a total life-style alternative. The focus on social reproduction in the movement, and its use of social reproduction tactics to educate, organize, and mobilize, also helped bring women to leadership positions in the open school, the commercial co-ops, the People's Center, and ultimately in the Minneapolis City Council.

The agency created by carefully organizing community social reproduction is demonstrated by the contradictory outcomes of the movement's third period. In this period the movement had increasing difficulty collectivizing social reproduction. For one thing, there were fewer community-building events just when they became most necessary because of the tensions created by disagreement over the redevelopment goals and the growing isolation of residents. Some new residents were poor, single women with children and had difficulties obtaining a family surplus, making them much less mobilizable. The ideological, cultural, and educational differences between old and new residents set up a problematic cycle: the differences created a lack of trust, the lack of trust prevented residents from getting together, and so on. The increasing involvement of young women leaders during this phase also fueled conflict as they saw themselves emphasizing the process of maximizing participatory decision making while they believed their male counterparts emphasized getting to the "product" of actual housing redevelopment.

From Movement Culture to Movement Structure

We have seen the unifying qualities of a highly elaborated and autonomous movement community culture, especially when that cultural elaboration extends to social reproduction activities. We have also seen the importance of countercultural values and practices in defining a sustainable urban community based on making the most of scarce resources through using participatory practices. These values and practices helped residents define exactly what they wanted their neighborhood to be and helped provide resources for the struggle. The Cedar-Riverside neighborhood movement was neither initially nor primarily a defensive movement. The young residents of Cedar-Riverside were intent on building a community from scratch, based in a critique of and an attempt to improve on the communities in which they had grown up.

Finally, the neighborhood ideology and social reproduction base had to be implemented through an *organized* social movement. It is at this point that the community begins to develop the political self-management component of Castells's (1983) model. Political self-management, especially when the community is being threatened from the outside, requires a level of organization beyond what can be provided by the informal networks created by social reproduction activities or even a highly developed ideology (Davis, 1991). The need for a more developed organizational structure is illustrated by the early movement structure's primary focus on social reproduction activities—with the single exception of the Community Union—and the failure of that structure to solve the recruitment, organizing, and tactical dilemmas to make the most of the structural weaknesses of the growth machine and prevent the construction of Cedar Square West.

It was in the second period of the movement, as CREDF, the Tenants Union, the PAC, and the CDC developed, that we can see the effect of a sophisticated movement structure. The federated frontstage structure, in which a single membership operated behind multiple organizational fronts, allowed the community to maintain unity while maximizing its ability to recruit participants, organize action, and implement tactics. But that organization structure could not have succeeded without an elaborate community ideology to bind members and a densely networked community social structure that inhibited factionalism. The collectivized social reproduction services provided through neighborhood organizations and activities created "multiplex relations," allowing people to interact in several different roles and contexts and establishing strong, broad, and deep community relationships (Pickvance, 1977).

And in the third period of the movement the strong community ideology that insisted on affordable housing and community control, prevented an imperfect organizational structure from having an even more destructive impact on democratic community-based redevelopment than had already occurred. The goals of community control and affordable housing were not contradictory in and of themselves. They were only *materially* contradictory within a political opportunity structure that took resources from one as it increased resources to the other. As the movement structure became more segmented, there was no longer a single constituency but, competing constituencies. And the goals and constituencies became separated into the PAC, which emphasized community control, and the CDC, which emphasized affordable housing. But the process of separation was gradual, and never total. The strength of the guiding ideology held the community together enough to finish the redevelopment.

Movement Structure, Movement Community, and Movement Agency

The evolving movement structure in Cedar-Riverside—from a base of social reproduction organizations to a sophisticated federated frontstage structure to a more segmented and fractured organization base—reflected a changing community. The movement structure of the first period reflected a community still forming and consciously guiding its formation. The second period's movement structure could exist only with a strong, unified community backstage. The movement structure in the third period shows what happens when community unity breaks down.

Throughout the history of the Cedar-Riverside neighborhood movement, then, community and movement were inextricably intertwined. Even in the third period, when the community began to factionalize, its institutions and movement organizations still provided reference points to remind residents what their neighborhood was all about and to hold the movement together to finish redevelopment. As the movement organizations withered away or lost their funding, something was still left underneath:

> The People's Center might go under. . . . We could lose that as a neighborhood resource. But we lost Dania Hall as a neighborhood resource twenty-five years ago, and the neighborhood survived. We think some things are linchpins or clothespins that hold the clothes on the line, like the PAC at this time, but maybe it's the legacy that keeps it on when those pins are gone. I don't think people can put this amount of energy in it and not leave a legacy—a mythology. (Ogren interview, 1991)

What remains of the community is its legacy—a legacy that is daily transformed and extended by new residents, new patrons at the New Riverside Cafe, new students seeking an alternative to alienated life. On its surface the community appears much more normal, much more average, much more typical than before. Perhaps that is its greatest sign of success. Many of the alternatives that seemed so outlandish and required so much careful ideological justification two decades ago have become the neighborhood's institutional base. The neighborhood seems so natural that its continuing alternative character goes nearly unnoticed.

Conclusion: Movement Community and Movement Agency in the Localized Social Movement

The sources of agency open to social movements—movement culture and movement structure—allow for more than a last-ditch response to apparently omnipotent political opportunity structures. Solidly developed and highly elaborated movement cultures that make seemingly outlandish demands can achieve a great deal. Cedar-Riverside activists brought down a solid growth coalition and demanded that urban redevelopment in their neighborhood be controlled by a grassroots community seen by the outside as a bunch of radicals, hippies, and freaks. But within that community there was a great deal of talent, vision, and knowledge that went into the movement's strategy.

In the first period it was countercultural vision that realized the New Riverside Cafe and the People's Center and that protected them from urban removal with very few resources. The strength of the community in bringing out large numbers to defend those institutions coerced advantageous arrangements with the University of Minnesota and Cedar-Riverside Associates. In the second period it was an innovative movement structure that was able to exploit fissures in the growth coalition through custom-designed organizations that stopped the New Town. And in the third period it was the community vision and the movement's ability to hold the course in unstable political seas that completed neighborhood redevelopment.

But the movement's agency was not total. Cedar Square West, now Riverside Plaza, still destroyed four blocks of the neighborhood, still cannot be organized as a community, and still is the source of many of the neighborhood's remaining problems. And the community relationships that were the basis for the movement, the source of the alternative, were strained in many cases to the breaking point in the third period. A clearer understanding of the roots of community tensions in the contradiction between affordable housing and community control, combined with a greater selectivity in bringing new residents into the neighborhood and more attention to the need to continue community organizing activities, would have helped prevent some of the community's disintegration. But other conflicts might have arisen. Adopting stricter guidelines for bringing new residents into the co-ops would have been seen by some as politically exclusionary or even racist. And continuing community organizing at the same level of skill that had been practiced in the neighborhood would have taken resources that were not readily available, requiring major shifts in the movement's structure. Ultimately, the problems of the third period were in the political opportunity structure, whose limits I explore in the next chapter.

What does Cedar-Riverside teach us about attempts to expand movement agency? By studying Cedar-Riverside, we learn a great deal about the unique qualities of a localized community movement. Although the national movements of the 1960s and 1970s had many of the community qualities of localized community movements, ideology and social reproduction exert a much more central role when the movement *is* the community. You can go home from a women's movement demonstration to a town or neighborhood that is perhaps sympathetic to the movement but is not often identified with it. In Cedar-Riverside, and in localized movements overall, the movement is home, and taking care of the community is also taking care of the movement. This reality has a unique influence on movement dynamics.

In attempting to understand agency for the localized social movement, we first see the importance of a developed ideology. A localized movement cannot simply organize for power, as Alinsky (1969, 1971) advocated. It must develop ideology, or culture, within the movement community to address sexism, racism, and other forms of illegitimate power that can be pervasive in movements avoiding ideology (Stein, 1986). This form of ideology is beyond populism and opposed to tradition, even its own traditions. Ideology in Cedar-Riverside was continually under discussion, even through the third period, when activists, as their children moved away from home and their incomes rose, increasingly supported housing for singles and those with higher incomes. But the core ideology—for community control, participatory planning, low densities, affordability, insulation from capitalist markets, and no displacement—remained stable from the beginnings of the struggle against the New Town through the completion of housing redevelopment. The importance of an educated and politically informed ideology as a source of community cohesion and a guide for political action cannot be overestimated.

Another thing we learn about localized social movement agency is the importance of providing for the social reproduction of the movement constituency. When ideology and social reproduction combine in a movement constituency, a movement *community* forms—no longer a group of isolated individuals, but a group of people who share a common culture and care for one another. Even the most well known recent national social movements—the civil rights movement, the student movement, the women's movement, and neighborhood movements—have been, to a large extent, *based* in communities. Members of these movements have done more than protest together. They have been neighbors, roommates, friends, lovers. They have been community members.

The third thing we learn about movement agency is how advantages are provided by a social movement structure that "fits" the political opportunity structure and how problems are created by a structure that does not fit. When judging the effectiveness of a movement's structure, we must take into account the extent to which the structure helps the movement engage in recruitment, organizing, and tactics that produce success in its particular political opportunity structure. In the case of a localized movement, that means we must take into account the geographic limitations on the movement's resource base. For localized movements, where there is only one issue and only one target, a centralized structure may work best. But those situations are rare. Where there are plentiful resources, diverse issues, and a large and diverse constituency, a DSR structure (or perhaps an umbrella structure if there is one overriding issue) inhibits factioning and allows strategic flexibility. But in cases where movements are isolated, are resource-poor, and must focus on multiple targets, and where core groups have time to maintain commitment, the federated frontstage structure likely offers the greatest advantage. This structure, which provides for highly specialized organizations to match the threats and resources in the political opportunity structure and is backed by a single unified membership, overcomes the limitations of the more well known movement structural models.

We must ask, however, whether Cedar-Riverside is somehow unique. Can other neighborhood movements be as successful in developing an alternative ideology, collectivizing social reproduction, and constructing unique movement structures as Cedar-Riverside? Can other neighborhoods then go on to create democratic community-based urban redevelopment that preserves the community and the rights of its citizens? The answer, as we see in the next chapter, is a hesitant yes, and the biggest barrier to a resounding yes is the political opportunity structure.

The Limits and the Potential of Community Control of Urban Redevelopment

Urban renewal has worsened the housing shortage and racial tensions. The overpaving of cities with expressways has fouled the air, destroyed communities, taxed our energy resources. The subsidy of housing has enriched builders and bankers but scarcely begins to meet the stated goal: decent, safe, sanitary housing for all. The attempts by government, from the White House to City Hall, to lessen racial antagonism have been so half-heartedly implemented that racist resistance to compliance with the laws of the land is encouraged. . . . The conventional analysis, which argues that the problem could be solved if one would but make the market work a bit better, seems as bankrupt as many of the older cities themselves. Everywhere the cry is heard for a new approach.
—*William Tabb and Larry Sawers*,
Marxism and the Metropolis

Success in Cedar-Riverside: Imaginary or Inevitable?

Both inside and outside the neighborhood there are those who argue that Cedar-Riverside was not all that successful in providing a positive exception to the miserable record of urban renewal. They point, first, to the failure of the neighborhood to stop the construction of Cedar Square West. They also point to the continuing encroachment of the educational and medical institutions: hospitals demolished housing for parking ramps, and Augsburg College did the same for parking lots and a campus building. Finally, they note the problems the newly created housing co-ops are experiencing in attempting to organize their members and purchase their buildings. The goals of the neighborhood movement—to develop affordable, community-controlled housing—have not been met to neighborhood activists' satisfaction. We have seen that, as a relatively homogeneous community is replaced by an increasingly diverse mixture of races, incomes, and political persuasions, the problem of maintaining "community control" has also become a problem of maintaining "community."

Some activists argue that the most successful period of the neighborhood movement was the early community-building phase. Residents practiced the most developed alternative lifestyles, the co-ops operated on a "pay what you can" basis, and residents lived and raised their children communally. The neighborhood movement succeeded wonderfully in creating a "community" in the fullest sense.

These activists also claim that, although the neighborhood movement stopped the New Town in Town during the second period, the community also began to splinter. There was not as much trust, not as much neighboring, more individualism, and more factioning. By the third period, in the 1980s, exlovers, excommunal partners, and expolitical allies began to take their frustrations out on one another.

Some neighborhood activists also argue that Keith Heller's scheme was a financial house of cards and would have come crashing down with or without neighborhood opposition. The city was desperate to do something to upgrade the image of the area, and the neighborhood did the planning work that the city would have done anyway. The argument concludes that the neighborhood movement just used up a lot of energy to reach an already determined outcome. In view of the restrictions imposed on the housing co-ops that forced the community to trade off affordability and control, it appears that the development that occurred in the neighborhood was the only development that could have occurred. This interpretation fits Frances Fox Piven and Richard Cloward's (1979:36) contention that "protesters win, if they win at all, what historical circumstances ha[ve] already made available to be conceded."

Is success in Cedar-Riverside imaginary? Does the loss of community cancel the victory of stopping the New Town in Town and creating affordable, low-density redevelopment? Or was success inevitable? Did the New Town collapse under its own economic weight with the city unloading the problem onto the neighborhood? And finally, even if there was real success in Cedar-Riverside, was the neighborhood so unique that we are unable to learn anything of use from its experience? In this chapter I explore these questions, looking at the limits imposed on Cedar-Riverside from the outside and the potential for generalizing the Cedar-Riverside experience to other neighborhoods under seige.

Did Cedar-Riverside Win?

Defining what success is for a community-based social movement, or indeed, for any social movement, is itself problematic. The topic is sorely understudied, and the measures of success include a wide range of variables (Weinberg, 1992). The most obvious standard for measuring success is, of course, achievement of movement goals (Gamson, 1975). But what does that mean? How much goal achievement is necessary to count as success? How long should it take to achieve those goals, and how indirect can the causal chain be? For example, does policy change that comes after the demise of the movement pushing for it (Goldstone, 1980; Killian, 1964) count as success? But even beyond the movement's own goals, should minor victories be considered success? Can we count ideological changes in the culture, or should only major structural changes be labeled success (Weinberg, 1992)?

Perhaps the most useful definition of social movement success comes from Sidney Tarrow (1983:5), who argues that evidence of success is "the unfolding of a process of policy innovation in the political system addressing the protestors' stated needs, if not their actual programs." To be more specific, this evidence includes changes in the *process* of policy development which increase the influence of the social movement constituency, and changes in the *substance* of policy outcomes which move toward meeting the needs of the movement's constituency. This process develops over time and can also disintegrate over time: the longer the impact lasts, the greater the success. Its extreme form is, of course, social revolution, but lesser forms exist as institutionalized citizen-participation mechanisms.

This argument does not mean that *any* changes in decision-making processes or in decisions necessarily provide for a more just distribution of material and political resources. Social movement collectivities can miscalculate the diverse consequences of their actions. They may, for example, actually serve to perpetuate inequality and domination by becoming incorporated into the political process, thereby rendered "harmless" (Mayer, n.d.; Gamson, 1975). The social movement's constituency may receive resources or power, but at the expense of other groups that have no state representation. We must distinguish between achievement of policy substance or process outcomes and achievement of progressive political change that actually results in more just distributions of power and wealth or heightened capacities to pursue such goals further.

Thus, protest movements may achieve *degrees of success*: from meeting their goals partially and producing minor progressive redistributions of power and wealth, to creating more change than they had intended. Movements may also succeed at one point in time only to watch those successes rolled back later on. A historical perspective is essential.

Employing the definition of success that emphasizes changes in policy substance and process reflecting social movement goals that have a long-term impact, we see that the Cedar-Riverside neighborhood movement had some rather significant successes. The community did indeed stop the remaining stages of the New Town in Town. It lost the first round, when Cedar Square West was constructed, but the next nine stages never got past the architect. Cedar-Riverside Associates probably would have gone bankrupt anyway, but local state managers, neighborhood activists, and members of the CRA staff believe that the project would have continued at least through Stage II and probably the Centrum, which the MHRA had approved. That would have meant destroying more housing, thus forcing activists out of the neighborhood, threatening community-based institutions, and perhaps leading to pressure to build the next stage to increase the population enough to support the Centrum mall. The other possibility is that, if CRA had stayed afloat through two or three more stages, the local state managers might have felt more compelled to bail out the project.

It is also important to note that the New Town in Town did not fail just because it caved in financially. The neighborhood movement's successful use of the new Environmental Protection Act also defined the project as environmentally unsound. If the neighborhood movement, through CREDF, had not brought the environmental impact statement lawsuit against the project, but had allowed the project to tumble financially, the city or another private developer could have simply picked up where CRA left off.

And would the city have scaled down the densities in the neighborhood without movement pressure? Probably not. The long struggle of local capitalists, City Hall, and the neighborhood movement over the new urban renewal plan showed how much both City Hall and local growth-oriented capital wanted higher densities than the residents wanted. A compromise was struck, with Seven Corners being reserved for medium high densities and the rest of the neighborhood for low densities.

In stopping the New Town, the residents also altered the *process* of urban renewal planning. In place of the top-down, capital-conscious planning that created the megadensity urban renewal plan of the 1960s, the residents instituted democratic, community-based planning that resulted in the passage of a very different urban renewal plan. The maximum densities of the new plan were the minimum densities of the old plan, and the new plan also protected residents from involuntary displacement, which was part and parcel of the old plan. And residents participated in the design and redevelopment of their housing, a complete reversal of the New Town in Town process. Moreover, the success of the movement in preserving the New Riverside Cafe and the People's Center from university expansion and in preserving some housing from Augsburg expansion makes it clear that the result is much better than the worst-case scenario.

Certainly, the loss of community is important in judging the degree of success of the Cedar-Riverside neighborhood movement, since defending and maintaining the community was one of the movement's goals. But how great was this loss and when did it occur? Although the greatest sense of community probably occurred in the first phase, it also existed in the second phase. Neighborhood movement success in stopping the New Town in Town could not have occurred without a strong community to unify the residents behind the federated front-stage structure in the second phase. But a strong community, by itself, would not have been enough to stop the New Town in Town before the plan did more damage to the neighborhood. Therefore, the decline of community is not a sign of failure as much as a sign of a social movement problem, a problem that reflects the social movement organizing dilemma. Community decline may lead to failure, since it may affect the process of community decision making by disabling community control. But that has not happened yet in Cedar-Riverside.

Success in Cedar-Riverside, then, is neither static nor either-or. Success, first of all, must be achieved and then maintained. The city government could still try to roll back changes in the urban renewal plan to create more high-density housing in the future. Without tender loving care, the co-ops could fail organizationally and/or financially. The neighborhood movement has won some and lost some, though its success in stopping the New Town in Town and in creating community-based housing argues for much more success than failure, up to now. Ultimately, the outcomes are contradictory. The community achieved tremendous success in creating affordable, democratic community-based redevelopment, but it failed to maintain the community social fabric.

Can Communities Always Win?

Can small communities, threatened with destruction either through disinvestment or through top-down, displacement-based urban renewal, beat the odds? The story of Cedar-Riverside shows they can. But victory for community movements is not easy. Urban political opportunity structures are organized to cater to capital—those who control profit-generating property (the rentier class) or the means of production (the capitalist class) (Logan and Molotch, 1987). The political opportunity structure, set into motion by the demands and contradictions of a capitalist economy, provides for only limited access by the powerless and propertyless. Those without property or power are rarely if ever invited to participate as equals in the policy-making process, and few if any structural mechanisms force policy makers to accept the participation of those groups. The economic leverage of the owners of property and production in the city forces policy makers to take into account the interests of these power holders even when they do not participate in the policy-making process (Molotch, 1979; Friedland, 1983). As Piven and Cloward (1979) have argued, sometimes the only option the excluded have is to withdraw their compliance, disrupting business as usual and using the elite's need for their compliance as a bargaining chip. In contrast to Piven and Cloward's pessimism about the exclusion of those groups from policy making, however, Cedar-Riverside shows that those groups can demand, and obtain, real and substantial influence over urban policy making.

But those communities do not always win. There is more than one story about communities that have failed to resist urban removal (Henig, 1982; Wylie, 1989; Gans, 1982 [1962]). And even Cedar-Riverside's success is not unqualified. The loss of four blocks of housing to Cedar Square West in the first period and the unraveling of community in the third period of the movement show the limits of community agency. But how do we understand those limits? Can we define the restrictions the political opportunity structure places on neighborhood movements struggling against displacement or for community-based redevelopment?

Capital, through its influence on the political opportunity structure, imposes limits on communities attempting to exert control over their fate. Communities can make significant strides in improving their social and physical environment, but ultimately they come up against the wall of capital. We first explore community defense movements, looking briefly at the Poletown case to understand the role of movement agency versus structural constraints in saving Cedar-Riverside and destroying Poletown. Then we shift focus to look at community development movements, using the example of Los Angeles's Route 2 community-based development project. Much of the danger in neighborhood-based mobilization hinges on a subtle shift within those movements from community organizing goals to community development goals, a shift encouraged by the political opportunity structure and a clear illustration of the dialectical nature of movement–political opportunity structure interaction.

Defending the Community: Against All Odds?

Sometimes the odds are too great. In those cases even the best efforts of the movement are unable to overcome the constraints imposed by the political opportunity structure. In the worst-case scenario, where the political opportunity structure is virtually inaccessible, alliances are lined up against the movement, and there is a great deal of political stability, even the most sophisticated movement likely faces failure. That appeared to be the case in Cedar-Riverside in the early period. As a small neighborhood with limited access to city government, few allies, and little sign that anything would change, West Bankers watched concrete rise out of the west side of the neighborhood. But Cedar-Riverside activists did discover vulnerabilities: a new and relatively undefined environmental impact statement requirement and a shaky financial base undergirding the New Town project.

One could take this outcome to indicate that even the worst-case political opportunity structure is not that bad and is in fact a sign that the system works. But we should not jump to such a hasty conclusion. Yes, communities can often prevail to stop a project that threatens them, but even in the case of Cedar-Riverside, success did not occur until residents went outside the system and its rules. The mass demonstration at the New Town dedication ceremony, the occupations of CRA's offices, the Tenants Union's rent strikes whose legality had to be decided by the Minnesota Supreme Court all showed that the system does not work.

And the worst-case political opportunity structure in Cedar-Riverside was only worst-case in a relative sense. When the forces of capital and the state rally together, there is virtually nothing a community can do to defend itself. Such a result was recorded in Poletown.

Poletown was a 465-acre Detroit neighborhood of 4,200 residents, bounded by railroad tracks and the Interstate 94 freeway (which, incidentally, also serves as Cedar-Riverside's southern boundary more than seven hundred miles away). A community of predominantly Polish and African-American residents, the neighborhood was wiped out by the City of Detroit and General Motors in 1980–81 for a Cadillac plant. The destruction of the neighborhood was accomplished with the complicity and, indeed, the blessing of the Detroit Catholic Archdiocese, the City of Detroit, and the United Auto Workers. The archdiocese removed Polish priest and neighborhood leader Father Joseph Karasiewicz from his neighborhood church and then sold the church to demolition. The United Auto Workers went door-to-door lobbying for the Cadillac plant and refused to support any criticism from residents. And the City of Detroit cleared the neighborhood site over the course of a single year. Even the traditional left, with the brief exception of the Workers' League, at best remained quiet, partly opposed to organizing on a community, as opposed to workplace, basis. Partly, they were not attracted by Poletown's populist, rather than socialist, appeal. Other community organizations, fearing antagonizing the archdiocese, Detroit city government, or General Motors, also stayed out of the fray (Wylie, 1989).

Poletown residents, with the aid of Ralph Nader's legal staff, filed lawsuit after lawsuit. They challenged the environmental impact statement that had been expedited specifically for the GM plant, the "quick take" condemnation law that allowed the City of Detroit to condemn and claim property with minimal administrative review, the "public purpose" requirements for that condemnation, and other factors. Their legal challenges moved all the way up through the Michigan Supreme Court, and all ended in failure in terms of the ultimate decision and even in their ability to delay the destruction of Poletown. Part of the failure of the lawsuits was due to the continuing deterioration of the neighborhood during the process. When the Detroit Archdiocese sold the Immaculate Conception Church—the pillar of the community—much of the argument behind the legal challenge became irrelevant. So resistant was GM to any impact from Poletown residents that the corporation refused even to consider a series of alternative proposals from resident-sponsored planners that would have preserved the majority of the neighborhood (Wylie, 1989; Clark and Dear, 1984).

In understanding how Poletown was crushed while Cedar-Riverside prevailed, we must first look at the different political opportunity structures the movements confronted. Poletown faced one of the world's strongest multinational corporations, which was promising thousands of union jobs to one of the country's most economically devastated rustbelt cities. GM could go literally anywhere to build cars, and Detroit and the UAW knew it. Cedar-Riverside faced a local developer, albeit a well-connected one. Cedar-Riverside Associates was not promising a hefty increase in long-term employment that would draw heavy union support. And the City of Minneapolis was not economically desperate enough to lunge at any urban redevelopment scheme regardless of the costs. In Minneapolis the political alliances supporting CRA were consequently much more volatile than in Detroit, and the neighborhood had access to allies such as unions and other neighborhoods. The Cedar-Riverside PAC and CDC staffs went so far as to unionize and to make certain that Snoose News was printed in a union shop. Moreover, in Detroit the City Council was then composed of only eight members, all elected at large in a city of a million people. Only council member Ken Cockrel remained a solid ally of Poletown (Wylie, 1989). Minneapolis's thirteen-member council, elected by districts in a city of under four hundred thousand, afforded dramatically greater representation. And the Poletown GM plant was developed with direct collaboration between the local state and capital, as the local state exerted its heavy hand in condemning the neighborhood housing. In Cedar-Riverside the local state remained at arm's length, becoming involved only in approving the original plan and providing some bail-out money. State participation at both the local and national levels was passive rather than active.

Fate played a role in the different outcomes as well. Poletown's legal challenges were thwarted at every turn by unsympathetic judges. Residents could achieve neither significant legal victories nor even significant delays. Cedar-Riverside received the support of sympathetic judges, particularly Federal Circuit Court Judge Miles Lord. Cedar-Riverside also had history on its side. At the time of CREDF's environmental impact statement suit, the Environmental Protection Act and the process for compiling an impact statement were still relatively undefined. Without precedents from a substantial amount of case law, the courts had to be cautious. A decade later Poletown faced a much more sophisticated growth coalition that knew the environmental ropes, and the courts had much more case law to work from. Additionally, the condemnation law had just been streamlined by the State of Michigan, leaving even less to chance.

It is also important to recognize, however, that Poletown was not made of the same political cloth as Cedar-Riverside. A more diverse, more traditional neighborhood, Poletown residents were not used to challenging the powerful and did not have experience with thinking about or building an alternative political system that would be more participatory. The Poletown Neighborhood Council seems to have quickly turned oligarchical, with a powerful central leader who, it appeared, was as interested in protecting his own status as he was in protecting the neighborhood. The disputes between the Poletown Neighborhood Council president and Ralph Nader's team, though kept quiet, inhibited movement action. And the shift to an almost exclusive reliance on legal strategies and symbolic demonstrations lost the movement the support of the Workers' League. By the time the residents of Poletown stepped up their resistance, it was too late. Much of the community had already been destroyed, residents had moved, neighborhood institutions had been decimated. The final and most militant act of resistance, when forty or so residents occupied the Immaculate Conception Church in an attempt to prevent its demolition, was far too little far too late (Wylie, 1989). In contrast, seven hundred or more people rioted in Cedar-Riverside early on in the struggle to save the neighborhood and thereby established a formidable threat to business as usual in the city. Poletown tried to promote alternative redevelopment plans at the beginning of the struggle, but they were not developed with the participatory planning process that Cedar-Riverside practiced and were not comprehensive.

It is doubtful, however, that even if Cedar-Riverside residents had lived in Poletown, they would have been able to succeed where Poletown residents failed. The assault on the community was so swift, massive, and merciless that there was barely time to gather any resistance. Even in Cedar-Riverside it took three years to develop an effective resistance. Poletown was gone in a year. If CRA had kept the bulldozers moving across Cedar Avenue, instead of stopping when the Cedar Square West site had been cleared, there would have been no celebration for me to attend on that warm summer day in 1986. Although the political opportunity structure was relatively insulated from Cedar-Riverside activists, its actors were neither as shrewd nor as brutal as in Detroit. And the political opportunity structure eventually provided small opportunities for movement challenges that were never available to Poletown activists. There were no shaky financial risks, legal trapdoors, or lukewarm growth-coalition allies in the destruction of Poletown.

Thus, the political opportunity structure is not a reification that either does or does not allow movements to win. It is made up of the relationships between powerful political actors who have to maintain allies, overall stability, and lack of accessibility to the system and then must take quick advantage of the structure. In the case of Poletown the political opportunity structure was more antagonistic to the community than in Cedar-Riverside, but that was because GM and the City of Detroit made it that way and rapidly exploited the opportunities that the structure provided. As much as the fight in both Cedar-Riverside and in Poletown was over neighborhood control, it was focused on the political opportunity structure—gaining accessibility to the policy-making process, building movement allies, and destabilizing politics. Community-capital struggles within any given political opportunity structure, then, are constantly making, unmaking, and remaking that political opportunity structure. Political opportunities appear and vanish rapidly in such a scenario, so the more quickly the movement can act, and the less quickly the target acts, the better the chances for community-based movement success.

It is difficult enough to stop community destruction. It is even more difficult to go on to build a community. Movements face subtle dangers as they shift from community defense to community development, dangers that are influenced by the role the political opportunity structure plays in community development movements.

The Dangers of the Shift from Community Organizing to Community Development

It is in the transition of the Cedar-Riverside neighborhood movement from a neighborhood defense movement to a neighborhood development movement that we see how the new political opportunity structure created by the successful defense movement in turn shaped the development movement to follow. The accumulation of city government support for activists' vision of democratic, community-based redevelopment provided the legitimacy and the resources to enact that vision. But the community's receipt of those advantages was contingent on its ability to adopt a development-implementation strategy that conformed to the requirements of bureaucratic timetables and decision-making processes of capital and state funding sources. As activists agreed to this price, the political opportunity structure changed further when national and international fiscal pressures led to increasing federal and city government belt-tightening and funding restrictions. Thus, continued development required greater and greater movement adaptation, until neighborhood redevelopment could no longer be accomplished without sacrificing either community control or housing affordability.

As we saw in Chapter 7, "community organizing" or "neighborhood defense" goals shift to "community development" or "neighborhood development" goals. Community organizing is literally that—organizing people into a self-sustaining, self-protecting community. Made famous by the late Saul Alinsky (1969, 1971), community organizing also became known as the practice of militant tactics to defend communities against direct and indirect threats (Reitzes and Reitzes, 1987). Community development, previously connected to rural development strategies, has become known as a set of strategies that attempts to revitalize decaying urban centers through the rehabilitation of housing and commercial property. Though seemingly complementary—how can you have successful development unless the community is organized to support the development?—community organizing and community development have become antagonistic activities in the contemporary political opportunity structure (Stoecker 1991c).

The same push away from community organizing and toward community development by the federal government and private foundations in the 1980s which disrupted the Cedar-Riverside community has had a general impact nationwide (McCarthy et al., 1991; Jenkins, 1985). Development, regardless of how participatory or affordable or comprehensive, is disruptive. The process of physical redevelopment disrupts patterns of interaction among neighbors, changes material interests, and brings out community diversity.[1] Wherever substantial community-based development has occurred—in East Toledo (Stoecker, 1991b), Toronto (Fraser, 1972), Montreal (Helman, 1986), Liverpool (McDonald, 1986), Los Angeles (Heskin, 1991), or Cedar-Riverside—the community social structure has been disturbed, internal conflicts have broken out, friendships have been shattered, and the community foundation has decayed. Development by itself, then, is not the answer, since the very process of development disrupts the relationships that are required to maintain the conditions of community.

Without adequate resources available from the political opportunity structure to support community organizing, these conditions lead the movement farther away from democratic community-based redevelopment and closer to "clientelism." The shift to community-based redevelopment is a shift to providing community-based services, which leads to community-based organizations "convert[ing] their constituents into clients" (Mollenkopf, 1983:292).

The problem of clientelism is best discussed by Allan Heskin (1991) in his study of the Route 2 community-based development project in Los Angeles. One of the few successful community-based development projects in the United States, the Route 2 project began out of a failed proposal to build a freeway through the Echo Park–Silverlake district of Los Angeles. Employing low- and moderate-income home-ownership and cooperative ownership programs, residents eventually took over control of the housing in the state-owned freeway corridor. As development progressed in the Route 2 project area and residents expanded their activities beyond housing development to neighborhood social services, a shift in neighborhood involvement took place that parallels the transition in Cedar-Riverside. Heskin argues that clientelism emerged as a dominant relationship between community leaders and other residents as development progressed. Rather than maintaining a relationship of fully enfranchised equals, which was pushed by the early leadership, new leaders began to behave as power holders who could choose how to distribute resources to residents. This transformation from the earlier participatory period was supported, Heskins argues, by Latino immigrant residents' familiarity with patron-peasant clientelism and their lack of familiarity with a more egalitarian and participatory process.

Although ethnicity appeared to shape the specific form of clientelism in the Route 2 project, a more general process is likely at work in establishing clientelism. In Cedar-Riverside, as activists expanded development beyond the old activist neighborhood and attempted to bring Cedar Square West under control, a similar clientelism emerged. Even in the old neighborhood, as people from backgrounds of educational and political disenfranchisement became residents, they were less familiar with what *participation* meant. There were continuous charges that "new residents act like the CDC is just another landlord." Participation became so difficult for the problem-plagued Sherlock Homes co-op that its board developed a policy to evict those residents who refused to provide four hours of co-op work each month. In Cedar Square West, as it was renamed Riverside Plaza and activists attempted to establish resident control, residents of the complex saw the PAC as a service provider rather than a means of political participation, and blamed the PAC for the lack of services and safety in the complex. The Committee for Open Government (COG) counter-movement tapped the frustration of Riverside Plaza residents in un-successfully demanding that the PAC behave as a service organiza-tion. The reality of these residents, trapped in the property class of tenants who lacked power to control the conditions of their tenancy, reinforced a clientelist attitude. The PAC leadership, hoping to over-come the pressures toward clientelism through the creation of RPTA, held steadfast to a different vision that emphasized people organizing themselves for change.

> They were constantly talking about what the PAC should be doing for us. . . . It was never them organizing to accomplish something. (Tim Ogren interview, 1991)

> We had a different perspective. An organization like the PAC is kind of like a bank account. Everybody puts their leadership into that bank. It builds, and it grows, and you have some strength. But if you don't make a deposit, you can't get anything. And we're sittin' around wonderin' "Well, where's your deposit?" And it's kind of like two different mindsets.   (Tim Mungavan interview, 1991)

The clientelism that was so frustrating to activists and residents and created such tensions was brought on by, and exacerbated by, the political opportunity structure. Nowhere but Cedar-Riverside were the ideals of socialism and anarchism, melded into a program of democratic community-based neighborhood redevelopment, so highly developed and frequently practiced. As CDC staff and co-op residents were drawn increasingly from outside the neighborhood, they brought their traditional political socialization, ranging from patronage to apathy, with them. As redevelopment became more com-plex to meet federal, state, and local funding requirements, higher and higher levels of knowledge were required of decision-making participants. At the same time, new residents came in with less basic knowledge of redevelopment bureaucracy and technology or of the neighborhood's history. And as control and affordability became contradictory goals, with control being sacrificed to affordability for the Sherlock Homes co-op, there was less to be gained from partici-pation. Try as they might, activists could not halt the slide toward clientelism in the neighborhood.

A greater awareness of the contradiction between community control and affordability, along with greater emphasis on educating new residents in the community culture, would have helped reduce the pressures toward clientelism and internal conflict in the third period of the movement. But the ultimate outcome may not have been much different, as people would have likely moved on anyway, the PAC would have still lived out its purpose, and the neighborhood would have settled down to become concerned with issues of keeping the streets safe and clean. The political opportunity structure demanded tremendous compromises. Some activists were skeptical from the beginning about the lease-hold co-op model, believing that unless the neighborhood residents actually owned their co-ops they could not have control. Others look at what was accomplished with deep disappointment in the transition of the neighborhood from a truly radical community to one that is no longer so militantly countercultural. In retrospect they would have all done many things differently. Some would have placed greater emphasis on developing homeownership to promote residential stability. Some would have placed stronger control on the CDC. Some would have been more selective in screening co-op housing applicants. But no one regrets having participated in the experiment. Ultimately, they won, and to have abandoned the opportunities because they required too many compromises would have meant losing.

> You're trying to implement a set of ideals that none of these programs were designed to address. So of course there isn't a perfect fit. And you can't get yourself in the position of saying, "Well, if it doesn't fit exactly the way I want it to, then fuck it, I'm not gonna do it," because essentially what that means is you're gonna lose. It means you'd rather walk away and let them do it. (Jack Cann interview, 1991)

Toward an Alternative Model for Urban Redevelopment

Even with all its problems, Cedar-Riverside succeeded in ways that few other neighborhood movements have. Cedar-Riverside activists changed not only the substance but also the process of urban redevelopment policy making in Minneapolis. Neighborhood redevelopment was literally turned over to the neighborhood. The possible outcomes were limited by the political opportunity structure at all levels, but within those limitations the movement was able to make urban redevelopment planning the result of the residents' collective vision and accountable to neighborhood residents. In how many neighborhoods do the residents themselves do the planning, obtain the financing, and oversee the implementation of urban renewal that actually serves their needs?

The neighborhood movement also succeeded well in balancing the contradictory goals of affordable housing and community control of housing, though many activists would disagree. The despair among activists for not gaining more control through the lease-hold co-op model must be taken into account, as a socialist perspective would argue that as long as capitalists actually *own* the housing, community control is in jeopardy. Yet the city retains title to much of the land, providing a source of influence that is at least partly accountable to a democratic process. And the amount of control afforded to residents is far greater than they could ever practice as renters, because the co-op model provides for greater resident autonomy and because the collective nature of a co-op offers greater political power against rentier capital than any individual renter could achieve. The most problematic example that activists still point to, however, is the Sherlock Homes co-op. At least a half dozen activists moved out of the neighborhood fearing they would have to leave the co-op once their children moved away from home or their incomes went up, making them ineligible to stay. Whether this would have happened and whether they could have been relocated within the neighborhood can never be known for certain. Many remaining activists believe that the community can still prevent displacement out of the neighborhood. Many others believe that the process of accomplishing displacement would be so disruptive, as families were shuffled from house to house to achieve the necessary economic mix, that the ideal of community control would become meaningless. Even in this case, however, it may have been the best the movement could do in the era of "conserving local government" (S. Fainstein and N. Fainstein, 1986), trying to stretch ever dwindling and more restrictive federal resources.

The neighborhood movement was least successful in maintaining its alternative community. But again, it was perhaps as successful as it could be. The movement could have worked harder at preventing the goal contradictions imposed by the political opportunity structure from being transformed into internal conflict. It is unlikely, however, that the movement could have maintained a stronger alternative local economy, for a healthy alternative community service base remains. In how many neighborhoods can you get organic produce from a worker-controlled co-op, serve your transportation needs through a bicycle co-op, eat out at a worker-controlled vegetarian restaurant, receive sliding-fee medical care for you and your companion animal, be entertained by a variety of local alternative theater troupes, and live in cooperatively controlled housing? And the neighborhood continues to work to build community. Cedar-Riverside activists still organize a variety of integrative events, including the annual neighborhood celebration, called "Cedarfest," which attracts musicians, artists, other performers, and crowds from throughout the Twin Cities. The heart of Cedarfest is the neighborhood-based parade, which typically features peace signs, multicultural dance troupes, and the neighborhood's lawnmower drill team—an anachronism in a community where middle-class standards of lawn care are all but ignored.

Any way you measure it, then, the story of Cedar-Riverside provides an alternative vision of urban renewal—of true community-based redevelopment that is focused on the community as much as on the neighborhood, and that is democratic. This vision is directly opposed to top-down, capital-conscious redevelopment, which demands much more centralized profit. What kind of alternative model of urban renewal can we build from the Cedar-Riverside experience? The model is, essentially, of an alternative political opportunity structure.

The Model

In the middle 1980s, when the negative effects of the Reagan economic restructuring were showing in cities around the country, Nancy Kleniewski (1984) provided a list of features necessary for a successful progressive urban policy. Her vision demanded that urban redevelopment be redistributive from the wealthy to the impoverished, emphasize public housing that is socially planned and controlled, reduce the influence of large-scale capital, and support locally based and locally controlled business. Little of that need has changed, except perhaps in emphasis. For we have also discovered that the big government that is produced under capitalism has become increasingly inaccessible, and the focus on public housing advocated by most progressive analysts brings with it the threat of centralized control in the hands of big government subservient to the demands of capital. Three components of Kleniewski's policy position on urban redevelopment should be emphasized: a whole neighborhood approach, a community approach, and a participatory democratic approach.

The whole neighborhood approach focuses redevelopment on an

entire neighborhood: its housing, its commercial buildings, its open spaces, its traffic patterns, its zoning restrictions. Cedar-Riverside did not just refurbish its housing. The commercial buildings also received treatment, ranging from facelifts to major structural rehabilitation. Intersections were redesigned, streets were closed, and parking regulations were changed. And the neighborhood was completely rezoned to prevent undesirable uses and also to accommodate and protect "nonconforming uses" such as North Country Co-op, which was located on a block zoned residential. The focus on commercial and residential renewal, though hotly disputed in the neighborhood and weighted perhaps too heavily in favor of small, capitalist-owned business, is important. David Daykin (1988:375) notes, "As long as districts of consumption (residential neighborhoods) are separated from districts of production (workplaces), urban residents are less likely to participate in neighborhood-centered networks." Cedar-Riverside was at its strongest when consumption and production were integrated in the community—intriguingly, before CDC-sponsored commercial redevelopment.

This approach to neighborhood redevelopment shows some interesting similarities to the old Model Cities urban renewal program. Those involved in Cedar-Riverside redevelopment note the similarities with some discomfort, even as they argue forcefully for part of this model:

> I believe very strongly that, in the inner cities of our country today, that doing spot development for low- and moderate-income persons is in and of itself a huge waste and that the lesson here is that you have to do things on a community, unit-by-unit, block-by-block basis, to make a fundamental improvement and stabilize a neighborhood—which is sort of the model of the old urban renewal days and you kinda hate to point to that. But what happened with the advent of the CDBG block grant money at the federal level was that, rather than focusing on a neighborhood, and doing what you had to do on a systematic basis, it got to be kind of a shotgun deal . . . but it does nothing for either stabilizing or turning around neighborhoods as such. (Dick Brustad interview, 1991)

The Cedar-Riverside approach is far different from the old "urban removal" days, however, when entire neighborhoods were wiped out from above to enhance the profit margin of capital. And those differences derive from the other two components of the alternative model. Cedar-Riverside activists adopted a community approach. The goal in the neighborhood became to develop not just buildings but community relationships, focused on the existing community. In stark contrast to traditional urban renewal, Cedar-Riverside redevelopment was conducted to *prevent* displacement. Urban redevelopment was to serve the neighborhood community, not the profit needs of capital-conscious, growth-oriented coalitions. And though the focus on service provision is reminiscent of the old Community Action Programs, it is not separated from physical redevelopment. Both the People's Center building and the New Riverside Cafe building underwent extensive renovation. The new daycare homes were funded in the last round of housing rehabilitation. Neither physical redevelopment of aging neighborhoods nor service provision in those neighborhoods will succeed without the two components working in tandem. And neither will succeed without continually organizing and reorganizing residents to take control of their neighborhood, the third component of the model.

Finally, both service provision and physical development was different in Cedar-Riverside than in traditional urban renewal because of real participatory democracy. Model Cities legislation, in practice, encouraged rational and efficient planning, requiring experts and limited participation, which contradicted the participatory demands of neighborhood-based groups (Judd and Mendelson, 1973). In contrast, Cedar-Riverside placed a strong emphasis on the actual participation of residents in the redesign of their block and their building. They talked and struggled and sweated over disputes on which houses to tear down, how to distribute scarce resources, and what to include in a park design. They held meeting after meeting. They knocked on doors and spread flyers to bring people to meetings and neighborhood elections. And even the PAC and CDC did not rely on their elected representatives alone, but invited residents who might be affected by any proposed policy or development in the neighborhood to speak at their meetings.

Can this model be generalized? Can any neighborhood be given control of the reigns of urban redevelopment and make it work? Cedar-Riverside was a peculiar neighborhood; its residents were young, highly educated and thoroughly radicalized. They had an abundance of specialized, home-grown talent in urban planning, architecture, and financial management, as well as time to devote to the community. What about a traditional working-class neighborhood, or a poor, minority neighborhood, lacking in education, political savvy, expertise, and spare time? Can the model also work there? Yes, it can, and it has. The Route 2 housing redevelopment project in Los Angeles shows that the model can work in a racially and economically diverse neighborhood—not without problems, but with better results than with top-down, capital-conscious redevelopment (Heskin, 1991). And the $15 million industrial street-widening project to boost reindustrialization in East Toledo, conceived of and designed through a participatory process spearheaded by the East Toledo Community Organization, shows that it can work in a traditional working-class neighborhood (Stoecker, 1991b). Other analysts have noticed that community-based development organizations in a diversity of settings around the country are beginning to increase their impact on urban neighborhoods (Peirce and Steinbach, 1990).

Accomplishing democratic, community-based redevelopment is more difficult in communities that do not have as strong a sense of political efficacy, as ready access to experts, or as much of a history in trying out the participatory democratic process as Cedar Riverside. But to the extent that those resources can be developed, urban redevelopment that focuses wholistically on an entire neighborhood rather than on spot rehab, that emphasizes developing community relationships as much as community buildings, and that is based in a process in which the citizens create and oversee the plan can be accomplished. Indeed, that may be the only kind of redevelopment that can succeed anymore. Spot rehab becomes invisible and falls into ruin without supporting redevelopment around it. Even substantial redevelopment is quickly trashed in neighborhoods where neighboring is absent and gangs and drugs rule the streets. And, finally, redevelopment done without the participation and support of the citizens to be affected by it has become more and more difficult.

The community side of the problem can be managed. A diversity of neighborhoods can conduct their own redevelopment. The question is, Can the political opportunity structure support it?

The Potential

Conducting urban redevelopment that takes a whole neighborhood approach, is community-focused, and practices a participatory democratic process requires a wholesale change of perspective among important actors in the political opportunity structure. First among those actors is city government. City government must be willing to provide neighborhoods with resources without demanding that they give up control. The activity of city planners changes from creating plans driven by visions from the top, to organizing neighborhood

Chapter 9

residents to create plans from the bottom up. The planner's job in this model is to find ways to make the residents' visions work, not to dictate what is not practical or what is not politically acceptable or what is not affordable, and definitely not to tell residents what they should think. The city council's and mayor's offices must also transform the urban governing structure. This restructuring, based on models developed in Hartford, Cleveland, Berkeley, Santa Monica, and Burlington, flattens and decentralizes the local state hierarchy. It also institutionalizes participation in overall urban planning and budgeting. From this restructuring, neighborhood-based organizations receive more support; more progressive policy initiatives, such as rent control and growth control, become reality (Clavel, 1986:215–216). This is easiest to accomplish, of course, in cities that already have decentralized government through ward-elected councils and other citizen boards, such as Cleveland, with its twenty-one-member, ward-elected City Council. In other places citizens have to push for local state restructuring first. But it can be accomplished even in such apparently traditional working-class cities as Pittsburgh, where citizen mobilization resulted in a local state restructuring from an at-large to a ward-elected council (Jezierski, 1988).

Accomplishing this local state restructuring, which capital opposes in general because such changes limit its influence (Stoecker and Schmidbauer, 1991), requires a redirection of the local state's mission from allowing the city's development to be guided by growth-machine politics and capital-conscious development pressures. This change is what Stone (1987:275) labels the "equality/efficiency tradeoff." Urban development that is most beneficial for citizens is probably not most efficient for the centralized accumulation of profit because it does not promote growth. But democratic, community-based redevelopment is most efficient from a perspective that values reduction of waste, according to the CDC's for-profit development partner:

> I sincerely do believe that in neighborhood urban renewal, the best decisions are made by the people in the community, number one. And number two, that using the lease co-op technique, truly given a free reign and the power and control to run their own housing destiny, that they will do a better job of, in effect, operating the housing than we would do, even though we don't do a bad job. And over the years, that clearly has been proven out. We own a lot of housing, a lot of it low-income around the city and in other cities, and the Cedar-Riverside projects are clearly the best by any objec-

tive measure—the most stable, the most efficient. In the operation of housing you measure costs on a per-unit basis. Electricity is x dollars per unit per month, that kind of thing. And the people living there have a stake in keeping those costs down. And they truly are lower. (Brustad interview, 1991)

The supposed "efficiency" of growth is irrelevant to neighborhood redevelopment and in fact makes it more difficult. The remaining problems of Cedar-Riverside center on the high-density Riverside Plaza, which was constructed out of a growth-motivated perspective. Alienation, crime, and service shortages are the main results of growth politics. Neither more nor bigger is better. Democratic, community-based redevelopment shifts the emphasis from growth to preservation. City politicians have to prevent profit-oriented growth demands from driving urban redevelopment planning. There is a basic agreement among progressive analysts that, until government is empowered to control capital mobility and redistribute wealth both locally and nationally, reforms attempting to return control of community life to community citizens will be vulnerable (Tabb, 1984; Kleniewski, 1984). On the one hand, then, all levels of government have to be brought back from the destruction visited on them by the Reagan and Bush administrations. But, on the other hand, at the same time that we make government more powerful, we also must make it more democratic.

Currently, however, since government cannot control the local and international capital that drives growth machines, capitalists can derail the process at any point. The increasing globalization of capital and internationalization of consumer markets undermines local identity and reduces local control over capital (Law and Wolch, 1983). General Motors certainly proved that in Poletown. Until there is true economic democracy in cities, so that capital cannot simply pick up and leave without any accountability whatsoever, city leaders are going to have to persuade capitalists that stable neighborhoods are the source of a more satisfied work force, a greater diversity of highly skilled talent, and an overall improved quality of life. Recently, much of the development backed by capitalists has been in decaying downtowns that housed the isolated poorest of the poor, who had far less voice than neighborhood residents, or in the hinterlands, where few if any people were displaced. But capitalists still have to be persuaded to pay taxes to support neighborhood development rather than taking hefty tax abatements. In cities such as Minneapolis, Boston, or San

Francisco, corporations see many locational advantages regardless of whether they have to pay more. Boston's "linkage" tax on downtown development, whose proceeds are put into a fund for neighborhood-based development, illustrates capital's lack of concern for increased costs when other advantages are available (Dreier, 1989).

Finally, the public must be supportive. And there are many risks in gaining their support. The most important one is that, with limited funds, neighborhoods will fight among themselves for a share of the redevelopment pie. The compromises that are likely to come from such struggles will require spot redevelopment projects that will not stem the tide of urban decline. Until adequate resources are available, neighborhoods will have to redevelop one at a time, and each will have to support the queuing of neighborhoods. Another danger is that the planning process may be abused by those in neighborhoods who wish to exclude others, enact their visions over the objections of others, or gain personally from redevelopment. Thus, the public can rally around such an alternative model for racist or other selfish purposes. This problem can be managed by careful training and structuring of the planning process, since practice with actual participatory, democratic decision making improves people's respect for others and the democratic process (Pateman, 1970; Evans and Boyte, 1986). But maintaining the training and the structure requires ongoing commitment from the local state and from capital.

In the wake of the successful implementation of this model in Cedar-Riverside, the City of Minneapolis has embarked on a project to expand the model throughout the city. It will likely provide the first test of whether the political opportunity structure will support whole-neighborhood, community-focused, participatory democratic urban redevelopment. Through its Neighborhood Revitalization Program, the city is attempting to refurbish itself neighborhood by neighborhood. Within each neighborhood, community-based organizations assisted by professional planners actually plan redevelopment. There are many concerns about the program, however. One is that the entire program is dependent on capital support and health, since it is funded out of tax-increment money. Another fear is that neighborhood-based planning may turn into right-wing populist attacks on the poor and minorities. In other words, community control of the planning process might mean that the community, or at least a few powerful members in the community, would exercise its prerogative to plan for the elimination of low-income housing (Rubenstein, 1991). The problem is that the vision supporting this planning process is much more populist than it is alternative. The idea is to give some control to the grass roots, without considering the need for leadership to focus that control toward meeting broader goals and maintaining a democratic process that is inclusive of *all* members of the neighborhood community who will be affected by it. And since the contradiction between control and affordability remains, the shift away from affordability is a real danger in many neighborhoods. The Minneapolis political opportunity structure is still not entirely supportive of either democratic, grass-roots control or affordable housing, since approval of the neighborhood plans is mediated by a board that is not controlled by either neighborhoods or the city but that has significant representation of local capital. This orientation will continue to influence grass-roots groups against the goals of affordability and community control, and perhaps also against one another, unless there are strong countervailing pressures at the neighborhood or city level (Rubenstein, 1991; DeWar, 1992).

Relying on community-based organizations to create the large-scale structural changes necessary to protect urban communities against capital is problematic. John Mollenkopf (1983) has noted the problems of attempting to build a mass movement for deep structural change on the energy of neighborhood-based organizations. For one thing, the local focus of neighborhood movements limits their ability to see the deeper and broader threats to community from the structural contradictions of capitalism. There is still a dearth of neighborhood organizing or even development movements in suburbia and in the southern or western parts of the United States. And because of the diversity of neighbors they represent, neighborhood-based organizations are often reduced simply to trying to prevent their own implosion from internal factioning, let alone attempting to maintain coalitions outside the neighborhood.

Conclusion: The Future of Community-controlled Urban Redevelopment

There are signs beyond Minneapolis that democratic, community-based urban redevelopment is gaining legitimacy, resources, and power. As far back as 1979 Joseph F. Timilty, the chair of the federally established National Commission on Neighborhoods, stated, "We conclude emphatically that much more authority can be better exercised, many programs can be better administered, and a higher proportion of public funds can be better spent at the neighborhood level." During the next decade community-based development groups expanded from almost none to an estimated nearly two thousand (Peirce and Steinbach, 1990), even while the federal housing budget was being slashed by 60 percent (U.S. Conference of Mayors, 1986). Support from foundations and state and local governments has grown dramatically with the increase in the number of organizations involved in community-based development (Peirce and Steinbach, 1990). These neighborhood-based movements have already influenced the national political agenda through organizing an identifiable voting block, creating "a political rhetoric of citizen participation, participatory planning, and community review which challenges the prevailing ideologies of pro-growth politics" and establishing a grass-roots organizational base (Mollenkopf, 1983:294).

As a result, even the federal government has come around to recognizing the role of community-based development in urban renewal. The 1990 National Affordable Housing Act, the first significant housing legislation passed since the beginning of the CDBG program in 1974, creates a block grant funding program for low-income housing. Cities obtain funds by completing a five-year plan for housing, called a Comprehensive Housing Affordability Strategy, or CHAS. Most important, within the provisions of the bill, state and local governments must provide at least 15 percent of their block grants to community-based, nonprofit developers (Center for Community Change, 1991).

Nevertheless, the proportion of housing constructed in the United States by nonprofits has still been minuscule compared to that of other countries—less than 1 percent of the total (Adams, 1990). There are many barriers to be overcome before the city is brought under citizen control. First is the overall disintegration of community. Fewer and fewer neighborhoods have the institutional infrastructure required for a strong community. Shopping malls and megamarkets springing up around the outskirts of the city have decimated neighborhood commercial centers, eliminating local gathering points and local employment. The exodus of even relatively nonpolluting light industry to the hinterlands has further taken the workplace out of the neighborhood. Community centers, neighborhood libraries, and other government-supported services have seen their hours curtailed or their doors padlocked as economic hard times settle in. Fewer places exist for neighborhood communities to gather and celebrate. And as there is less infrastructural support for community, there is also less financial support for the community-organizing activity that can help rebuild that infrastructure.

The threats facing neighborhood communities today are also much different from those facing neighborhoods in the 1960s. In the 1960s the enemies were visible and the cause was clear. Neighborhoods were threatened with clearance, by either a developer or a government, or a coalition of the two. In the 1990s the threat is not capital in the form of the rogue speculative investor but capital as the blank face of *disinvestment*. The closure of neighborhood businesses and churches, the abandonment of neighborhood housing, and the arson and vandalism those conditions encourage can be as devastating to a neighborhood community as a bulldozer. And the enemy is much harder to fight. The community cannot go to one target and demand that it stop destroying the neighborhood. Defending the neighborhood means defending it from multiple threats, all of which operate in the shadows or behind closed doors. The strategy must be a complex demand for complex resources—to bring back neighborhood commerce, local jobs, habitable housing, residential stability, and community control.

That means a demand for resources at a time when they are at their shortest. Even the new federal National Affordable Housing Act is sorely underfunded. And the requirements for the construction of the CHAS are far too weak to require any meaningful community participation in writing the plans. Groups are organizing to have an impact on the CHAS (Omaha Housing Equity Project, 1991; Center for Community Change, 1991), but it is not clear that the outcome will be any more significant than it was for Model Cities planning unless there is a strong community organizing push. At a time when city leaders perceive it to be less expensive and less politically difficult simply to let neighborhoods deteriorate than to open themselves to the public scrutiny that a whole-neighborhood, community-focused, participatory, democratic urban planning process would require, it is difficult to imagine an alternative. And when the citizens themselves do not have an alternative vision of community and do not have the sense of political efficacy that allows them to demand that city and national leaders respond, a vicious cycle ensues.

Yet an alternative vision is what we must pursue. Every urban redevelopment program up to now has shown itself to be a dismal failure. Exploited by speculators, controlled by bureaucrats, manipulated by capitalists, derailed by politicians, urban redevelopment has caused unimaginable anguish, split up communities, displaced entire populations, and bulldozed history. There are only a few alternatives, the best example of which is perhaps Cedar-Riverside. There have been other whole-neighborhood renewal projects, other examples of participatory planning, and many stories of community-focused organizing. But Cedar-Riverside brought it all together, not perfectly, but extremely comprehensively. That is why Cedar-Riverside stands as a real alternative. With luck, the most important thing about the outcome of Cedar-Riverside will be its legacy.

CHAPTER **10**

The Legacy of
Cedar-Riverside

I N THE SUMMER of 1991, as the neighborhood redevelopment
wound to a conclusion and I returned to Minneapolis to prepare
this book, I visited those who had been most active in the movement
to save and rebuild Cedar-Riverside. I asked them to reflect on what
they thought they had accomplished, what they thought they had
failed to accomplish, and what, if any, legacy they had left behind.
Here is a sampling of what they said. For some, their achievements
brought a quiet sense of pride.

> I'm really glad I got to take some of those things that were gleams in
> our eye, and make them happen, and that was fun. (Kathy O'Brien
> interview, 1991)

For others, the enormity of the movement's accomplishments and the
transition of the movement were not completely real. The transformation of the neighborhood from a slum to a model of redevelopment
paralleled the transformation of the activists from ignored outsiders to
respected insiders. Some still were not quite used to the idea of being
power holders, having moved into important positions in city government, the MCDA, management companies, unions, and other areas.

> I suppose "Anything is possible" is the legacy everybody has been
> telling me because of the irony of what's transpired in a reasonably
> short period of time from the late sixties to now with a small band
> of yahoo radicals who now own the neighborhood and have set up
> all these institutions and . . . are partners in Riverside Plaza when
> they were out in the streets being maced and protesting against the

war and against this building all at the same time not very many years ago. (Steve Parliament interview, 1991)

Some were not sure if they had succeeded or not. To a certain extent, their compromises had reduced the alternative character of their mission—and it was the struggles over those compromises that helped to create cracks in the community foundation.

It's the American way of doing things as opposed to the way we envisioned. And I think, invariably, if the community is really organized in the first place . . . and you've gotten a reasonable amount of, let's say, control over your destiny socially, then you have to get control over your destiny physically. And the way to do that is to start acquiring the property. And at that point, you've bought the system. So what happens is . . . you become a development company, and development becomes the issue, not community. No matter how much rhetoric and how many good things are done, the emphasis changes at that point. (Ralph Wittcoff interview, 1991)

Good things were done, and the emphasis did change. But as the movement goals shift once again to emphasize maintaining the neighborhood, the diverse interests are beginning to coalesce. The tensions created by goal contradiction are being replaced by more common concerns:

What we've become is, fortunately or unfortunately, we've become a mature neighborhood, and we're dealing with typical neighborhood issues—real issues—that deal with keepin' a neighborhood that's decent to live in, beautifying it, and trying to run it with the diverse population we have. And see, these people here are not politically interested, but they certainly are domestically and environmentally interested because they want their lawn, they want their garbage can, they want this and they want that. And the mothers, they don't want lead paint here. . . . And they don't want cocaine freaks running up and down. And they don't want crime. . . . So we are in a successful mode right now, and because of that we are somewhat lost, because there's nothing driving us anymore. And now there's a sense of floundering, a sense of who are we, what are we gonna do, a sense of what is our role now, and a sense of who's the future leadership? (Hal Barron interview, 1991)

For yet others, the outcome was a vindication, a sense that they had indeed done what everyone said could not be done, should not be done, and would not be done. They had stuck to their principles, and even though not everything they had tried worked, they were able at least to try to make it work.

> The fact that an entire neighborhood was redeveloped in a thorough-going way—virtually every single unit was substantially treated—really with involuntary displacement from the neighborhood drastically minimized, I think is unusual and suggests (A) that it can be done, and (B) that it ought to be done.   (Jack Cann interview, 1991)

> I think it demonstrated you can do some things. You can develop a neighborhood with a democratic process. Painful as it is, you can use democratic process and make change happen. You can integrate a neighborhood in such a way as to deal with some of the basic fundamental racial issues. . . . And we were able to do that with all union labor, with the exception of the very recent thing. And to a large extent we made our own mistakes. We didn't do it all right, but it wasn't somebody else that did it for us wrong.   (Tim Mungavan interview, 1991)

The self-criticism notwithstanding, many who were involved have no regrets. They accomplished much of what they had set out to accomplish and far more than they had ever hoped to accomplish, despite heavy odds.

> I'd do the same thing again; I'd just do it better. That's my legacy. I'd do the same thing over again. It was one of the most exciting times in my life. It was just wonderful beating the powers to be, and not stopping there, but going on to fulfill the dreams and the ideas we had. And we did fulfill them. . . . So basically I'd do it all over again except I'd do it better.   (Barron interview, 1991)

And for others, the chance simply to try was the real legacy. In a nation that celebrates a "thousand points of light" without ever providing the fuel needed to keep them burning, the chance to make the most of rather substantial resources was a rarity.

> Maybe that is a legacy there, that we had an opportunity to experiment. Some things worked. Some things we don't know if they worked yet or not. Some worked for the time that they needed to work. And we need to accept that this has been an experiment and find out what did work, improve on that, and not be dogmatic. (Tim Ogren interview, 1991)

The influence and legacy of Cedar-Riverside extends far beyond the boundaries of the neighborhood, creating a mythology and an aura that is hard for neighborhood activists to live down. Anyone who came of age in the 1960s and 1970s knows Cedar-Riverside. In my travels, when I meet baby boomers who are current or former Minneapolitans, and I tell them that I am researching the Cedar-Riverside neighborhood, their eyes get that faraway look brought on by the memory of a once-in-a-lifetime experience. People remember, and they enjoy remembering. And even though some old friends have become enemies, old foes have the opportunity to become friends.

> Another thing that's really wonderful about Cedar-Riverside—
> it's so funny. This neighborhood belongs to everybody in the city.
> Somehow this neighborhood touched everybody's lives. I get into
> arguments with people. They just come here to drink, and they
> know all there is to—it's like a little neighborhood where anybody
> can project whatever they want onto it. And it's very mythological
> to lots of people. . . . It's really funny. I was hiring a secretary. And
> this woman came in; I was interviewing her. And I said, "I don't
> know you." And she said, "Well, I know you quite well." And I
> went, "Oh?" And I said, "How do you know me?" And she said, "I
> used to work for Keith Heller." I just about fell off the chair. I went,
> "Oh yeah?" "Yeah, I hope you won't hold that against me." But we
> hired her, and she and I had a lot of fun—we've got a lot to talk
> about.   (Dorothy Jacobs interview, 1991)

I also talked with Ralph Wittcoff. Ralph had been interviewed in 1978 about the neighborhood movement, when it appeared that the New Town plan was on the skids. When the interviewer asked him what the movement would do now that the New Town plan was dead, he responded, "I don't know that it's dead yet." He was right, of course, for in 1980 Cedar-Riverside Associates came back with the First National Bank of St. Paul and almost revived the New Town. So I asked him what he saw for the future of the neighborhood now. At a time when many activists were discouraged because of what they had not accomplished—they did not control the land, they did not actually own the co-ops—and many old activists had left the neighborhood altogether, he said:

> And as the century rolls around, and the notes are paid off, what
> then? And the grass roots might rise again. It wouldn't surprise
> me if the wheel turns and the people who now live there actually

do end up reclaiming their neighborhood. I can see them mounting a large campaign against the West Bank CDC and maybe they'd win. . . . Because that's the real legacy.   (Wittcoff interview, 1991)

Finally, we must not forget that the process was as important as the end product. In many ways it was the disruption in the process that discouraged activists in the end. For what they most often cite as the important legacy in their movement is not the housing, or the alternative service base, or any of the physical development. What they identify, without exception, is the sense of fulfillment, empowerment, and pleasure gained from the struggle itself: "Gee, we had fun" (Ogren interview, 1991).

Interviewees and Interviews

This list includes all interviewees who allowed their names or their quotations to be used. For various reasons, many others requested that their names or their words not appear in the book. The information provided by interviewees who did not want their names to be used was checked against other sources; information that could not be confirmed elsewhere was eliminated. Interviewees cited in the manuscript are those who made specific charges or were directly quoted. Interviewees who provided general historical information available through outside sources or recognized as common knowledge are not cited. Many informal discussions, which were not taped, do not appear in this list. Quotations from all interviews dated 1978 are cited or quoted with permission from the Minnesota Historical Society's Sound and Visual Collections.

Interviews Obtained from the Minnesota Historical Society

WILLIAM BETZLER (CRA employee)—Interviewed by Jon Kerr, May 24, 1978.

JOHN (JACK) CANN (Minnesota Tenants Union organizer and Cedar-Riverside activist)—Interviewed by Claire Cunningham and Sheila Jordan, May 8, 1978.

ROBERT DREW (MHRA planner)—Interviewed by Jon Kerr, May 22, 1978.

THOMAS FEENEY (HUD regional official)—Interviewed by Jon Kerr, May 19, 1978.

KEITH HELLER (CRA founder)—Interviewed by Jon Kerr, May 25, 1978.

STEVE PARLIAMENT (Cedar-Riverside activist and founder of Parliament Management Company)—Interviewed by Claire Cunningham, May 23, 1978.

RALPH RAPSON (CRA architect)—Interviewed by Jon Kerr, May 16, 1978.

DAVID RAYMOND (CRA employee)—Interviewed by Jon Kerr, May 19, 1978.

CHARLES WARNER (HUD representative)—Interviewed by Jon Kerr, May 23, 1978.

RALPH WITTCOFF (Cedar-Riverside activist and New Riverside Cafe member)—Interviewed by Claire Cunningham, May 23, 1978.

JOYCE YU (Cedar-Riverside activist and People's Center organizer)—Interviewed by Claire Cunningham, May 18, 1978.

Formal Interviews Conducted by the Author

HAL BARRON (Cedar-Riverside activist and founding CDC board member)—Interviewed July 17, 1991.

HOWARD BILLIAN (Cedar-Riverside resident and B-PAC organizer)—Interviewed November 1985.

DICK BRUSTAD (MHRA executive director and Brighton Development Corporation executive director)—Interviewed July 19, 1991.

JOHN (JACK) CANN—Interviewed July 1, 1991.

LEE GREENFIELD (Minnesota state representative for Cedar-Riverside area)—Interviewed November 28, 1984.

DOROTHY JACOBS (Cedar-Riverside activist, PAC staff member, MCDA official)—Interviewed October 30, 1984; February 9, 1988; July 18, 1991.

TIM MUNGAVAN (Cedar-Riverside activist and PAC architect/organizer)—Interviewed November 1, 1984; February 7, 1985; February 13, 1986; March 26, 1991; July 18, 1991.

KATHY O'BRIEN (Cedar-Riverside activist and Minneapolis City Council member)—Interviewed March 26, 1991.

TIMOTHY J. (TIM) OGREN (Cedar-Riverside activist, PAC chair, Neighborhood Priorities Coalition chair)—Interviewed December 4, 1984; February 8, 1985; March 27, 1985; December 3, 1987; March 26, 1991; July 18, 1991.

STEVE PARLIAMENT—Interviewed July 18, 1991.

ALLAN SPEAR (Minnesota state senator)—Interviewed December 1984.

REV. WILLIAM (BILL) TESKA (Cedar-Riverside activist and Episcopal priest)—Interviewed October 31, 1984.

RALPH WITTCOFF—Interviewed November 7, 1984; February 6, 1988; July 16, 1991.

Notes

Chapter 1: Capital, Community, and Cedar-Riverside

1. There seems to be no particular preference among activists for one or the other label. More recently arrived residents tend to refer to the area as the West Bank; older residents call it Cedar-Riverside. It is interesting that the main resident planning organization in the neighborhood is referred to as the "Cedar-Riverside Project Area Committee," while the development organization, which became a political rival, is called the "West Bank Community Development Corporation."

2. In mid-1992 the co-op board voted to sell the store to a private grocer to retire the store's accumulated debt.

3. Čapek and Gilderbloom (1992) also advocate the integration of these two perspectives, and they provide the first attempt to accomplish that goal. Although they probably err on the side of emphasizing social movement theory over new urban sociology, they have gone farther than anyone before them in bringing the two perspectives together.

4. Cox (1981) and Čapek and Gilderbloom (1992) refer to the conflict between use values and exchange values as "commodity" versus "community." Since commodification is the result of the actions of capital, however, rather than a source of the conflict, I believe the conflict is better portrayed as a struggle between *capital* and community.

5. *Growth coalition*, like all catchy terms, has become a disputed item. Mollenkopf (1978) used the term *pro-growth coalition* to refer to those urban elites who organized to back specific urban development projects. When Molotch (1979) and Logan and Molotch (1987) popularized the term along with the metaphor of "the city as a growth machine," it became increasingly unclear whether the city power structure and the growth coalition could be separated (see Friedland and Palmer, 1984). On the other hand, Fleischmann and Feagin (1987) limit *growth coalition* to "business centered, mayor-led coalitions," which seems too narrow. Some clarity of the concept has been

returned by Houghton (1991), who argued for a clear separation of the concepts of *growth coalition* and *growth machine*. My use of the term is more variable, as expressed further in Chapter 1, from a coalition of elites supporting a particular project outside government, to the complete dominance of urban governance by the growth-oriented elite.

6. Fleischmann and Feagin (1987) advocate more research to determine just what affects growth-machine outcomes, hypothesizing that the outcomes may vary historically, by type of capital involved, according to the city's position in the urban hierarchy, or because of other variables.

7. The typical Marxist elaboration of this problem refers to a contradiction between "accumulation" and "legitimation," or "production" and "reproduction." Regime theorists such as Elkin (1987) and Stone (1987) describe a tension between "equality" and "efficiency." In the regime characterization, though essentially the same as the Marxist, *efficiency* can be defined in several ways, and what is efficient for the accumulation of capital in the short term will likely not be efficient for community maintenance in the long term. Thus, the source of the problem is more accurately depicted as a tension between *accumulation* and the need to *legitimize* that accumulation to citizens who will not likely gain from it and will likely lose out. There is also a debate among local state theorists over whether the local state is more involved in supporting legitimation through providing social reproduction services such as housing and unemployment compensation (Cockburn, 1977; Saunders, 1981; Boddy, 1983), or may variably attempt to support both accumulation and legitimation (Duncan and Goodwin, 1982; Clark and Dear, 1984). In the case of U.S. cities the evidence is strong that the local state, through its ability to provide tax abatements and other incentives, strongly supports capital accumulation as well as legitimation functions (Lauria, 1986; Fainstein et al., 1986; Squires, 1989b). Swanstrom's (1985) work on the attacks of capital against the Kucinich mayoral administration in Cleveland shows just how vulnerable the local state becomes when its managers refuse to use it to support capital.

8. Core activists are motivated by their commitment to the collective good, or "purposive incentives" (Wilson, 1973; Oliver, 1983, Williams, 1985). But a movement can rarely run on only its core group and must expand its base with less committed members.

9. Gerlach (1976) has also referred to this model as "segmented," "polycentric," and "networked," and (Gerlach, 1983), along with Dwyer (1983), as "segmentary," "polycephalous," and "reticulate."

10. *Snoose News* has been an extremely valuable source and is very accurate as a historical document. In my continuous reevaluation of *Snoose News*, I was able to compare it to other sources, especially the mainstream Minneapolis newspapers. When both reported on neighborhood events, the descriptions were nearly identical. It was only in the analysis that *Snoose News* diverged. Thus, as a source of descriptive information, *Snoose News* is per-

fectly adequate and provides details and checks for residents' memories that otherwise would be unavailable.

11. Some interviewees declined to be identified for specific quotations. In most cases, however, interviewees are identified in the text or in a parenthetical citation. These interviewees are listed in the appendix.

Chapter 2: Capital Invades Cedar-Riverside

1. Berger et al. (1992) recognize the existence of these partnerships long before the 1980s but argue that it was only recently that they were promoted as a model for urban redevelopment.

2. The local state became more politicized in the 1980s with an increase in mayoral powers and a reinstatement of partisan ballots in local elections.

3. Ultimately, however, the luxury units were segregated in one building because of cost and code concerns, making for far less class integration than had been initially hoped (Martin, 1978).

4. Apparently, shots of Cedar Square West appeared in the opening credits of the "Mary Tyler Moore Show," and occasional descriptions of the complex Mary moved into on the show made it seem as if it could only be Cedar Square West. "Mary Tyler Moore" producers, publicists, and studio staff could not confirm that any of this association to Cedar Square West was purposeful, however.

5. The various units of the state can also be considered support decision makers, but since the state is not a fraction of capital, it has different interests and thus does not occupy the same role as capital actors. Thus, we must consider the state a separate kind of actor in this analysis.

Chapter 3: A New Community Forms Against the New Town

1. Crowd estimates are always difficult to verify and often vary widely among different observers even when they have the same political perspective. I have chosen to provide the range of estimates of crowd size for demonstrations, meetings, and other events when there is no way to verify any single estimate.

2. In reviewing the original book manuscript, Ralph Wittcoff recalled that the original poster drawn by Zack was an adaptation of a poster from the Industrial Workers of the World, or "Wobblies"—a militant labor movement active in the early twentieth century—which had a black cat in the center and "BEWARE SABOTAGE" at the top and bottom. Zack deleted the original slogan and replaced it with "STOP HELLER TONITE" on the body of the cat.

3. Neighborhood residents say that one of the injured was Don Fraser's daughter. Don Fraser went on to become mayor of Minneapolis and a supporter of the neighborhood. This demonstration expanded over to the East

Bank of the University of Minnesota, blocking the bridge connecting the two campuses and ultimately closing the university.

4. Ralph Wittcoff, in his comments on the original manuscript, recalled the story of the night before the Cedar Square West dedication ceremony when the neighborhood beat cops discovered the evidence of the New Riverside Cafe's stenciling activity: "After we finished stenciling the 'hood, sneaky-pete-ing around avoiding the beat cops, and were sitting in the cafe surrounded by empty paint cans, the beat cops knocked on the door. We thought they were about to bust us—we were smoking dope. Instead, they said, 'We know where you can get some more paint. Maybe you guys should go out to one of your farms and bring back a truckload of manure and drop it in the middle of the intersection of Cedar and Riverside.' "

Chapter 4: Building on Community

1. Ralph Wittcoff suggested the term *liberation* to me when I asked him questions about what I called the "PAC takeover." In retrospect, I agree with him, as the PAC was "liberated" from the control of capital and placed under the control of neighborhood residents.

2. The newspaper was named after "Snoose Boulevard" before it became Cedar Avenue. "Snoose" was the anglicized version for *snus*, referring to the chewing tobacco the original Scandinavian immigrants used (*Snoose News*, April 1975:1). *Snoose News* provided an enormous amount of historical documentation and corroboration of interview-based information from the middle 1970s to the early 1980s.

3. The PAC's 1986–87 fiscal year budget from the MCDA was $77,821, reported at the July 1987 PAC meeting, added to $39,410 donated funds reported at the December 1986 PAC meeting. The budget had been topping $100,000 since the early 1980s.

4. The June 1986 CDC board meeting reported the CDC annual income at $323,200 and listed thirteen staff members, including part-time staff and in-house consultants.

Chapter 5: The Growth Coalition Falters

1. The connections to the Stern Fund came from a Stern family member who had "dropped out" of society and had a farm in Wisconsin near a farm owned by Steve Parliament and Bill Teska. Some West Bank activists, including members of the New Riverside Cafe collective for a time, escaped to farms in Wisconsin.

2. In order to show the absurdity of purchasing "air rights" above Cedar Square West, activists held a contest for plans for what the city could do with

its air rights. As expected, the suggestions were as absurd as the air-rights purchase itself.

3. Ralph Wittcoff, in his comments on the original manuscript, related that one of the consequences of the saving of the firehouse for Mixed Blood theater was that the building was then developed specifically for Mixed Blood productions and thus was no longer practical as a site for neighborhood "boogies." That was perhaps one of the earliest signs of the neighborhood differentiation that would create problems in the 1980s.

4. There is an interesting distinction here between the coverage of *Snoose News* and that of the *Minneapolis Star*. The front-page headline of the October 29, 1976, *Star* read, "Tenant 'Union' Strikes Illegal, Top Court Says." The front-page headline of the December 1976 *Snoose News* read, "Tenant Strikes Still Legal," preserving the legitimacy of the idea of a tenants' union and recognizing that the court had ruled against rent strikes for collective bargaining actions, but not to protest code violations.

5. Ralph Wittcoff, in his comments on the rough draft of this manuscript, noted that Judge Albrecht used to play with "The Balding Banjo Company" at the New Riverside Cafe.

Chapter 6: Building the Foundation for Community-based Development

1. From the perspective of activist residents, the WBBA was associated with a business owner who was believed to be an "agent provocateur" on CRA's payroll and was a frequent antagonist to the PAC.

2. The concern for energy efficiency was not simply for the sake of political correctness or environmental sensitivity. The monthly costs for the housing would have been too high for many residents unless the homes were made more energy efficient.

3. Some residents did not see this first project as perfectly following the community-based planning model, since there were no existing residents on the site to be involved in the planning and the architect of the project exerted more influence than would be the case in later planning.

4. The Section 8 units were originally funded so that residents paid no more than 25 percent of their income on housing. The neighborhood practiced a policy that no one should pay more than 30 percent of their income for rent. When it became clear that the policy would sometimes mean unaffordably low rents, the neighborhood switched to a policy for residents that made their pre-rehab rent their minimum.

5. Brian Coyle ran for Jackie Slater's reapportioned seat after Slater chose not to pursue reelection. Slater died of cancer at an early age in late 1984. Ironically, Coyle, who took over her seat in her reapportioned ward, also died early, of complications from AIDS.

6. Philanthropic donations came from foundations and corporations such as Dayton-Hudson, General Mills, the Northwest Area Foundation (NAF), and MNSHIP. Grants ranged as high as $75,000 from NAF.

Chapter 7: The Struggle Within

1. Probably no issue generated more tension in the neighborhood during the late 1980s than the bar question, partly because the theater district idea was generated through the CDC more than through neighborhood-based planning. Additionally, radical residents who had come of age with drugs, sex, and (loud) rock 'n' roll now had children and full-time jobs. They did not like their children watching drunken bar patrons urinating on their lawns, vandalizing their cars, and waking everyone up at closing time. Thus, radical residents took a hard line against any bar license upgrades or expansions, out of an attempt to maintain resident control over local small capitalists and to preserve the quality of life in the neighborhood. Others, however, especially a new generation of younger and less radical residents, were attracted to the West Bank specifically for the entertainment available. Though a smaller number, they were as vocally in favor of the bars as radical residents were opposed. PAC meetings over whether to support license upgrades were at times barely kept under control, and radical residents tended to prevail in maintaining restrictions over the bars. Their influence was blamed, perhaps erroneously, for the closing of one restaurant whose liquor license was delayed and restricted.

2. The headline on page 7 of the CDC's October–November 1984 *West Bank Newsletter* read, "CDC to Emphasize Economic Development in '85." It was seen as another sign that local businesses were exerting undue influence over neighborhood policy. Though some of the impulses leading the CDC in this direction were compatible with the interests of radical residents, such as helping to create more community-based businesses to provide more local jobs, the CDC also was pursuing more traditional paths to economic development which looked too much like an endorsement of capitalism.

3. Conscious efforts to integrate the neighborhood resulted in an increase of racial minorities from almost none to about 20 percent of the neighborhood population. The new residents of color were primarily African American and included both poor and middle-class residents.

4. Pruitt-Igoe was a public housing complex built in St. Louis in 1954–55 that replaced 57.5 acres of "slum" housing with thirty-three eleven-story towers. The high-density complex quickly became a war zone of violence seemingly without solution. By the middle 1970s much of the complex had been razed (McCue, 1973).

5. Activists made many attempts to improve life in the complex, helping to organize the Oromo Cultural Society, Vietnamese Social Services of Min-

nesota, Person to Person Inc., Youth Programs, Childrens Home Society at Cedar-Riverside, the East Side Regional Support Program, Currie Neighborhood Center, "How to Start Your Own Business" classes, and other daycare, mental health, and cultural services.

6. Cedar-Riverside activists involved with other neighborhood organizations in Minneapolis report that a combined PAC-CDC does not necessarily prevent the conflict from disrupting the organization.

7. This vote tally is disputed, but all tallies give the motion at least a majority.

8. Most estimates place "voluntary displacement"—residents who chose to leave the neighborhood permanently when their unit was scheduled for rehab—at 50 to 60 percent. A survey conducted of the neighborhood in 1987 showed that 46 percent of residents in the old neighborhood east of Cedar Avenue had lived there more than three years (Mack, 1988).

9. On September 11, 1992, the MCDA approved the last $1.4 million of the $2.5 million needed to begin construction of the center, which will include a full-size gym, library, classrooms, food shelf, and teen center and will expand the social service and community programs previously provided through Currie Center.

Chapter 8: The Role of Community in Urban Insurgency

1. This focus on "agency" developed in the late 1980s in reaction to the Marxist structuralism of Louis Althusser (1969, 1970), which seemed to imply that human actors had no agency but only occupied structural locations that already had their own dynamics. The reaction was led by E. P. Thompson (1978:161), who argued for seeing "men and women as subjects of their own history." As agents, individuals could resist being propelled by social forces if they understood them and actively strategized against them. The agency-structuralism dualism is also problematic in social movement theory, where sometimes theorists emphasize the structural limits on social movements and other times emphasize the movements' own organizing, recruitment, and tactical choices. In this chapter I try to ground the implied agency in much of social movement theory by specifying the sources of agency.

2. There is some question whether "new social movements" are even all that new. Though the cultural critique believed to characterize these movements may be more prominently expressed in the 1990s than it was in the 1960s, past social movements were not bereft of cultural critique. Even the civil rights movement, especially as it led to a rediscovery and reclamation of black African culture, held characteristics of a new social movement. But the civil rights movement was split between the early movement that pushed for political inclusion and the later black power movement that pushed for more cultural autonomy.

Chapter 9: The Limits and the Potential of Community Control of Urban Redevelopment

1. Ralph Wittcoff reminded me that the early "community development" on the West Bank—the rise of the New Riverside Cafe, People's Center, North Country Co-op, and so on—*built* rather than disrupted community. That really was *community* development, as opposed to *physical* development, which too often pays little or no attention to the human community.

References

Abler, Ronald, and John Adams. 1976. *America's Great Cities: Twenty Metropolitan Regions*. Minneapolis: Association of American Geographers and University of Minnesota Press.

Adams, Carolyn. 1990. "Non-Profit Housing in the U.S.: Why So Rare?" Paper presented at the Urban Affairs Association annual meeting.

Alford, Robert R., and Eugene C. Lee. 1971. "Voting Turnout in American Cities." In *Community Politics: A Behavioral Approach*, ed. Charles M. Bonjean, Terry N. Clark, and Robert L. Lineberry, pp. 87–105. New York: Free Press.

Alinsky, Saul D. 1969. *Reveille for Radicals*. New York: Vintage Books.

———. 1971. *Rules for Radicals*. New York: Vintage Books.

Althusser, Louis. 1969. *For Marx*. Trans. Ben Brewster. London: Allen Lane.

———. 1970. *Reading Capital*. London: New Left Books.

Armitage, Dan, and the West Bank History Collective. 1973. "The Curling Waters: A West Bank History." Publication updated by the Cedar-Riverside PAC staff.

Bailis, Lawrence N. 1974. *Bread or Justice: Grassroots Organizing in the Welfare Rights Movement*. Lexington, Mass.: Lexington Books.

Baldinger, Stanley. 1971. *Planning and Governing the Metropolis: The Twin Cities Experience*. New York: Praeger.

Banfield, Edward, and James Q. Wilson. 1963. *City Politics*. Cambridge, Mass.: Harvard University Press.

Barkan, Steven E. 1979. "Strategic, Tactical, and Organizational Dilemmas of the Protest Movement Against Nuclear Power." *Social Problems* 27:19–37.

———. 1986. "Interorganizational Conflict in the Southern Civil Rights Movement." *Sociological Inquiry* 56:190–209.

Barnes, Donna. 1987. "Organization and Radical Protest: An Antithesis?" *Sociological Quarterly* 28:575–594.

Bellush, Jewel, and Murray Hausknecht. 1967. *Urban Renewal: People, Politics, and Planning*. Garden City, N.Y.: Anchor Books.

Bennett, Larry. 1989. "Postwar Redevelopment in Chicago: The Declining Politics of Party and the Rise of Neighborhood Politics." In *Unequal Partnerships: The Political Economy of Redevelopment in Postwar America*, ed. Gregory D. Squires, pp. 161–177. New Brunswick, N.J.: Rutgers University Press.

Bennett, Larry, Kathleen McCourt, Philip Nyden, and Gregory Squires. 1988. "Chicago's North Loop Redevelopment Project: A Growth Machine on Hold." In *Business Elites and Urban Development: Case Studies and Critical Perspectives*, ed. Scott Cummings, pp. 183–202. Albany: SUNY Press.

Bennett, Tom, David Boss, Jim Campbell, Seymour Siwoff, Rick Smith, and John Wiebusch (eds.). 1977. *Official Encyclopedic History of Professional Football*. New York: Macmillan.

Benson, J. Kenneth. 1977. "Organizations: A Dialectical View." *Administrative Science Quarterly* 22:1–21.

———. 1983. "A Dialectical Method for the Study of Organizations." In *Beyond Method: Strategies for Social Research*, ed. Gareth Morgan, pp. 331–346. Beverly Hills, Calif.: Sage.

Berger, Annette, Shobha Das, Tony G. Fox, Joseph Galaskiewicz, Celia Kamath, Bill McEvily, and Ray Sinclair. 1992. "Public-Private Partnerships in the Urban Community: An Example of an Interorganizational Action." Paper presented at the American Sociological Association annual meeting.

Berkowitz, Bruce D. 1985. "Justice with a Spin on It." *National Review*, August 9, pp. 35–36.

Berndt, Harry E. 1977. *New Rulers in the Ghetto: The Community Development Corporation and Urban Poverty*. Westport, Conn.: Greenwood Press.

Bjarkman, Peter C. 1991. "Washington Senators—Minnesota Twins: Expansion-era Baseball Comes to the American League." In *Encyclopedia of Major League Baseball Team Histories: American League*, ed. Peter C. Bjarkman, pp. 437–534. Westport, Conn.: Meckler.

Blakely, Edward, and Armando Aparicio. 1990. "Balancing Social and Economic Objectives: The Case of California's Community Development Corporations." *Journal of the Community Development Society* 21:115–128.

Bloom, Jack M. 1987. *Class, Race, and the Civil Rights Movement*. Bloomington: Indiana University Press.

Boddy, Martin. 1983. "Central-Local Government Relations: Theory and Practice." *Political Geography Quarterly* 2:119–138.

Boggs, Carl. 1986. *Social Movements and Political Power*. Philadelphia: Temple University Press.

Boise Peace Quilt Project. 1987. *A Stitch for Time* (film). Los Angeles: Direct Cinema Limited.

Boyte, Harry C. 1980. *The Backyard Revolution: Understanding the New Citizen Movement*. Philadelphia: Temple University Press.

———. 1982. "Neighborhood Politics: The Building Blocks." *Social Policy* 12:2–4.

———. 1984. *Community Is Possible: Repairing America's Roots*. New York: Harper and Row.

———. 1986. "Beyond Politics as Usual." In *The New Populism and the Politics of Empowerment*, ed. Harry C. Boyte and Frank Riessman, pp. 3–15. Philadelphia: Temple University Press.

———. 1989. *Commonwealth: A Return to Citizen Politics*. New York: Free Press.

Boyte, Harry C., Heather Booth, and Steve Max. 1986. *Citizen Action and the New American Populism*. Philadelphia: Temple University Press.

Boyte, Harry C., and Frank Riessman (eds.). 1986. *The New Populism: The Politics of Empowerment*. Philadelphia: Temple University Press.

Breines, Wini. 1980. "Community Organization: The New Left and Michels' 'Iron Law.'" *Social Problems* 27:419–429.

———. 1989. *Community and Organization in the New Left, 1962–1968*. New Brunswick, N.J.: Rutgers University Press.

Brighton Development Corporation. 1990. Housing Development Data: Cedar-Riverside Urban Renewal Project Data. (spreadsheet printout).

Broadbent, Thomas Andrew. 1977. *Planning and Profit in the Urban Economy*. London: Methuen.

Brown, L. David, and Rajesh Tandon. 1983. "Ideology and Political Economy in Inquiry: Action Research and Participatory Research." *Journal of Applied Behavioral Science* 19:277–294.

Browning, Harley, and Joachim Singleman. 1978. "The Transformation of the U.S. Labor Force: The Interaction of Industry and Occupation." *Politics and Society* 8:481–509.

Buechler, Steven M. 1990. *Women's Movements in the United States: Woman Suffrage, Equal Rights, and Beyond*. New Brunswick, N.J.: Rutgers University Press.

Business Week. 1984. "A. H. Robins Hauls a Judge into Court." July 16, pp. 27–28.

Camilleri, Joseph A. 1984. *The State and Nuclear Power: Conflict and Control in the Western World*. Seattle: University of Washington Press.

Čapek, Stella M., and John I. Gilderbloom. 1992. *Community versus Commodity: Tenants and the American City*. Albany: SUNY Press.

Castells, Manuel. 1977. *The Urban Question: A Marxist Approach*. Cambridge, Mass.: MIT Press.

———. 1978. *City, Class, and Power*. New York: St. Martin's Press.

———. 1981. "Local Government, Urban Crisis, and Political Change." In *Political Power and Social Theory*, vol. 2, ed. Maurice Zeitlin, pp. 1–19. Greenwich, Conn.: JAI Press.

———. 1983. *The City and the Grassroots: A Cross-Cultural Theory of Urban Social Movements*. Berkeley: University of California Press.

Center for Community Change. 1988. "Report of Activities, June through September, 1988." Washington, D.C.: Center for Community Change.

———. 1991. "Housing Bill Calls for Big Changes, More $, But Administration Says No." *Community Change*, Issue 10 (Winter/Spring): 7–10.

Checkoway, Barry. 1985. "Neighborhood Planning Organizations: Perspectives and Choices." *Journal of Applied Behavioral Science* 21:471–486.

Citizens' Clearinghouse for Hazardous Wastes, Inc. 1989. Annual Convention Preregistration Packet. Arlington, Va.

Clapp, James A. 1971. *New Towns and Urban Policy*. New York: Dunellen.

Clark, Gordon L., and Michael Dear. 1984. *State Apparatus: Structures and Language of Legitimacy*. Boston: Allen and Unwin.

Clark, Terry N. 1971. "Community Structure, Decision Making, Budget Expenditures, and Urban Renewal." In *Community Politics: A Behavioral Approach*, ed. Charles M. Bonjean, Terry N. Clark, and Robert L. Lineberry, pp. 293–313. New York: Free Press.

Clavel, Pierre. 1986. *The Progressive City: Planning and Participation, 1969–1984*. New Brunswick, N.J.: Rutgers University Press.

Clavel, Pierre, and Nancy Kleniewski. 1990. "Space for Progressive Local Policy: Examples from the United States and the United Kingdom." In *Beyond the City Limits: Urban Policy and Economic Restructuring in Comparative Perspective*, ed. John R. Logan and Todd Swanstrom, pp. 199–234. Philadelphia: Temple University Press.

Cockburn, Cynthia. 1977. *The Local State: Management of Cities and People*. London: Pluto Press.

Cohen, Jean. 1985. "Strategy or Identity: New Theoretical Paradigms and Contemporary Social Movements." *Social Research* 52:663–716.

Cox, Kevin. 1981. "Capitalism and Conflict Around the Communal Living Space." In *Urbanization and Urban Planning in Capitalist Society*, ed. Michael Dear and Allen J. Scott, pp. 431–455. New York: Metheun.

CRA (Cedar-Riverside Associates). 1972. "Cedar-Riverside New Community Narrative Description." Booklet.

Crenson, Matthew A. 1974. "Organizational Factors in Citizen Participation." *Journal of Politics* 36:356–378.

Dahl, Robert. 1961. *Who Governs? Democracy and Power in an American City*. New Haven: Yale University Press.

Davidson, Leonard. 1983. "Countercultural Organizations and Bureaucracy: Limits on the Revolution." In *Social Movements of the Sixties and Seventies*, ed. Jo Freeman, pp. 162–176. New York: Longman.

Davis, John Emmeus. 1991. *Contested Ground: Collective Action and the Urban Neighborhood*. Ithaca, N.Y.: Cornell University Press.

Daykin, David S. 1988. "The Limits to Neighborhood Power: Progressive Politics and Local Control in Santa Monica." In *Business Elites and Urban Development: Case Studies and Critical Perspectives*, ed. Scott Cummings, pp. 357–387. Albany: SUNY.

Dearlove, John. 1979. *The Reorganization of British Local Government*. Cambridge: Cambridge University Press.

Delgado, Gary. 1986. *Organizing the Movement: The Roots and Growth of ACORN*. Philadelphia: Temple University Press.

DeWar, Tom. 1992. "Minneapolis: Whittier Plan Tests City Commitment." *Neighborhood Works*, April/May, p. 8.

Domhoff, G. William. 1983. *Who Rules America Now: A View for the Eighties*. Englewood Cliffs, N.J.: Prentice-Hall.

Draheim, Kirk, Richard Howell, and Albert Shapero. 1966. *The Development of a Potential Defense R&D Complex: A Study of Minneapolis-St. Paul*. California: Stanford Research Institute.

Dreier, Peter. 1989. "Economic Growth and Economic Justice in Boston: Populist Housing and Jobs Policies." In *Unequal Partnerships: The Political Economy of Redevelopment in Postwar America*, ed. Gregory D. Squires, pp. 35–58. New Brunswick, N.J.: Rutgers University Press.

Duncan, S. S., and Goodwin, M. 1982. "The Local State and Restructuring Social Relations: Theory and Practice." *International Journal of Urban and Regional Research* 6:157–186.

Durkheim, Emile. 1964 [1893]. *The Division of Labor in Society*. Trans. George Simpson. New York: Free Press.

Dwyer, Lynn E. 1983. "Structure and Strategy in the Antinuclear Movement." In *Social Movements of the Sixties and Seventies*, ed. Jo Freeman, pp. 148–161. New York: Longman.

Edelstein, David, and Malcolm Warner. 1976. *Comparative Union Democracy: Organization and Opposition in British and American Unions*. New York: Wiley.

Eisinger, Peter K. 1973. "The Conditions of Protest Behavior in American Cities." *American Political Science Review* 67:11–28.

Elkin, Stephen L. 1987. *City and Regime in the American Republic*. Chicago: University of Chicago Press.

Engstrom, Richard L., and Michael D. McDonald. 1981. "The Election of Blacks to City Councils: Clarifying the Impact of Electoral Arrangements of the Seats/Population Relationship." *American Political Science Review* 75:344–354.

Estep, Rhoda. 1979. "The Effect of Interorganizational Ties on the Contemporary Consumer Cooperative Movement in Minnesota." Ph.D. dissertation, University of Minnesota.

Evans, Sara. 1979. *Personal Politics: The Roots of Women's Liberation in the Civil Rights Movement and the New Left*. New York: Knopf.

Evans, Sara, and Harry C. Boyte. 1986. *Free Spaces: The Source of Democratic Change in America*. New York: Harper and Row.

Fainstein, Norman I., and Susan S. Fainstein. 1974. *Urban Political Movements*. Englewood Cliffs, N.J.: Prentice-Hall.

———. 1986a. "New Haven: The Limits of the Local State." In *Restructuring the City*, ed. Susan S. Fainstein, Norman I. Fainstein, Richard Child Hill, Dennis R. Judd, and Michael Peter Smith, pp. 27–79. White Plains, N.Y.: Longman.

———. 1986b. "Regime Strategies, Communal Resistance, and Economic Forces." In *Restructuring the City*, ed. Susan Fainstein, et al., pp. 245–282. White Plains, N.Y.: Longman.

Fainstein, Susan S. 1987. "Local Mobilization and Economic Discontent." In *The Capitalist City: Global Restructuring and Community Politics*, ed. Michael Smith and Joe Feagin, pp. 323–342. Cambridge: Basil Blackwell.

Fainstein, Susan S., and Norman I. Fainstein. 1986. "Economic Change, National Policy, and the System of Cities." In *Restructuring the City*, ed. Susan S. Fainstein et al., pp. 1–26. White Plains, N.Y.: Longman.

Fainstein, Susan S., Norman I. Fainstein, Richard Child Hill, Dennis Judd, and Michael Peter Smith (eds.). 1986. *Restructuring the City*. White Plains, N.Y.: Longman.

Feagin, Joe R., and Robert Parker. 1990. *Building American Cities: The Urban Estate Game*. 2d ed. Englewood Cliffs, N.J.: Prentice-Hall.

Feldman, Roberta M., and Susan Stall. 1991. "The Politics of Space: A Case Struggle of Women's Struggles for Homeplace in Chicago Public Housing." Paper presented at the Society for the Study of Social Problems annual meeting.

Fine, Gary Alan, and Randy Stoecker. 1985. "Can the Circle Be Unbroken? Small Groups and Social Movements." In *Advances in Group Processes: A Research Annual*, vol. 2, ed. Edward J. Lawler, pp. 1–28. Greenwich, Conn.: JAI Press.

Fischer, Claude S. 1982. *To Dwell among Friends: Personal Networks in Town and City*. Chicago: University of Chicago Press.

Fish, John H. 1973. *Black Power/White Control*. Princeton: Princeton University Press.

Fisher, Robert. 1981. "From Grass-Roots Organizing to Community Service: Community Organization Practice in the Community Center Movement, 1907–1930." In *Community Organization for Urban Social Change: A Historical Perspective*, ed. Robert Fisher and Peter Romanofsky, pp. 33–58. Westport, Conn.: Greenwood Press.

———. 1984. *Let the People Decide: Neighborhood Organizing in America*. Boston: G. K. Hall.

Fleischmann, Arnold, and Joe R. Feagin. 1987. "The Politics of Growth-

Oriented Urban Alliances: Comparing Old Industrial and New Sunbelt Cities." *Urban Affairs Quarterly* 23:207–232.

Fraser, Graham. 1972. *Fighting Back: Urban Renewal in Trefann Court.* Toronto: A. M. Hakkert.

Fraser, Ronald. 1988. *1968, A Student Generation in Revolt: An International Oral History.* New York: Pantheon Books.

Freeman, Jo. 1972–73. "The Tyranny of Structurelessness." *Berkeley Journal of Sociology* 17:151–164.

——. 1975. *The Politics of Women's Liberation.* New York: Longman.

——. 1983a. "On the Origins of Social Movements." In *Social Movements of the Sixties and Seventies,* ed. Jo Freeman, pp. 8–30. New York: Longman.

——. 1983b. "A Model for Analyzing the Strategic Options of Social Movement Organizations." In *Social Movements of the Sixties and Seventies,* ed. Jo Freeman, pp. 193–210. New York: Longman.

Friedland, Roger. 1980. "Corporate Power and Urban Growth: The Case of Urban Renewal." *Politics and Society* 10:203–224.

——. 1983. *Power and Crisis in the City: Corporations, Unions, and Urban Policy.* New York: Schocken Books.

Friedland, Roger, and Donald Palmer. 1984. "Park Place and Main Street: Business and the Urban Power Structure." *Annual Review of Sociology* 10:393–416.

Frug, Geral E. 1980. "The City as a Legal Concept." *Harvard Law Review* 93:1057–1154.

Galaskiewicz, Joseph. 1985. *Social Organization of an Urban Grants Economy: A Study of Business Philanthropy and Nonprofit Organizations.* Orlando, Fla.: Academic Press.

Gamson, William. 1975. *The Strategy of Social Protest.* Homewood, Ill.: Dorsey Press.

Gans, Herbert J. 1982 [1962]. *The Urban Villagers: Group and Class in the Life of Italian Americans.* New York: Free Press.

Gardner, Hugh. 1973. "Crises and Politics in Rural Communes." In *Communes: Creating and Managing the Collective Life,* ed. Rosabeth Moss Kanter, pp. 150–166. New York: Harper and Row.

Gerlach, Luther P. 1976. "Developer, Resistor, Mediator, and Manager Networks in Conflict over Energy Development: Disintegration or a New Kind of Integration?" Paper presented at the American Political Science Association annual meeting.

——. 1983. "Movements of Revolutionary Change: Some Structural Characteristics." In *Social Movements of the Sixties and Seventies,* ed. Jo Freeman, pp. 133–147. New York: Longman.

Gerlach, Luther P., and Virginia H. Hine. 1970. *People, Power, Change: Movements of Social Transformation.* Indianapolis: Bobbs-Merrill.

Giloth, Robert. 1985. "Organizing for Neighborhood Development." *Social Policy* 15 (Winter): 37–42.

Giloth, Robert P., and Robert Mier. 1989. "Spatial Change and Social Justice: Alternative Economic Development in Chicago." In *Economic Restructuring and Political Response*, ed. Robert A. Beauregard, pp. 181–208. Beverly Hills, Calif.: Sage.

Gitlin, Todd. 1980. *The Whole World Is Watching: Mass Media in the Making and Unmaking of the New Left*. Los Angeles: University of California Press.

Goffman, Erving. 1959. *The Presentation of Self in Everyday Life*. New York: Anchor Books.

Goldsmith, William W., and Edward J. Blakely. 1992. *Separate Societies: Poverty and Inequality in U.S. Cities*. Philadelphia: Temple University Press.

Goldstone, Jack A. 1980. "The Weakness of Organization: A New Look at Gamson's *The Strategy of Social Protest*." *American Journal of Sociology* 85:1017–1042.

Gottdeiner, M., and Joe Feagin. 1988. "The Paradigm Shift in Urban Sociology." *Urban Affairs Quarterly* 24:163–187.

Granovetter, Mark S. 1973. "The Strength of Weak Ties." *American Journal of Sociology* 78:1360–1380.

Greer, Scott. 1965. *Urban Renewal and American Cities*. Indianapolis: Bobbs-Merrill.

Halfmann, Jost. 1988. "Risk Avoidance and Sovereignty: New Social Movements in the United States and West Germany." *Praxis International* 8:14–25.

Handler, Joel F. 1978. *Social Movements and the Legal System*. New York: Academic Press.

Hannigan, John. 1985. "Alain Touraine, Manuel Castells, and Social Movement Theory: A Critical Appraisal." *Sociological Quarterly* 26:435–454.

Hartmann, Heidi. 1981. "The Family as the Locus of Gender, Class, and Political Struggle: The Example of Housework." *Signs* 6:366–394.

Hartsock, Nancy. 1979. "Feminism, Power, and Change: A Theoretical Analysis." In *Women Organizing: An Anthology*, ed. Bernice Cummings and Vicky Schuck, pp. 2–24. Metuchen, N.Y.: Scarecrow Press.

Harvey, David. 1978. "The Urban Process under Capitalism: A Framework for Analysis." *International Journal of Urban and Regional Research* 2:101–131.

———. 1985. *The Urbanization of Capital: Studies in the History and Theory of Capitalist Urbanization*. Baltimore: Johns Hopkins University Press.

Helman, Claire. 1986. *The Milton Park Affair: Canada's Largest Citizen Development Organization*. Montreal: Vehicle Press.

Henig, Jeffrey R. 1982. *Neighborhood Mobilization: Redevelopment and Response*. New Brunswick, N.J.: Rutgers University Press.

Heskin, Allan D. 1991. *The Struggle for Community*. Boulder, Colo.: Westview Press.

Hollander, Zander (ed.). 1979. *The Modern Encyclopedia of Basketball*, 2d rev. ed. Garden City, N.Y.: Doubleday.

hooks, bell. 1990. *Yearning: Race, Gender, and Cultural Politics*. Boston: South End Press.

Houghton, John. 1991. "Urban Development and Elite Adaption: Toward a Theory of the Growth Machine." Paper presented at the American Sociological Association annual meeting.

Hunter, Floyd. 1953. *Community Power Structure*. Garden City, N.Y.: Anchor Books.

Janowitz, Morris. 1967. *The Community Press in an Urban Setting*. Chicago: University of Chicago Press.

Jenkins, J. Craig. 1977. "Radical Transformation of Organizational Goals." *Administrative Science Quarterly* 22:568–586.

———. 1983. "Resource Mobilization and the Study of Social Movements." *Annual Review of Sociology* 9:527–553.

———. 1985. "Foundation Funding of Progressive Social Movements." In *Grant Seekers Guide*, ed. Jill R. Shellow, pp. 7–18. Mt. Kisko, N.Y.: Moyer Bell.

Jenkins, J. Craig, and Barbara G. Brents. 1989. "Social Protest, Hegemonic Competition, and Social Reform." *American Sociological Review* 54:891–909.

Jezierski, Louise. 1988. "Political Limits to Development in Two Declining Cities: Cleveland and Pittsburgh." In *Research in Politics and Society*, vol. 3, ed. Michael Wallace and Joyce Rothschild, pp. 173–180. Greenwich, Conn.: JAI Press.

Jonasdóttir, Kristin. 1988. "Oligarchy and/or Goal Transformation: The Case of the National Organization for Women." Paper presented at the Midwest Sociological Society annual meeting.

Judd, Dennis R., and Robert Eugene Mendelson. 1973. *The Politics of Urban Planning: The East St. Louis Experience*. Urbana: University of Illinois Press.

Kanter, Rosabeth Moss. 1977. *Men and Women of the Corporation*. New York: Basic Books.

Karnig, Albert K. 1975. " 'Private-Regarding' Policy, Civil Rights Groups, and the Mediating Impact of Municipal Reforms." *American Journal of Political Science* 19:91–106.

Katovich, Michael, Marion W. Weiland, and Carl J. Couch. 1981. "Access to Information and Internal Structures of Partisan Groups: Some Notes on the Iron Law of Oligarchy." *Sociological Quarterly* 22:431–445.

Katz, Steven, and Margit Mayer. 1985. "Gimme Shelter: Self-Help Housing Struggles Within and Against the State." *International Journal of Urban and Regional Research* 9:15–46.

Katznelson, Ira. 1981. *City Trenches: Urban Politics and the Patterning of Class in the United States*. New York: Pantheon Books.

Keating, Dennis, Norman Krumholz, and John Metzger. 1989. "Cleveland: Post-Populist Public-Private Partnerships." In *Unequal Partnerships: The Political Economy of Urban Redevelopment in Postwar America*, ed. Gregory D. Squires, pp. 121–141. New Brunswick, N.J.: Rutgers University Press.

Kelly, Rita M. 1977. *Community Control of Economic Development: The Board of Directors of Community Development Corporations*. New York: Praeger.

Killian, Lewis M. 1964. "Social Movements." In *Handbook of Modern Sociology*, ed. Robert E. L. Faris, pp. 426–455. Chicago: Rand McNally.

Kitschelt, Herbert P. 1986. "Political Opportunity Structures and Political Protest: Anti-Nuclear Movements in Four Democracies." *British Journal of Political Science* 16:57–85.

Klandermans, Bert. 1986. "New Social Movements and Resource Mobilization: The European and the American Approach." *International Journal of Mass Emergencies and Disasters* 4:13–37.

Klehr, Harvey. 1984. *The Heyday of American Communism: The Depression Decade*. New York: Basic Books.

Kleniewski, Nancy. 1984. "From Industrial to Corporate City: The Role of Urban Renewal." In *Marxism and the Metropolis: New Perspectives in Urban Political Economy*, 2d ed., ed. William Tabb and Larry Sawers, pp. 205–222. New York: Oxford University Press.

Kutner, Bernard. 1950. "Elements and Problems of Democratic Leadership." In *Studies in Leadership*, ed. Alvin Gouldner, pp. 459–467. New York: Harper and Brothers.

Lamb, Curt. 1975. *Political Power in Poor Neighborhoods*. New York: John Wiley and Sons.

Lancourt, Joan E. 1979. *Confront or Concede: The Alinsky Citizen-Action Organizations*. Lexington, Mass.: Lexington Books.

Laslett, Barbara. 1981. "Production, Reproduction, and Social Change: The Family in Historical Perspective." In *Sociology: Problems and Prospects*, ed. James F. Short, Jr., pp. 239–258. Beverly Hills, Calif.: Sage.

Laslett, Barbara, and Rhona Rapoport. 1975. "Collaborative Interviewing and Interactive Research." *Journal of Marriage and the Family* 37:968–977.

Lather, Patti. 1986. "Research as Praxis." *Harvard Educational Review* 5:257–277.

Lauria, Mickey. 1980. "Community-Controlled Redevelopment: South Minneapolis." Ph.D. dissertation, University of Minnesota.

———. 1986. "Toward a Specification of the Local State: State Intervention Strategies in Response to a Manufacturing Plant Closing." *Antipode* 18:39–63.

Law, Robin M., and Jennifer R. Wolch. 1983. "Social Reproduction in the City: Restructuring in Time and Space." In *The Restless Urban Landscape*, ed. Paul L. Knox, pp. 165–206. Englewood Cliffs, N.J.: Prentice-Hall.

Lawson, Ronald. 1983. "A Decentralized but Moving Pyramid: The Evolution and Consequences of the Structure of the Tenant Movement." In *Social Movements of the Sixties and Seventies*, ed. Jo Freeman, pp. 148–161. New York: Longman.

Lawson, Ronald, and Stephen E. Barton. 1980. "Sex Roles in Social Movements: A Case Study of the Tenant Movement in New York City." *Signs* 6:230–247.

Lebedoff, David. 1972. *Ward Number Six*. New York: Charles Scribner's Sons.

Lenz, Thomas J. 1988. "Neighborhood Development: Issues and Models." *Social Policy* 18 (Spring): 24–30.

Levine, Marc V. 1989. "The Politics of Partnership: Urban Redevelopment since 1945." In *Unequal Partnerships: The Political Economy of Urban Redevelopment in Postwar America*, ed. Gregory D. Squires, pp. 12–34. New Brunswick, N.J.: Rutgers University Press.

Lineberry, Robert L., and Edmund P. Fowler. 1971. "Reformism and Public Policies in American Cities." In *Community Politics: A Behavioral Approach*, ed. Charles M. Bonjean, Terry N. Clark, and Robert Lineberry, pp. 277–292. New York: Free Press.

Lipietz, Alain. 1988. "Building an Alternative Movement in France." *Rethinking Marxism* 1:80–99.

Lo, Clarence. 1982. "Countermovements and Conservative Movements in the Contemporary U.S." *Annual Review of Sociology* 8:107–134.

Logan, John R., and Harvey L. Molotch. 1987. *Urban Fortunes: The Political Economy of Place*. Berkeley: University of California Press.

Lowe, Stuart. 1986. *Urban Social Movements: The City after Castells*. New York: St. Martin's Press.

Luxton, Meg. 1980. *More than a Labour of Love: Three Generations of Women's Work in the Home*. Toronto: Women's Press.

Lyon, Larry. 1987. *The Community in Urban Society*. Philadelphia: Temple University Press.

Lyon, Larry, Lawrence G. Felice, M. Ray Perryman, and E. Stephen Parker. 1981. "Community Power and Population Increase: An Empirical Test of the Growth Machine Model." *American Journal of Sociology* 86:1387–1400.

McAdam, Doug. 1982. *Political Process and the Development of Black Insurgency, 1930–1970*. Chicago: University of Chicago Press.

———. 1986. "Recruitment to High-Risk Activism: The Case of Freedom Summer." *American Journal of Sociology* 92:64–90.

McCarthy, John D., David W. Britt, and Mark Wolfson. 1991. "The Institutional Channeling of Social Movements by the State in the United States." In *Research in Social Movements, Conflicts, and Change*, vol. 13, ed. Louis Kriesberg, pp. 45–76. Greenwich, Conn.: JAI Press.

McCarthy, John D., and Mayer Zald. 1977. "Resource Mobilization and Social

Movements: A Partial Theory." *American Journal of Sociology* 82:1212–1241.

McCue, George. 1973. "$57,000,000 Later." *Architectural Forum* 138 no. 4 (May):42–45.

McDonald, Alan. 1986. *The Weller Way*. London: Faber and Faber.

Mack, Edward. 1988. "Cedar-Riverside Residents' Survey: A Summary of Results." Research Report, Cedar-Riverside Project Area Committee.

Mansbridge, Jane. 1980. *Beyond Adversary Democracy*. New York: Basic Books.

———. 1984. "Feminism and the Forms of Freedom." In *Critical Studies in Organization and Bureaucracy*, ed. Frank Fischer and Carmen Siriani, pp. 472–481. Philadelphia: Temple University Press.

Markusen, Ann. 1978. "Class and Urban Social Expenditure: A Marxist Theory of Metropolitan Government." In *Marxism and the Metropolis: New Perspectives in Urban Political Economy*, ed. William K. Tabb and Larry Sawers, pp. 90–111. New York: Oxford University Press.

———. 1980. "City Spatial Structure, Women's Household Work, and National Urban Policy." *Signs* 5:523–544.

Martin, Judith A. 1978. *Recycling the Central City: The Development of a New Town in Town*. Minneapolis: University of Minnesota Press.

Mayer, Margit. n.d. "Restructuring and Opposition in West German Cities." Unpublished manuscript.

Melville, Keith. 1972. *Communes in the Counter Culture: Origins, Theories, and Styles of Life*. New York: William Morrow.

Michels, Roberto. 1962 [1915]. *Political Parties: A Sociological Study of Oligarchical Tendencies of Modern Democracy*. Trans. Eden Paul and Cedar Paul. New York: Free Press.

Minneapolis City Planning Commission. 1965–66. *Riverside: Challenge and Opportunity*. Publication no. 168.

———. 1966. *Riverside—The Next Twenty Years: A Staff Report to the Minneapolis City Planning Commission*. Preliminary Plan Report, Publication no. 169, Neighborhood Series no. 11.

Minneapolis Housing and Redevelopment Authority. 1968. *Cedar-Riverside Urban Renewal Plan*. March 1; revised September 12.

Mitchell, J. Clyde. 1983. "Case and Situation Analysis." *Sociological Review* 31:187–211.

Mollenkopf, John H. 1978. "The Postwar Politics of Urban Development." In *Marxism and the Metropolis: New Perspectives in Urban Political Economy*, ed. William K. Tabb and Larry Sawers, pp. 117–152. New York: Oxford University Press.

———. 1981. "Community and Accumulation." In *Urbanization and Urban Planning in Capitalist Society*, ed. Michael Dear and Allen J. Scotts, pp. 319–338. New York: Metheun.

———. 1983. *The Contested City*. Princeton: Princeton University Press.

Molotch, Harvey. 1976. "The City as Growth Machine: Toward a Political Economy of Place." *American Journal of Sociology* 82:309–332.

———. 1979. "Capital and Neighborhood in the United States." *Urban Affairs Quarterly* 14:289–312.

———. 1988. "Strategies and Constraints of Growth Elites." In *Business Elites and Urban Development: Case Studies and Critical Perspectives*, ed. Scott Cummings, pp. 25–48. New York: SUNY.

Molotch, Harvey, and John Logan. 1984. "Tensions in the Growth Machine: Overcoming Resistance to Value-Free Development." *Social Problems* 31:483–499.

Morlock, Laura L. 1974. "Business Interests, Countervailing Groups, and the Balance of Influence in Ninety-One Cities." In *The Search for Community Power*, 2d ed., ed. Willis D. Hawley and Frederick M. Wirt, pp. 309–328. Englewood Cliffs, N.J.: Prentice-Hall.

Morris, Aldon. 1984. *The Origins of the Civil Rights Movement: Black Communities Organizing for Change.* New York: Free Press.

Moya-Raggio, Eliane. 1984. "Arpilleras: Chilean Culture of Resistance." *Feminist Studies* 10:277–282.

National Commission on Neighborhoods. 1979. *People Building Neighborhoods: Final Report to the President and the Congress of the United States.* Washington, D.C.: U.S. Government Printing Office.

Neubeck, Kenneth J., and Richard E. Ratcliff. 1988. "Urban Democracy and the Power of Corporate Capital: Struggle over Downtown Growth and Neighborhood Stagnation in Hartford, Connecticut." In *Business Elites and Urban Development: Case Studies and Critical Perspectives*, ed. Scott Cummings, pp. 299–332. New York: SUNY Press.

Norman, Jack. 1989. "Congenial Milwaukee: A Segregated City." In *Unequal Partnerships: The Political Economy of Urban Redevelopment in Postwar America*, ed. Gregory D. Squires, pp. 178–201. New Brunswick, N.J.: Rutgers University Press.

Northern States Power Co., First Bank of Minneapolis, Northwestern National Bank of Minneapolis, and Minneapolis Area Development Corporation. 1959. *Minnesota's Case for the Electronics Industry: A Plant Location Report.* Minneapolis: Northern States Power Company.

Novack, David R. 1987. "Forced Busing in South Boston: Class, Race, and Power." *Journal of Urban Affairs* 9:277–292.

Noyelle, Thierry, and Thomas Stanback, Jr. 1984. *The Economic Transformation of American Cities.* Totowa, N.J.: Rowman and Allanheld.

Oberschall, Anthony. 1973. *Social Conflict and Social Movements.* Englewood Cliffs, N.J.: Prentice-Hall.

O'Connor, James. 1973. *The Fiscal Crisis of the State.* New York: St. Martin's Press.

Offe, Claus. 1985. "New Social Movements: Challenging the Boundaries of Institutional Politics." *Social Research* 52:817–868.

Oliver, Pamela. 1983. "The Mobilization of Paid and Volunteer Activists in the Neighborhood Movement." In *Research in Social Movements, Conflict, and Change*, vol. 5, ed. Louis Kriesberg, pp. 133–170. Greenwich, Conn.: JAI Press.

Olson, Mancur. 1965. *The Logic of Collective Action: Public Goods and the Theory of Groups*. Cambridge, Mass.: Harvard University Press.

Omaha Housing Equity Project. 1991. "Affordable Housing Strategies for Low-Income Families in Omaha: Recommendations for the CHAS Plan." Unpublished manuscript.

Pascal, Erica, and Stephen Parliament. 1977. "NEPA and the Human Environment: The Case of Cedar-Riverside." *Land Use Law and Zoning Digest* (May), 5–10.

Pateman, Carole. 1970. *Participation and Democratic Theory*. London: Cambridge University Press.

Pecorella, Robert F. 1987. "Fiscal Crises and Regime Change: A Contextual Approach." In *The Politics of Urban Development*, ed. Clarence N. Stone and Heywood T. Sanders, pp. 52–72. Lawrence: University Press of Kansas.

Peirce, Neal, and Carol Steinbach. 1990. *Enterprising Communities: Community-Based Development in America, 1990*. Washington, D.C.: Council for Community-Based Development.

Pickvance, C. G. 1977. "From 'Social Base' to 'Social Force': Some Analytical Issues in the Study of Urban Protest." In *Captive Cities: Studies in the Political Economy of Cities and Regions*, ed. Michael Harloe, pp. 175–186. New York: John Wiley and Sons.

Piven, Frances Fox, and Richard A. Cloward. 1977. *Poor People's Movements: Why They Succeed, How They Fail*. New York: Pantheon Books.

———. 1979. *Poor People's Movements: Why They Succeed, How They Fail*. New York: Vintage Books.

Platt, Adam. 1990. "A House Divided: Minneapolis's West Bank Is at War with Itself—Again." *Twin Cities Reader*, June 18–24, pp. 10–13.

Posner, Prudence, S. 1990. "Introduction." In *Dilemmas of Activism: Class, Community, and the Politics of Local Mobilization*, ed. Joseph M. Kling and Prudence S. Posner, pp. 3–20. Philadelphia: Temple University Press.

Ratcliff, Richard. 1980. "Banks and Corporate Lending: An Analysis of the Impact of the Internal Structure of the Capitalist Class on the Lending Behavior of Banks." *American Sociological Review* 45:553–570.

Reitzes, Donald C., and Dietrich C. Reitzes. 1987. *The Alinsky Legacy: Alive and Kicking*. Greenwich, Conn.: JAI Press.

Riessman, Frank. 1986. "The New Populism and the Empowerment Ethos." In *The New Populism: The Politics of Empowerment*, ed. Harry C. Boyte and Frank Riessman, pp. 53–63. Philadelphia: Temple University Press.

Rivlin, Leanne G. 1980. "Group Membership and Place Meanings in an Urban Neighborhood." *Journal of Social Issues* 38:75–93.

Roelofs, Joan. 1987. "Foundations and Social Change Organizations: The Mask of Pluralism." *Insurgent Sociologist* 14:31–72.

Rosa, Eugene A., and William A. Freudenberg. 1984. "Nuclear Power at the Crossroads." In *Public Reaction to Nuclear Power: Are There Critical Masses?* ed. William R. Freudenberg and Eugene A. Rosa, pp. 3–37. Boulder, Colo.: Westview Press.

Ross, Murray G. 1955. *Community Organization: Theory and Principles.* New York: Harper and Brothers.

Ross, Robert J. S. 1976. "The Impact of Social Movements on a Profession in Process: Advocacy in Urban Planning." *Sociology of Work and Occupations* 3:429–454.

Rothschild-Whitt, Joyce. 1979. "The Collectivist Organization: An Alternative to Rational-Bureaucratic Models." *American Sociological Review* 44:509–527.

Rubenstein, Bruce. 1991. "Leap of Faith." *City Pages,* July 17, pp. 10–15.

Rucht, Dieter. 1988. "Themes, Logics, and Arenas of Social Movements: A Structural Approach." *International Social Movement Research* 1:305–368.

———. 1989. "Environmental Movement Organizations in West Germany and France: Structure and Interorganizational Relations." *International Social Movement Research* 2:61–94.

Rupp, Leila J., and Verta A. Taylor. 1987. *Survival in the Doldrums: The American Women's Rights Movement, 1945 to the 1960's.* New York: Oxford University Press.

Saint-Jean, Armande. 1986. "From Counterculture to Feminist Culture." In *Old Passions, New Visions: Social Movements and Political Activism in Quebec,* ed. M. Raboy, pp. 39–59. Toronto: Between the Lines.

Saltman, Juliet. 1990. *A Fragile Movement: The Struggle for Neighborhood Stabilization.* Westport, Conn.: Greenwood Press.

Sanbonmatsu, John. 1989. "Animal Liberation: Should the Left Care?" *Zeta Magazine* (October), 101–110.

Sargent, Lydia. 1981. "New Left Women and Men: The Honeymoon Is Over." In *Women and Revolution: A Discussion of the Unhappy Marriage of Marxism and Feminism,* ed. Lydia Sargent, pp. xi–xxxi. Boston: South End Press.

Saunders, Peter. 1978. "Domestic Property and Social Class." *International Journal of Urban and Regional Research* 2:233–251.

———. 1981. *Social Theory and the Urban Question.* London: Hutchinson.

Sayer, Andrew. 1984. *Method in Social Science: A Realist Approach.* London: Hutchinson.

Sbragia, Alberta. 1989. "The Pittsburgh Model of Economic Development:

Partnership, Responsiveness, and Indifference." In *Unequal Partnerships: The Political Economy of Urban Redevelopment in Postwar America*, ed. Gregory D. Squires, pp. 103–120. New Brunswick, N.J.: Rutgers University Press.

Schultze, William A. 1974. *Urban and Community Politics*. North Scituate, Mass.: Duxbury Press.

Schulz, Ann. 1979. *Local Politics and Nation States: Case Studies in Politics and Policy*. Santa Barbara, Calif.: Clio Books.

Schumacher, Paul D. 1978. "The Scope of Political Conflict and the Effectiveness of Constraints in Contemporary Urban Protest." *Sociological Quarterly* 19:168–184.

Serrill, Michael S. 1984. "A Panel Tries to Judge a Judge." *Time*, July 23, p. 88.

Shlay, Anne B., and Robert R. Faulkner. 1984. "The Building of a Tenants Protest Organization: An Ethnography of a Tenants Union." *Urban Life* 12:445–465.

Simmel, Georg. 1950 [1905]. "The Metropolis and Mental Life." In *The Sociology of Georg Simmel*, trans. Kurt Wolff, pp. 409–424. New York: Free Press.

Smith, Michael, and Robert Tardanico. 1987. "Urban Theory Reconsidered: Production, Reproduction, and Collective Action." In *The Capitalist City: Global Restructuring and Community Politics*, ed. Michael Smith and Joe Feagin, pp. 87–110. Cambridge: Basil Blackwell.

Smith, Robert T. 1988. *Minneapolis-St. Paul: The Cities, Their People*. Helena, Mont.: American Geographic Publishing.

Snow, David A., E. Burke Rochford, Jr., Steven K. Worden, and Robert D. Benford. 1986. "Frame Alignment Processes, Micromobilization, and Movement Participation." *American Sociological Review* 51:464–481.

Snow, David A., Louis A. Zurcher, and Sheldon Ekland-Olson. 1980. "Social Networks and Social Movements." *American Sociological Review* 45:787–801.

Squires, Gregory D. 1989a. "Public-Private Partnerships: Who Gets What and Why." In *Unequal Partnerships: The Political Economy of Urban Redevelopment in Postwar America*, ed. Gregory D. Squires, pp. 1–11. New Brunswick, N.J.: Rutgers University Press.

———, ed. 1989b. *Unequal Partnerships: The Political Economy of Redevelopment in Postwar America*. New Brunswick, N.J.: Rutgers University Press.

Stack, Carol. 1974. *All Our Kin*. New York: Harper and Row.

Staggenborg, Suzanne. 1988. "The Consequences of Professionalization and Formalization in the Pro-Choice Movement." *American Sociological Review* 53:585–606.

———. 1989a. "Organizational and Environmental Influences on the Development of the Pro-Choice Movement." *Social Forces* 68:204–240.

———. 1989b. "Stability and Innovation in the Women's Movement: A Comparison of Two Movement Organizations." *Social Problems* 36:75–92.

Stallings, Robert. 1973. "Patterns of Belief in Social Movements: Clarifications from an Analysis of Enviromental Groups." *Sociological Quarterly* 14:465–480.

Steedly, Homer, and John Foley. 1979. "The Success of Protest Groups: Multivariate Analyses." *Social Science Research* 8:1–15.

Stein, Arlene. 1986. "Between Organization and Movement: ACORN and the Alinsky Model of Community Organizing." *Berkeley Journal of Sociology* 31:93–115.

Stein, Maurice R. 1960. *The Eclipse of Community: An Interpretation of American Studies.* Princeton: Princeton University Press.

Sternlieb, George, and James W. Hughes. 1981. *Shopping Centers: USA.* Piscataway, N.J.: Center for Urban Policy Research, Rutgers University.

Stever, James A. 1978. "Contemporary Neighborhood Theories: Intergration Versus Romance and Reaction." *Urban Affairs Quarterly* 13:263–284.

Stoecker, Randy. 1990. "Taming the Beast: Maintaining Democracy in Community-Controlled Redevelopment." *Berkeley Journal of Sociology* 35:107–126.

———. 1991a. "Evaluating and Redefining the Case Study." *Sociological Review* 39:88–112.

———. 1991b. "Community Organizing and Community Development: The Life and Times of the East Toledo Community Organization." Research Report, University of Toledo Urban Affairs Center.

———. 1991c. "Community Organizing and Community Development in Cedar-Riverside and East Toledo: A Comparative Study." Research Report, University of Toledo Urban Affairs Center.

———. 1992. "Who Takes Out the Garbage? Social Reproduction and Social Movement Research." In *Perspectives on Social Problems*, ed. Gale Miller and James A. Holstein, pp. 239–264. Greenwich, Conn.: JAI Press.

———. 1993. "The Federated Front-Stage Structure and Localized Social Movements: A Case Study of the Cedar-Riverside Neighborhood Movement." *Social Science Quarterly* 74:169–184.

Stoecker, Randy, and David Beckwith. 1992. "Advancing Toledo's Neighborhood Movement Through Participatory Action Research: Integrating Activist and Academic Approaches." *Clinical Sociology Review* 10:198–213.

Stoecker, Randy, and Mary Schmidbauer. 1991. "Local State Reform and Class Struggle: The Case of Toledo, Ohio." *Critical Sociology* 18:99–123.

Stone, Clarence N. 1987. "Summing Up: Urban Regimes, Development Policy, and Political Arrangements." In *The Politics of Urban Development*, ed. Clarence N. Stone and Heywood T. Sanders, pp. 269–290. Lawrence: University Press of Kansas.

——— . 1989. *Regime Politics: Governing Atlanta, 1946–1988*. Lawrence: University Press of Kansas.

Strange, John H. 1973. "Local Strategies for Attaining Neighborhood Control." In *Neighborhood Control in the 1970's: Politics, Administration, and Citizen Participation*, ed. George Fredrickson, pp. 167–178. New York: Chandler.

Swanstrom, Todd. 1985. *The Crisis of Growth Politics: Cleveland, Kucinich, and the Challenge of Urban Populism*. Philadelphia: Temple University Press.

Szabó, Máté. 1988. "New Factors in the Political Socialization of Youth in Hungary: The Alternative Social Movements and Subcultures." *Praxis International* 8:26–33.

Tabb, William. 1984. "A Pro-People Urban Policy." In *Marxism and the Metropolis: New Perspectives in Urban Political Economy*, 2d ed., ed. William Tabb and Larry Sawers, pp. 367–382. New York: Oxford University Press.

Tabb, William, and Larry Sawers. 1978. "Editors' Introduction." In *Marxism and the Metropolis: New Perspectives in Urban Political Economy*, ed. William Tabb and Larry Sawers, pp. 3–19. New York: Oxford University Press.

Tarrow, Sidney. 1983. *Struggling to Reform: Social Movements and Policy Change During Cycles of Protest*. Western Societies Program Occasional Paper No. 15, Center for International Studies, Cornell University. Ithaca, N.Y.

——— . 1992. "Mentalities, Political Cultures, and Collective Action Frames: Constructing Meanings Through Action." In *Frontiers in Social Movements Theory*, ed. Aldon D. Morris and Carol McClurg Mueller, pp. 174–202. New Haven: Yale University Press.

Taylor, Verta. 1989. "Social Movement Continuity: The Women's Movement in Abeyance." *American Sociological Review* 54:761–775.

Taylor, Verta, and Leila J. Rupp. 1991. "Women's Culture and Lesbian Feminist Activism: A Reconsideration of Cultural Feminism." Paper presented at the Society for the Study of Social Problems annual meeting.

Thompson, E. P. 1978. *The Poverty of Theory and Other Essays*. New York: Monthly Review Press.

Tilly, Charles. 1984. "Social Movements and National Politics." In *State-making and Social Movements: Essays in History and Theory*, ed. Charles Bright and Susan Harding, pp. 297–317. Ann Arbor: University of Michigan Press.

Töennies, Ferdinand. 1963 [1887]. *Community and Society*. New York: Harper and Row.

Touraine, Alain. 1988. *Return of the Actor: Social Theory in Post-Industrial Society*. Trans. Myrna Godzich. Minneapolis: University of Minnesota Press.

Traugott, Mark. 1978. "Reconceiving Social Movements." *Social Problems* 26:39–49.

Trubek, David M. 1977. "Complexity and Contradiction in the Legal Order: Balbus and the Challenge of Critical Social Thought about Law." *Law and Society Review* 11:529–569.

Turner, Ralph H. 1970. "Determinants of Social Movement Strategies." In *Human Nature and Collective Behavior: Papers in Honor of Herbert Blumer*, ed. Tamotsu Shibutani, pp. 145–164. Englewood Cliffs, N.J.: Prentice-Hall.

Turner, Ralph H., and Lewis M. Killian. 1972. *Collective Behavior*. 2d ed. Englewood Cliffs, N.J.: Prentice-Hall.

Twelvetrees, Alan. 1989. *Organizing for Neighborhood Development*. Brookfield, Vt.: Avebury.

U.S. Conference of Mayors. 1986. *Rebuilding America's Cities*. Cambridge, Mass.: Ballinger.

Useem, Bert, and Mayer Zald. 1982. "From Pressure Group to Social Movement: Organizational Dilemmas of the Effort to Promote Nuclear Power." *Social Problems* 30:144–156.

Useem, Michael. 1975. *Protest Movements in America*. Indianapolis: Bobbs-Merrill.

Valelly, Richard M. 1989. *Radicalism in the States: The Minnesota Farmer Labor Party and the American Political Economy*. Chicago: University of Chicago Press.

Vogel, Jennifer. 1991. "Faulty Towers." *City Pages*, September 4, pp. 8–15.

Von Eschen, Donald, Jerome Kirk, and Maurice Pinard. 1971. "The Organizational Sub-Structure of Disorderly Politics." *Social Forces* 49:529–543.

Walsh, Edward J. 1986. "The Role of Target Vulnerabilities in High Technology Protest: The Nuclear Establishment at Three Mile Island." *Sociological Forum* 1:199–218.

Walsh, Edward J., and Rex H. Warland. 1983. "Social Movement Involvement in the Wake of a Nuclear Accident: Activists and Free Riders in the TMI Area." *American Sociological Review* 48:764–780.

Wandersman, Abraham, Paul Florin, Robert Friedmann, and Ron Meier. 1987. "Who Participates, Who Does Not, and Why? An Analysis of Voluntary Organizations in the United States and Israel." *Sociological Forum* 2:534–555.

Ward, Jean, and Cecilie Gaziano. 1976. "A New Variety of Urban Press: Neighborhood Publications." *Journalism Quarterly* 53:61–67.

Weaver, Clyde Mitchell. 1990. "Community Development in North America: Survey and Prospects for the 1990's." *Community Development Journal* 25:345–355.

Weinberg, Adam. 1992. "Defining the Success of a Social Movement: The Adopt-a-Planet Project—A Case Study." Paper presented at the Midwest Sociological Society annual meeting.

Weissman, Steven. 1981. "Environmental Constraints on Neighborhood Mobilization for Institutional Change: San Francisco's Mission Coalition Organization, 1970–1974." In *Community Organization for Urban Social Change: A Historical Perspective*, ed. Robert Fisher and Peter Romanofsky, pp. 187–216. Westport, Conn.: Greenwood Press.

Wellman, Barry, and Barry Leighton. 1979. "Networks, Neighborhoods, and Communities: Approaches to the Study of the Community Question." *Urban Affairs Quarterly* 14:363–390.

West, Cornel. 1986. "Populism: A Black Socialist Critique." In *The New Populism: The Politics of Empowerment*, ed. Harry C. Boyte and Frank Riessman, pp. 207–212. Philadelphia: Temple University Press.

Wheeler, Charlene Eldridge, and Peggy L. Chinn. 1984. *Peace and Power: A Handbook of Feminist Process*. Buffalo, N.Y.: Margaretdaughters.

Whyte, William F. 1943. *Street Corner Society*. Chicago: University of Chicago Press.

Williams, Michael R. 1985. *Neighborhood Organizations: Seeds of a New Life*. Westport, Conn.: Greenwood Press.

Wilson, James Q. 1973. *Political Organizations*. New York: Basic Books.

Wirth, Louis. 1938. "Urbanism as a Way of Life." *American Journal of Sociology* 44:1–24.

Workers of the Writers' Program. 1944. *The Story of a City: Minneapolis*. Minneapolis: Minnesota Writers' Project of the Works Projects Administration.

Worthy, William. 1976. *The Rape of Our Neighborhoods*. New York: William Morrow.

Wright, Erik Olin. 1978. *Class, Crisis, and the State*. London: New Left Books.

———. 1985. *Classes*. London: Verso.

Wylie, Jeanie. 1989. *Poletown: Community Betrayed*. Chicago: University of Illinois Press.

Yates, Douglas. 1973. *Neighborhood Democracy: The Political Impact of Decentralization*. Lexington, Mass.: Lexington Books.

Zablocki, Benjamin. 1971. *The Joyful Community*. Baltimore: Penguin.

Zald, Mayer, and Roberta Ash. 1966. "Social Movement Organizations: Growth, Decay, and Change." *Social Forces* 44:327–341.

Zald, Mayer, and John D. McCarthy. 1980. "Social Movement Industries: Competition and Cooperation among Movement Organizations." In *Research in Social Movements, Conflicts, and Change*, vol. 3, ed. Louis Kriesberg, pp. 1–20. Greenwich, Conn.: JAI Press.

Zald, Mayer N., and Bert Useem. 1987. "Movement and Countermovement Interaction: Mobilization, Tactics, and State Involvement." In *Social Movements in an Organizational Society: Collected Essays*, ed. Mayer N. Zald and John D. McCarthy, pp. 247–272. New Brunswick, N.J.: Transaction Books.

Zukin, Sharon. 1980. "A Decade of the New Urban Sociology." *Theory and Society* 9:575–601.

Bibliography of Newspapers and Newsletters

Minneapolis Star, Minneapolis Tribune, and *Star-Tribune*

Ackerberg, Peter. "HRA ODs Cedar-Riverside Commercial Plan Despite Objection." *Minneapolis Star,* October 4, 1974, p. A16.

"Battle Lost, Fight Goes On." *Minneapolis Star,* September 11, 1973, p. C1.

"Cedar-Riverside Development Plans Attacked." *Minneapolis Tribune,* December 22, 1967, p. 13.

Coleman, Nick. "Cedar-Riverside Opponents to Make 'Alternative' Plans." *Minneapolis Tribune,* October 19, 1974, p. B4.

———. "Corporations Reject Plan to Save Cedar-Riverside from Financial Calamity." *Minneapolis Tribune,* November 1, 1974, p. A1.

———. "HUD Report Indicates that C-R Project Is 'Not Viable.'" *Minneapolis Tribune,* December 16, 1974, p. A1.

Erickson, Howard. "Crowd of 400 Angrily Protests Cedar-Riverside Renewal Plan." *Minneapolis Tribune,* August 15, 1968, p. 21.

Hartgen, Stephen. "17 Arrested in West Bank Disorder." *Minneapolis Star,* May 10, 1972, p. B2.

Jones, Gwenyth. "Tenant 'Union' Strikes Illegal, Top Court Says." *Minneapolis Star,* October 29, 1976, p. A1.

Kaszuba, Mike. "Cedar-Riverside Finds Itself in a Midlife Crisis." *Star-Tribune,* April 8, 1988, pp. 1, 14A.

"Residents Assail HRA Cedar-Riverside Plan." *Minneapolis Tribune,* December 11, 1967, p. 21.

"Suit Opposes Renewal Plan for Riverside." *Minneapolis Tribune,* December 6, 1967, p. 19.

"200 Youths Protest Dania Hall Closing." *Minneapolis Tribune,* July 4, 1968, p. 24.

"U.S. Mines N. Vietnam's Coastline." *Minneapolis Star,* May 9, 1972, pp. A1, 3.

Waterhouse, Ann, and Bruce Rubenstein. "Community Control of Cedar-Riverside Planning." *Minneapolis Tribune,* June 29, 1975, p. A13.

"West Bank Residents Agree to Police Center." *Minneapolis Tribune*, March 5, 1971, p. B3.

Snoose News

I relied heavily on *Snoose News* for neighborhood detail. Below are only those articles I have directly discussed or quoted in the text. Numerous other authors of *Snoose News* articles that informed this book also deserve recognition: Jeanne Brockway, Jack Cann, Steve Eide, Larry Glenn, Warren Hanson, Kirk Hill, Beryle Miller, Devi S. Nadiri, Ann Norton, Steve Parliament, Diane Rackowski, Joan Scully, Jean Simmons, Jackie Slater, Reverend William J. Teska, and Barb Yonda.

Andre, Billy, Heather Baum, Dorothy Jacobs, Bruce Rubenstein, Matt Shuth, Tim Strick, Ralph Wittcoff. "Yes." *Snoose News*, February 1988, p. 6.

Baum, Heather. "Who Owns the West Bank?" *Snoose News*, November 1987, p. 8.

Cato, Chris, Chip Halbach, Al Haug, Kay Heinz, Lucian Marsh, Claudia Parliament, Mary Alice Smalls. "Should the CDC Be Dissolved: NO." *Snoose News*, February 1988, p. 7.

"Council Cuts Low-Income Projects." *Snoose News*, December 1977, p. 6.

Currier, Ross. "More Boos." *Snoose News*, February 1988, p. 4.

"Eulogy for Cedar-Riverside Associates." *Snoose News*, November 1977, p. 3.

"Evictions Threatened." *Snoose News*, December 1977, p. 1.

Fisketti, Charlotte. "Snoose Lost to Budget Cuts." *Snoose News*, January/February 1983, p. 1.

Foos, Rickey. "PAC Activities: What Are We Doing?" *Snoose News*, March 1975, p. 2.

"Judge Lord Signs Suit." *Snoose News*, April 1976, p. 1.

"Lack of Maintenance Forces Housing Condemnations." *Snoose News*, April 1978, p. 1.

"Legislators, Council Members Rebuke CRA." *Snoose News*, July 1976, p. 6.

" 'Listen to the People.' " *Snoose News*, April 1977, p. 2.

"Million for C-R?" *Snoose News*, July 1975, p. 1.

Mungavan, Tim. "Cedar East Block Meetings." *Snoose News*, August 1981, pp. 1, 2.

"Negotiating with Thorpe Continues." *Snoose News*, July/August 1978, p. 7.

"Neighborhood Committees Form." *Snoose News*, January 1977, p. 7.

Norton, Ann. "CREDF Wins Lawsuit." *Snoose News*, September 1975, p. 1.

O'Brien, Kathy. "West Bank Beginnings." *Snoose News*, April 1975, p. 1.

"PAC Study Finds Rehab. Key to Affordable Housing." *Snoose News*, January 1977, p. 6.

"PAC Workshops to Review '68 Plan." *Snoose News*, July 1975, p. 1.

"Rent Strikes Begin." *Snoose News*, October 1977, p. 1.

"Riverside Park Meetings Continue." *Snoose News*, April 1978, p. 8.

"Riverside Park Plan Adopted." *Snoose News*, December 1978, pp. 1, 4–5.

"Taxpayers Stuck for $20 Million." *Snoose News*, January 1976, p. 3.

"Tenant Strikes Still Legal." *Snoose News*, December 1976, p. 1.

"Threatening Letter to Tenants Revoked." *Snoose News*, November 1977, p. 2.

"University Demolition Delayed." *Snoose News*, November 1975, p. 3.

"Who Caused This Mess." *Snoose News*, June 1976, p. 1.

"Who Caused This Mess." *Snoose News*, August 1976, p. 4.

Wittcoff, Ralph. "Business Closings Sign of CDC Misdirection." *Snoose News*, December 1987, pp. 1, 3.

The Surveyor

"For a Tenant Partnership at Cedar Square West" (editorial). *The Surveyor*, December 1987, p. 2.

Share, Steve. "Lawsuit Seeks More Low-Income Units at Cedar Square West." *The Surveyor*, July 1987, pp. 1, 3.

West Bank Newsletter

"CDC to Emphasize Economic Development in '85." *West Bank Newsletter*, October–November 1984, p. 7.

Wittcoff, Ralph (as told to Elaine Wynne). "West Bank History: The Everlasting Watch Cat." *West Bank Newsletter*, March 1986.

Index

Italicized page numbers refer to illustrations.

Chicago, Illinois, 104, 149, 214

Citizens' Clearinghouse for Hazardous Wastes, Inc., 217

Civil rights movement, as based in localized movements, 76

Class: and background of Cedar-Riverside residents, 8, 27, 32, 52; influence of contradictory class locations on Cedar-Riverside, 146–148; as a limited concept, 214; and transition in social movement mobilization, 5–6

Class consciousness, role of, in Cedar-Riverside neighborhood movement, 47–48

Cleveland, Ohio, 149, 168, 169, 249

Clientelism, 241–243; and affordable housing/community control contradiction, 242–243; in Cedar-Riverside, 241–243; and COG, 242; and PAC, 242; in Route 2 project, 241; and RPTA, 242

Cloward, Richard A., 230, 234

Coalition for the Defense of Neighborhood Priorities, 112, 116, 164–165

Cockburn, Cynthia, 43–44

COG (Committee for Open Government), 195–198, 212, 242

Collective identity. See Culture; Ideology; Social movements

Committee for Open Government, 195–198, 212, 242

Communities Organized for Public Service (COPS), 149, 177–178

Community: in Cedar-Riverside, x–xi, 45, 61–62, 74, 244–245; decline of, in Cedar-Riverside, 182–184, 199; defined, 16–17; as goal of counterculture, 51; historical changes in, 17–19; organization of, compared to organization of capital, 100; relation of, to social movement, 19–23, 62. See also Counterculture; Culture; Democratic, community-based redevelopment; Social reproduction.

Community-based movements. See Social movements: localized variant

Community development, and disruption of community, 240–241. See also Community; Democratic, community-based redevelopment in Cedar-Riverside

Community Development Block Grant. See CDBG

Community Development Corporation, in Cedar-Riverside. See CDC

Community Development Corporations, distrust of, nationally, 178–179

Community organizing movement, United States, 50

Community organizing, shift of, to community development, 177–179, 239–243; role of foundations in, 177

Community Union: founding of, 53–55; and rent strike tactic, 143–144; role of, in Cedar-Riverside neighborhood movement, 67–68, 77, 88, 93, 95, 147, 181; structure of, 54, 58

Co-op wars, 208, 219

Counterculture: in Cedar-Riverside, x, 8, 52, 63, 148, 182, 208, 219; and communes, 51; goals of, 215–216; Haight-Ashbury as, 51; and participatory democracy, 152; and split with New Left in Cedar-Riverside, 51–52. See also Culture; Democratic, community-based redevelopment; Ideology; Social reproduction

Countermovements, 194–195; in Cedar-Riverside, 195–198, 212

Coyle, Brian, 165, 185, 196, 200, 219, 269n.5

CRA (Cedar-Riverside Associates): conflict of, with Tenants Union, 80–84; financial problems of, 101, 102–103, 105, 109, 121, 143, 148; founding of, 39; and MHRA bail-out plans, 105; and settlement agreement of 1980, 120–122. See also Cedar Square West

CREDF (Cedar-Riverside Environmental Defense Fund): founding of, 77–79; and lawsuit against New Town, 78–79, 105, 107–109; organizational structure of, 89; role of, in Cedar-

CREDF (cont'd)
Riverside neighborhood movement, 86, 88, 89, 91, 92, 93, 95, 96, 97, 99, 101, 104, 216, 217, 222, 232; and social movement tactical dilemma, 93. See also Environmental impact statement

Culture: and early Cedar-Riverside residents, 27, 32; relation of social movement culture to social movement structure in Cedar-Riverside, 221–223; in social movements, 19, 204–206. See also Community; Counterculture; Democratic, community-based redevelopment; Ideology; Social reproduction

Dania Hall, 52, 200
Davidov, Marv, 69, 70
Davis, John, 145–146
Dedication ceremony uprising. See Cedar Square West
DeMars, Lou, 122
Democratic, community-based redevelopment, 11; community approach of, 246–247; compared to top-down, capital-conscious redevelopment, 11–12; and dependence on capital, 250–251; model for, 245–248; and need for local state restructuring, 249; and need for public support, 251; participatory democracy in, 247; whole neighborhood approach for, 245–246. See also Democratic, community-based redevelopment in Cedar-Riverside; Tax increment financing
Democratic, community-based redevelopment in Cedar-Riverside, 154–160; and affirmative action hiring in construction, 162; and affordable housing/community control contradiction, 188–192; and Brighton Development Corporation, 161, 163; and Canadian Financial Corporation, 161, 200; cost of, 9, 162, 200; and daycare houses, 197;

and energy efficiency planning, 157–159, 269n.2; and first groundbreaking, 136, 161; and housing co-ops, 161, 163, 171, 174–176, 179, 197; and housing rehabilitation, 137; and in-fill housing strategy, 158; and internal conflict, 184–187, 192–196, 270n.2; and "no-displacement" policy, 150; and number of housing units, 9, 200; and planning process, 85, 92, 113, 136, 156–160, 207; and problems with economic redevelopment, 138, 179–182, 270n.2; and reevaluation of 1968 urban renewal plan, 106; and Section 8 housing, 158–159, 160, 163, 171, 182; tax increment funding for, 113, 142; and townhome development, 173. See also Cedar-Riverside; Cedar-Riverside neighborhood movement; Democratic, community-based redevelopment; Exchange values versus use values
Democratic Farmer Labor Party, 30, 32, 165
Democratic Party, 30, 32, 165
Detroit, Michigan, and Poletown, 236–239
DFL (Democratic Farmer Labor Party): historical background of, 30, 32; in Minneapolis city government, 165
Dialectical methodology, 172
Disinvestment and urban decline, 254
Domestic property classes: defined, 145–146; role of, in Cedar-Riverside, 146–148
Drew, Robert, 37, 39, 40
"Dr. Judy," 56, 57
Durable Goods, 138, 146, 181, 207
Durkheim, Emile, 17

East-West Bank Tenants Union. See Tenants Union
Economic development in Cedar-Riverside. See Democratic, community-based redevelopment in Cedar-Riverside
Economic Opportunity Act of 1965,

role of, in Cedar-Riverside neighborhood movement, 59

Economic Research Action Project, 50–51, 211

EIS. See Environmental impact statement; National Environmental Policy Act

EIS lawsuit. See CREDF; National Environmental Policy Act, role of, in Cedar-Riverside

Electric Fetus, 61

Elliot Park Surveyor, 164, 186

Energy efficiency. See Democratic, community-based redevelopment

Environmental impact statement (EIS): general use of, by social movements, 94; in Cedar-Riverside, 66–67, 78–79, 94–95, 105, 107–109, 216, 232

Evans, Sara, 57, 183, 220

Exchange values versus use values, 11; influence of, on Cedar-Riverside redevelopment, 146–148; in relation to local state, 43; in top-down, capital-conscious redevelopment, 13. *See also* Capital versus community in urban development; Democratic, community-based redevelopment; Top-down, capital-conscious redevelopment

Feagin, Joe R., 16, 46–47, 103

Federal government: criticisms of role in urban redevelopment, 34; role of, in Cedar-Riverside, 41, 46, 59, 68, 72, 102, 109, 110, 113, 117, 120–122, 185–186; role of, in undermining community, 177. *See also* CDBG; Environmental impact statement; HoDAG, in Cedar-Riverside redevelopment; HUD; National Environmental Policy Act, role of, in Cedar-Riverside

Federated frontstage structure, 86–97; in Cedar-Riverside neighborhood movement, 86–97; and community ideology, 222; compared to DSR structure, 87; and frontstage and backstage characteristics, 87–88;

and growth coalition fissures, 96; and localized social movements, 226; and organizational overlap problem in Cedar-Riverside neighborhood movement, 90; and organizing dilemma in Cedar-Riverside neighborhood movement, 88–90; and recruitment dilemma in Cedar-Riverside neighborhood movement, 90–93; and relative autonomy of the local state, 96–97; and tactical dilemma in Cedar-Riverside neighborhood movement, 93–95

Firehouse, 111

First National Bank of St. Paul: role of, in Cedar-Riverside, 112, 120; and settlement agreement of 1980, 121

Flynn, Raymond, 169

Fraser, Don, 114, 116, 165

Free rider problem in social movements, 20, 91–92

Free spaces: in Cedar-Riverside, 57, 183; defined, 57; and social reproduction, 220

Free Store, 143

Friedland, Roger, 14

General Motors, role of, in destruction of Poletown, 236–239

Gerlach, Luther, 21, 67, 75, 86, 188, 266n.9

Government. See Local state

Government of Minneapolis. See Minneapolis city government

Greenfield, Lee, 116

Growth coalition, 12–16; and capital fractions, 15–16; CRA-led, in Cedar-Riverside, 39, 43, 100–109; defined, 13; and effect of capital fractions on CRA, 45–48; problems of, generally, 14–16; in relation to urban regime, 14; role of, in urban redevelopment, 13–14; and role of rentier class, 103–104; source of term, 265–266n.5; unraveling of, in Cedar-Riverside, 100–109

Growth perspective, and conflicts

North Country Co-op, 57, 84, 90, 96, 146, 199, 207, 208, 209, 246

O'Brien, Kathy, 122, 164, 165, 196, 197, 200, 257
Ogren, Tim, ix, xi, 89, 93, 110, 117, 118, 119, 120–121, 123, 164, 187, 196, 198, 201, 219, 223, 242, 259, 261
Oligarchy in social movements, 153–154
Organic intellectuals, 154–155

PAC (Project Area Committee): and affordable housing/community control contradiction, 187–192; budget of, 89, 113, 164, 187, 268n.3; disbanding of, 198; founding of, 58–61; internal conflict in, 186–187; liberation of, by Cedar-Riverside residents, 79–80; organizational structure of, 89; and overlap with CDC activity, 188–189; and participatory democracy, 155–160; and Riverside Plaza social problems, 189, 196; role of, in Cedar-Riverside neighborhood movement, 67, 71, 77, 85, 91, 95, 97, 102, 108, 110, 111, 144, 181, 185, 194, 195, 197; and social movement tactical dilemma, 93; structure of, 89, 93, 147
"Parcel B" development, 194–195, 197
Parker, Robert, 16, 46–47, 103
Parliament, Steve, 53, 54, 55, 59, 66–67, 77, 78, 84, 99, 148, 192, 201, 216, 257–258
Participatory democracy, 151–160; in redevelopment planning in Cedar-Riverside, 153–160. See also Democratic, community-based redevelopment in Cedar-Riverside
People's Center: budget cuts in, 201; founding of, 56–58; and mobilization to defend against university expansion, 64–65; and purchase of building, 110; and rehab of building, 162; role of, in Cedar-Riverside neighborhood movement, 70, 91, 199, 208, 209, 213; and social repro-

duction, 96, 216, 219, 220–221, 223
People's Pantry, 57, 129, 216
Peterson, Norman, 132
Pittsburgh, Pennsylvania, 44, 249
Piven, Frances Fox, 230, 234
Planning, for democratic, community-based redevelopment in Cedar-Riverside, 85, 92, 113, 156–157. See also Democratic, community-based redevelopment in Cedar-Riverside
Poletown, 48, 236–239; compared to Cedar-Riverside, 237–239
Political opportunity structure: and changes in relation to Cedar-Riverside, 100–101; defined, 22–23; and federated frontstage structure in Cedar-Riverside neighborhood movement, 95–97; in Minneapolis in 1960s, 32; role of, in Cedar-Riverside, 42–45, 65–68, 109–117; and shift to supporting democratic, community-based redevelopment, 148–151; and social movement agency, 226. See also Local state; Minneapolis city government
Press. See News media
Project Area Committee. See PAC
Pruitt-Igoe, 185, 270n.4
Public-private partnership: in Cedar-Riverside, 34–35; history of, 267n.1

Rapson, Ralph, 38, 80
Raymond, David, 42, 46
Reaganomics, impact of, on Minneapolis city government, 163–164
Redevelopment authorities, role of, in insulating urban renewal from accountability, 35–36
Reform Caucus, 147
Riverbluff housing co-op, 158–159, 161, 179, 200
Riverside Park: location of, in Cedar-Riverside, 2, 8; redevelopment planning for, 156
Riverside Plaza: purchase of, 186; and social problems, 196, 270–271n.5. See also Cedar Square West; PAC

Riverside Plaza Tenants Association, 186–187, 196
Romney, George, 40, 68–70, 208
Route 2 community-based development movement, 241
RPTA (Riverside Plaza Tenants Association), 186–187, 196
Rubenstein, Bruce, 144, 251, 252

St. Paul. *See* Minneapolis
San Antonio, Texas, 149, 177–178
San Francisco, California, 178, 250–251
Santa Monica, California, 165–166
Savran's Bookstore, 181
Sawers, Larry, 229
Scallon, Tony, 107, 114, 149, 165, 167, 196
Section 8 housing. *See* Democratic, community-based redevelopment in Cedar-Riverside
Segal, Gloria, 38–39, 42, 82
Service industries, role of, in urban redevelopment, 150–151
Settlement agreement of 1980, 120–122; and democratic, community-based redevelopment, 142
Seven Corners: location of, in neighborhood, 2, 6–7; redevelopment of, 111, 162–163
Seward neighborhood, 212
Sherlock Homes co-op, 174–176, 179, 192–193, 244
Sign house, 159, 160
Single-room occupancy housing, 171–172
Slater, Jackie, 112, 114, 119, 144, 164, 269n.5
Snoose News: comparison of coverage to mainstream press, 266–267n.10, 269n.4; origin of name, 268n.2; role of, in Cedar-Riverside neighborhood movement, 79, 82–83, 91, 118, 119, 156, 192
Social movement agency, 204–206, 223–227, 271n.1
Social movement community, 19–23, 62

Social movement organizing dilemma, 20–22, 75–76, 221–223; and CDC structure, 89–90; in Cedar-Riverside, 65–68, 188–189; and CREDF structure, 89; and decentralization of neighborhood organizations in Cedar-Riverside, 57–58; and decentralized, segmentary, reticulate structure, 21, 67, 75, 76, 86–87, 188, and federated frontstage structure, 86–97; and federated frontstage structure in Cedar-Riverside neighborhood movement, 88–90; and localized movements, 76; and PAC structure, 89; and participatory democracy, 152–160; and Tenants Union structure, 81, 89. *See also* Social reproduction
Social movement recruitment dilemma, 20, 189–190; in Cedar-Riverside, 63–65; and federated frontstage structure in Cedar-Riverside, 90–93. *See also* Social reproduction
Social movements: dilemmas of, 19–22; localized variant of, 4–6, 205–206, 210, 224–229; new social movement theory, 205. *See also* Neighborhood movements; Social movement organizing dilemma; Social movement recruitment dilemma; Social movement success; Social movement tactical dilemma; Social reproduction
Social movements and social reproduction. *See* Social reproduction
Social movement structure. *See* Social movement organizing dilemma
Social movement success: in Cedar-Riverside, 229–234; defined, 231–232
Social movement tactical dilemma, 22; in Cedar-Riverside neighborhood movement, 68–72, 190–191; and electoral tactics in Cedar-Riverside, 79, 95; and federated frontstage structure in Cedar-Riverside neighborhood movement, 93–95; and

Social movmnt. tact. dil. (cont'd)
National Environmental Policy Act,
94–95; and rent strike tactic, 81–83,
117–120; and use of uncontrollable
elements in Cedar-Riverside neighborhood movement, 93, 110, 121,
181. See also Social reproduction
Social movement theory and new
urban sociology, 9–10
Social reproduction: in Cedar-
Riverside neighborhood movement,
63, 64, 183–184, 217–218; collectivization of, 215; and counterculture,
215–216; defined, 213; and goals
of Cedar-Riverside neighborhood
movement, 216–217; and "homeplace," 213; and role of Cedar-
Riverside neighborhood movement
organizations, 216–221; and social
movement goals, 215–217; and
social movement recruitment, 218–
220; and social movement structure,
217–218; and social movement tactics, 220–221; and struggle over the
surplus, 214–215
Spear, Allan, 112, 116, 118
Stage I. See Cedar-Square West
Staggenborg, Suzanne, 57–58
Stone, Clarence N., 14–15, 35, 103,
165, 168, 249
Student Nonviolent Coordinating
Committee (SNCC), 50
Students for a Democratic Society
(SDS), 50–51
Surveyor, 164, 186

Tabb, William, 229
Tarrow, Sidney, 22, 231
Tax increment financing: and democratic, community-based redevelopment in Cedar-Riverside, 113, 142;
redirection of funds by Minneapolis
city government, 173
Tenants Union, 117–120; and Cedar
Square West rent strike, 119; demonstration tactic of, 81, 83, 119;
founding of, 80–81; organizational
structure of, 81, 88, 89; rent strike

poster of, 133; rent strike tactic of,
81–83, 117–120; role of, in Cedar-
Riverside neighborhood movement;
91, 93, 95, 96, 97; symbol of, 132
Teska, Bill, 53, 109, 123, 125, 193
Toënnies, Ferdinand, 17
Top-down, capital-conscious redevelopment, 11, 116–117; compared to
democratic, community-based redevelopment, 11–12; defined, 13. See
also Capital; Capital versus community in urban development; Growth
coalition
Trinity block redevelopment, 194, 200
Twin Cities. See Minneapolis

UCPI (University Community Prop-
erties Incorporated), 80–84; and
firehouse, 111
Uncontrollable elements. See Social
movement tactical dilemma
Unicorn Fund, 198
Union Homes co-op, 163; role of, in
CDC dissolution vote, 193
University Community Properties
Incorporated (UCPI), 80–84; 111
University of Minnesota: location of,
in relation to Cedar-Riverside, 2, 6;
1960s expansion of, 32, 64; role of,
in Cedar-Riverside, 62, 64–66, 83,
110
Urban regime: activist regime in 1960s
Minneapolis, 35; defined, 14; problems of progressive regimes, 168;
in relation to growth coalition, 14;
shift toward progressive regime in
Minneapolis, 166
Urban renewal plan: in 1968, 37; reevaluation of, in Cedar-Riverside,
105–106; revised plan, 150
Use values versus exchange values.
See Exchange values versus use
values

Vietnam war, role of, in Cedar-
Riverside neighborhood movement,
68–70
Vreeland, Scott, 194

"War council," in Cedar-Riverside, 118
Warner, Charles, 39, 40, 46
Watchcat, 56, *130*, *140*, 267n.2
Watchcat committee, 161
Watchcat co-op, 171
West Bank. *See* Cedar-Riverside
West Bank Business Association
  (WBBA), 147
West Bank Community Development
  Corporation. *See* CDC
West Bank Co-op Grocery, 84–85, 102,
  110; sale of, 182, 265n.2
West Bank Homes Co-op, 161
West Bank Tenants Union. *See* Tenants Union

Whale, The, 61, *125*
Wittcoff, Ralph, xi, xii, 42, 53, 55, 56,
  63, 64–65, 69, 71, 79, 85, 86, 91, 92,
  125, 147, 160, 199, 207, 208, 258,
  260, 267n.2, 268nn.1, 4, 269nn.3, 5,
  272n.1
Wolking, Debbie, xii, *131*, *135*, *138*,
  139, *140*
Wylie, Jeanie, 236–238

Yu, Joyce, 53, 57, 58, 59–60, 65, 68–
  69, 70, 72, 73

Zniewski, Zack, 56, *129*, *130*, 267n.2

1. self. interest

2. holding comm. contact ? possible?

3. must comm. pol. be id. pol.

   (good ends ⟺ good means)

4. 'agency' ⟺ successful action